Barnes & Noble Shakespeare

David Scott Kastan
Series Editor

BARNES & NOBLE SHAKESPEARE features newly edited texts of the plays prepared by the world's premiere Shakespeare scholars. Each edition provides new scholarship with an introduction, commentary, unusually full and informative notes, an account of the play as it would have been performed in Shakespeare's theaters, and an essay on how to read Shakespeare's language.

DAVID SCOTT KASTAN is the Old Dominion Foundation Professor in the Humanities at Columbia University and one of the world's leading authorities on Shakespeare.

Barnes & Noble Shakespeare
Published by Barnes & Noble
122 Fifth Avenue
New York, NY 10011
www.barnesandnoble.com/shakespeare

Image on page 334:
William Shakespeare, *Comedies, Histories, & Tragedies*, London, 1623, Bequest of Stephen Whitney Phoenix, Rare Book & Manuscript Library, Columbia University.

Library of Congress Cataloging-in-Publication Data

Shakespeare, William, 1564–1616.
 Henry V / William Shakespeare.
   p. cm. — (Barnes & Noble Shakespeare)
 Includes bibliographical references.
 ISBN-13: 978-1-4114-9996-6
 ISBN-10: 1-4114-9996-4
 1. Henry V, King of England, 1387–1422—Drama. 2. Great Britain—History—
   Henry V, 1413–1422—Drama. I. Title. II. Title: Henry the Fifth.

 PR2812.A1 2007
 822.3'3—dc22

                      2007021949

Printed and bound in the United States
  3 5 7 9 10 8 6 4 2

HENRY V

William

SHAKESPEARE

BENEDICT S. ROBINSON
EDITOR

Barnes & Noble Shakespeare

Contents

Introduction to *Henry V*
by Benedict S. Robinson

enry V is the last of Shakespeare's major history plays—that is, the last of the plays he wrote during the vogue for history plays in the 1590s. As such, we might expect it to be triumphant, climactic, grandiose. And, in many ways, it is: it narrates the English conquest of France, showing us an English "band of brothers" united against a common enemy in a difficult war. That phrase has given us the name of an HBO miniseries about World War Two, and the image of a small, embattled group of brothers struggling against overwhelming odds virtually defines a whole genre of patriotic war movies, movies that imagine national unity in terms of a small but tough community of men. Both of the major film versions of this play, one by Laurence Olivier in 1944 and the other by Kenneth Branagh in 1989, offer Henry's army as a synecdoche for an England united in military struggle—even if to do so they must dispense with some of the more problematic passages in the play, passages that complicate or even call into question the story of heroic nationalism.

An intensely political play, *Henry V* concentrates most of its energies on the public face of its titular central figure: Henry delivers only one soliloquy in the play, and even then what he thinks about is his father's "fault" in "compassing the crown"—that is, in rebelling against Richard II and setting himself on the throne (4.1.285–286). Even Henry's private moments are resolutely political. The fact that he thinks back to this moment, recalling the larger narrative of what is sometimes called the "second tetralogy"—*Richard II; Henry IV, Part One; Henry IV, Part Two;* and *Henry V*—reveals that what is at stake in this play is, in large measure, the nature of English political life in the aftermath of civil war. Because its subject matter is war and politics, and because so much rides on our response to its central figure, this is a play that has been intensely debated: Does it depict a king who unites a divided England with a strong foreign policy, or a king with no real claim to the throne who tries to distract attention from that fact by waging a dubious war? Is Henry a strong monarch or a master manipulator? The answer, of course, may be both: Shakespeare's Henry is a complex figure, not reducible to simple responses.

E. M. W. Tillyard famously argued that Shakespeare's purpose in writing the history plays was "to dramatize the whole stretch of English history from the prosperity of Edward III, through the disasters that succeeded, to the establishment of civil peace under the Tudors"—that is, to chronicle England's escape from civil war and rebellion with the arrival of the Tudor dynasty, the dynasty still in power when Shakespeare wrote his histories. Certainly, that was the point of one of Shakespeare's sources, Edward Hall's *The Union of the Two Noble and Illustrious Families of Lancaster and York*, in which the union of the rival factions in the Tudors gives the narrative its goal, its telos. But Shakespeare did not end his version of English history with the arrival of the Tudors; in fact, the sequence in which he wrote these plays is strikingly at odds with actual chronology. He first dramatized the reign of Henry VI in three plays of that name and culminated with *Richard III*, the play that does in fact conclude with the coronation of the first Tudor king, Henry VII. But in the second tetralogy he went back to the beginning of the troubles to dramatize Bolingbroke's revolt against Richard II; his troubled reign as Henry IV; and, finally, the reign of his son,

Henry V. At the moment that *Henry V* ends, in other words, the victory over France is shadowed by disasters still to come, disasters already chronicled in previous Shakespeare plays, as the epilogue reminds us: Henry's son "lost France and made his England bleed" (12).

The history plays probably don't fit together into the kind of total design Tillyard imagined: Shakespeare was a professional dramatist writing for a commercial theater company, responding to the popularity of plays based on English history by writing more such plays—he almost certainly did not set out to tell a single story all the way through eight plays. Tillyard's disappointment with *Henry V* is perhaps conditioned by the excessive coherence he seeks from the histories as a whole. But we should perhaps also expect this kind of refusal of single explanations and single purposes from Shakespeare, who is often celebrated for his ability to render multiple and even conflicting perspectives. *Henry V* might be the emblem for this perspectival quality of Shakespearean drama. Critics of the play have been divided about whether it is a heroic play or whether it offers a darker, more complicated, more uncomfortable truth about political life: if the play invites us to take pleasure in English victories and to enjoy the rhetoric of patriotism, it also hints at the limits of patriotism, at the distortions it imposes, the divisions and differences it fails to acknowledge, and the violence on which it depends.

In *Henry V*, Shakespeare constantly asks us to contrast different versions of history: we are given an official story, sponsored by Henry and the Chorus, but we are also confronted with a series of other perspectives that do not easily confirm what Henry and the Chorus tell us. For example, throughout the play, Henry insists that God is on his side. He exhorts his soldiers to cry "God for Harry, England, and Saint George!" (3.1.34), interprets the discovery of a conspiracy against him as a providential sign that "every rub" will be "smoothèd on our way" (2.2.186), and insists that the battle of Agincourt is God's own victory—even enforcing this claim with a harsh punishment:

"be it death proclaimèd through our host / To boast of this or take that praise from God / Which is his only" (4.8.110–112). But in a crucial speech Henry also gives a very different perspective on what this war means. Before the walls of Harfleur, he threatens that, if the citizens do not surrender, his soldiers will rape and murder them, dragging women by their hair and old men by their beards, even spitting infants on pikes. He concludes by comparing his soldiers to those of Herod, massacring the first-born sons of Israel (3.3.38–41). When the city yields, Henry commands his soldiers to "Use mercy"; but the violence of his rhetoric, and his invocation of war as "impious," unholy, necessarily complicates his later insistence that God fights for him (4.8.102–108). It is no accident that many performances of the play cut this speech quite radically: we necessarily come away from it with a more complex, more ambivalent understanding of what is taking place.

The rhetoric of heroic war also often collides awkwardly with what we actually see in this play. The first two scenes of Act One show some of the deliberations that precede Henry's decision to go to war. In Act One, scene two, Henry asks the Archbishop of Canterbury about the legitimacy of his claim to France: "justly and religiously unfold / Why the law Salic that they have in France / Or should or should not bar us in our claim" (1.2.10–12). Here we see a king ordering his policy according to the most truthful advice he can seek, a king who will not undertake war unless it is justified by both human and divine law. Just before this, however, in Act One, scene one, we see Canterbury consulting with another bishop about a law in parliament that proposes to strip the church's temporal lands. Wondering what is to be done, the two churchmen recall the king's wild youth—dramatized in the *Henry IV* plays—and his sudden "reformation" when he inherited the throne. They praise him as a scholar, an analyst of government policy, a compelling rhetorician, and "a true lover of the holy Church" (24). But they appeal not to his sense of justice or his love of the church but to his financial need: they offer to subsidize the war. The advice that Canterbury gives in Act One, scene two, as we know by the time we get there, is given out of financial motives. Instead of epic action we get compromising intrigue.

Henry himself has other motives for going to war than those spelled out by Canterbury in Act One, scene two. At the end of *Henry IV, Part Two*, the dying king advised his son to "busy giddy minds / With foreign quarrels"(4.3.342–343). Both Henry IV and Henry V had ample reason to want to keep "giddy minds" busy. The older king came to power by taking it, and neither of them could easily claim, as Richard II had done, that they ruled England by God's will: "Not all the water in the rough rude sea / Can wash the balm off from an anointed king." It turned out not to be true for Richard, but the fact of his deposition, if it brought Henry IV and his son to power, also faced them with a problem of legitimacy: on what basis, other than force alone, could they claim rightful rule?

There is no civil war in *Henry V*, but there is the possibility of one. In Act Two, scene two, Henry confronts Cambridge, Scroop, and Grey, claiming that they have betrayed him for "foreign hire" (2.2.98). Cambridge denies that money had anything to do with his actions—"For me, the gold of France did not seduce"—although he does not spell out his real motives, and Henry does not follow up on this cryptic remark (2.2.153). In fact, Cambridge was the brother-in-law of a rival claimant to the English throne, Edmund, Earl of March, and both he and Scroop were related to close adherents of Richard II. In *Henry VI, Part One*, Shakespeare gave a very different explanation for Cambridge's execution: there, the Earl of March tells Cambridge's son that his father "Levied an army, weening to redeem / And have installed me in the diadem" (2.5.88–89). In other words, this is a conspiracy to restore the monarchy to the House of York; that Henry refuses to see it as such, calling it instead "Another fall of man," perhaps tells us something about his particular combination of earnest moralism and willful blindness (2.2.140).

Henry clearly wants to tell a story about English heroism, and the Chorus collaborates with him; but Shakespeare also gives us enough material to tell a rather different story. Henry has by this point in the tetralogy long shown himself to be an able manipulator of public images. In the _Henry IV_ plays, the young Prince Hal reveled in various kinds of role play and performance; the culminating performance takes place at the end of _Henry IV, Part Two_, when the young prince, who has spent his life in the taverns of Eastcheap, presents himself to the court as the new king. It is a nervous moment, both because of England's recent history of civil war and because of Henry's own reputation. Henry plays the part fully, announcing that he will rule by law, and demonstrating how he has changed by publicly dismissing Falstaff, the companion of his Eastcheap life, with a cold, "I know thee not, old man" (5.5.46).

Perhaps Falstaff had to be turned away for Henry to rule well: just before their final encounter, he was joyfully imagining the life of criminal impunity he would lead as the best friend of a king. Certainly, for the _appearance_ of good government, Falstaff must be banished. But this is also a cruel demand, and its memory lingers painfully in _Henry V_. In Act Two, scene one, the Hostess tells us that Falstaff is sick, perhaps dying, and lays the blame on Henry: "The King has killed his heart" (2.1.83). In Act Two, scene three, she quite movingly describes Falstaff's death, confronting us again with the personal cost of Henry's transformation (2.3.8–24). The memory of this abandonment pursues the king even at Agincourt, where Fluellen compares Henry and Alexander the Great, not for military skill but for their responsibility for the deaths of friends: "As Alexander killed his friend Cleitus, being in his ales and his cups, so also Harry Monmouth, being in his right wits and his good judgments, turned away the fat knight with the great-belly doublet" (4.7.42–46).

The issue here concerns more than just how we respond to Henry as a character: Henry's repudiation of Falstaff is motivated by his deep investment in *playing the part* of king, in performing what it is to be a king. This sense of performance effectively defines his understanding of politics. Henry is a consummate actor, a rhetorician. And it may be that power, after the deposition of Richard II, is necessarily a performance. Political legitimacy is no longer a question of God-given authority but a matter on the one hand of armies, strategy, and calculation, and on the other hand of charismatic leadership—that is, finally, of role playing. To be king one must be able to play the role of king. The Chorus articulates this as a principle from the very beginning: "'tis your thoughts that now must deck our kings" (1.0.28). This is, on the one hand, a point about the distance between reality and theater, an insistence that the audience must participate in creating the play in their imagination—"be kind, / And eke out our performance with your mind" (3.0.34–35). The Chorus focuses on the limits of theater, even if, paradoxically, it thereby invites our recognition of the theater's power to solicit the imagination, its "imaginary puissance" (1.0.25). But it also implies that kings, like actors, are "decked"—dressed, presented, turned into meaningful figures—by the imaginations of the public. Kingship becomes theater, in this most self-consciously theatrical of Shakespeare's plays.

In some ways, Henry has been preparing for this role all his life. In the opening scene, the bishops marveled at his "reformation," but we know from the *Henry IV* plays that this is a deliberately cultivated effect. In his first soliloquy in *Henry IV, Part One,* Henry anticipates the wonder his transformation will inspire: "like bright metal on a sullen ground, / My reformation, glitt'ring o'er my fault, / Shall show more goodly" (1.2.201–203). From the first time we see him, Henry shows himself aware of what it is to play a role. In Eastcheap, he learned to "drink with any tinker in his own language," a skill that stays with him as king: he calls his soldiers "dear friends" and "brothers," and himself "Harry." Richard II thought himself chosen to be king by God, and Henry IV stayed nervously out of public view to increase the people's awe. Henry V cultivates his public, earning its love by seeming to min-imize the distance between king and subject.

This populism is what the great battlefield speeches—the most memorable parts of the play—especially emphasize: the Eng-lish army is a "band of brothers" struggling together in the same cause (4.3.60). The struggle, Henry promises, will equalize them: "he today that sheds his blood with me / Shall be my brother; be he ne'er so vile, / This day shall gentle his condition" (4.3.61–63). What Henry imagines is not only a dynastic state held together by the claims of genealogical legitimacy but also a nation-state, a state unified by horizontal bonds and affections: whatever the differences between them, Henry urges, his army is united in a shared Englishness. National sentiment enables him to sidestep the question of legitimacy in order to turn himself into a symbol of English unity, imagined not in terms of fathers and sons but of brothers: in this way, he seeks to evade the memory of his father's crime.

But when Agincourt is over, the English dead are counted not as brothers but in terms of continuing social divisions: only the titled gentlemen are listed, while the others are dismissed with a cold phrase: "None else of name" (4.8.101). Henry's promises before the battle, like his violent threats at Harfleur, turn out to be mere rheto-ric. The question of class divisions among the English "brothers" is also opened by the scene in which Henry, on the eve of Agincourt, goes in disguise among his soldiers, ostensibly to encourage them, as the Chorus says; but in fact he gets into a heated debate with a sol-dier named Williams over the question of the king's responsibility for those who die in battle: Williams argues that if Henry has let so many die in a bad cause, he will have to answer for it at the "Latter Day," when the dead will appear to accuse him, "some swearing, some crying for a surgeon, some upon their wives left poor behind them, some upon the debts they owe, some upon their children rawly left" (4.1.133–136).

In Williams we get one more perspective calling this war into question, although it is one that seems to make no impact on Henry: he evades Williams's question, and in the ensuing soliloquy never worries about the justice of this war, only asking God not to think today of his father's "fault," the usurpation. But from Williams, we—if not Henry—learn that despite the rhetoric of fraternal unity, the English army is in fact significantly divided. Other fractures are revealed in Act Three, scene two, in which we see an at times acrimonious conversation between four captains, Gower, Fluellen, Macmorris, and Jamy—an Englishman, a Welshman, an Irishman, and a Scot, representing the four nations that made up the British islands and that, with the accession of James VI of Scotland as Elizabeth's probable successor already on the horizon in 1599, would in one way or another all owe their allegiance to the monarch in London. But if Wales embodies a supposedly comfortable merging of peoples—the Tudors claimed Welsh descent, although they also passed laws banning official uses of the Welsh language—Ireland embodies an intractable problem. Under Elizabeth, English armies were almost constantly at war in Ireland, suppressing what they saw as rebellions; *Henry V* was probably first performed during one such Irish war, in the summer of 1599. The problem of Ireland led English authors sometimes to fantasize that the difference between English and Irish might disappear, especially if certain Irish cultural practices were eradicated, and sometimes to advocate virtually genocidal political projects. The appearance of MacMorris among Henry's soldiers opens up an enormous problem for any understanding of national identity in this play: this, perhaps, is the meaning of MacMorris's inscrutable but angry question to Fluellen, "What ish my nation?" (3.2.114).

The question of cultural difference haunts the end of the play, where we are offered the hope of a resolution of Henry's war that moves beyond victory on the battlefield to a real union of two peoples, a "spousal" of kingdoms, so that "English may as French, French

Englishmen, / Receive each other," as Queen Isabel puts it (5.2.348, 353–354). Henry similarly, if more bluntly, proposes to Katherine that they will "compound a boy, half French, half English," who will go abroad and fight a common enemy, "the Turk"—apparently learning from Henry's own strategy of creating unity through foreign wars and perhaps also fulfilling Henry IV's dream of leading a new crusade (201–203). Not only must Irish, Scots, and Welsh merge into English, but the difference of French and English must also be accommodated.

The play's insistent rendering of accented speech quietly suggests the limits of such cross-cultural translation. We are several times invited to laugh at comically distorted versions of English and are thereby reminded that not all of Henry's soldiers participate equally in Englishness. After the scenes at Harfleur, we also see Katherine learning to speak English, apparently understanding that if France loses this war she herself will be one of the terms of the treaty: she is, as Henry says in Act Five, "our capital demand," since it is through his marriage to her that his heirs will be kings of France (5.2.96). But the English that Katherine speaks is constantly marred by inadvertent sexual puns—puns that remind us that this woman's body is one of the spoils of war. That this scene comes so soon after Henry's threats of rape at Harfleur invites us to see the conquest itself as a kind of rape, both metaphorical—in a way that early modern readers were ready to perceive, given the insistent metaphors of love as conquest in the literature of the time—and even literal. When Henry asks her in Act Five whether she will take him as her husband, she answers that this depends on her father; Henry's reply—"Nay, it will please him well, Kate. It shall please him, Kate"—reminds us that the wills of both father and daughter have been overruled by war (5.2.241–242).

The fifth act, scene two, has often seemed a strange coda for the action of this most military of Shakespeare's histories. The play suddenly shifts to a new dramatic idiom, the romantic comedy, as it shows us Henry courting a woman he has already "won" on the battlefield. The appeal to romance seeks to end the play on a note of reconciliation: if the dominant image of Henry's speech at Harfleur is rape, here romance becomes the basis of a new language of unity. But the kingdoms will not stay united, as the epilogue tells us. Moreover, although in Act Five, scene two, we see Henry convincingly playing his new role of awkward lover, we cannot forget that this would-be romance is really the result of a military victory, as Katherine reminds us when she asks, "Is it possible dat I should love de *ennemi* of France?" (166). Henry tries to step around this question with a piece of sophistry—"Kate, when France is mine and I am yours, then yours is France and you are mine"—but she responds with a question that may simply indicate her inability to understand his English but may also dismiss his words as mere rhetoric: "I cannot tell wat is dat" (173). As she tells him earlier, *"Les langues des hommes sont pleines de tromperies"*— the speech of men is full of tricks (114). That may be the most telling comment of all about this player-king, who seeks to keep his rule by the power of his own rhetorical performances. It is a testament to the breadth of Shakespeare's dramatic vision that he lets us see both Henry's consummate skill as linguist and actor and the questions, conflicts, and violence that Henry would have us forget as we listen to him.

Shakespeare and His England
by David Scott Kastan

hakespeare is a household name, one of those few that don't need a first name to be instantly recognized. His first name was, of course, William, and he (and it, in its Latin form, *Gulielmus*) first came to public notice on April 26, 1564, when his baptism was recorded in the parish church of Stratford-upon-Avon, a small market town about ninety miles northwest of London. It isn't known exactly when he was born, although traditionally his birthday is taken to be April 23rd. It is a convenient date (perhaps too convenient) because that was the date of his death in 1616, as well as the date of St. George's Day, the annual feast day of England's patron saint. It is possible Shakespeare was born on the 23rd; no doubt he was born within a day or two of that date. In a time of high rates of infant mortality, parents would not wait long after a baby's birth for the baptism. Twenty percent of all children would die before their first birthday.

Life in 1564, not just for infants, was conspicuously vulnerable. If one lived to age fifteen, one was likely to live into one's fifties, but probably no more than 60 percent of those born lived past their mid-teens. Whole towns could be ravaged by epidemic disease. In 1563, the year before Shakespeare was born, an outbreak of plague claimed over one third of the population of London. Fire, too, was a constant threat; the thatched roofs of many houses were highly flammable, as well as offering handy nesting places for insects and rats. Serious crop failures in several years of the decade of the 1560s created food shortages, severe enough in many cases to lead to the starvation of the elderly and the infirm, and lowering the resistances of many others so that between 1536 and 1560 influenza claimed over 200,000 lives.

Shakespeare's own family in many ways reflected these unsettling realities. He was one of eight children, two of whom did not survive their first year, one of whom died at age eight; one lived to twenty-seven, while the four surviving siblings died at ages ranging from Edmund's thirty-nine to William's own fifty-two years. William married at an unusually early age. He was only eighteen, though his wife was twenty-six, almost exactly the norm of the day for women, though men normally married also in their mid- to late twenties. Shakespeare's wife Anne was already pregnant at the time that the marriage was formally confirmed, and a daughter, Susanna, was born six months later, in May 1583. Two years later, she gave birth to twins, Hamnet and Judith. Hamnet would die in his eleventh year.

If life was always at risk from what Shakespeare would later call "the thousand natural shocks / That flesh is heir to" (*Hamlet*, 3.1.61–62), the incessant threats to peace were no less unnerving, if usually less immediately life threatening. There were almost daily rumors of foreign invasion and civil war as the Protestant Queen Elizabeth assumed the crown in 1558 upon the death of her Catholic half sister, Mary. Mary's reign had been marked by the public burnings of Protestant "heretics," by the seeming subordination of England to Spain, and by a commitment to a ruinous war with France, that, among its other effects, fueled inflation and encouraged a debasing of the currency. If, for many, Elizabeth represented the hopes for a peaceful and prosperous Protestant future, it seemed unlikely in the early days of her rule that the young monarch could hold her England together against the twin menace of the powerful Catholic monarchies of Europe and the significant part of her own population who were reluctant to give up their old faith. No wonder the Queen's principal secretary saw England in the early years of Elizabeth's rule as a land surrounded by "perils many, great and imminent."

In Stratford-upon-Avon, it might often have been easy to forget what threatened from without. The simple rural life, shared by about 90 percent of the English populace, had its reassuring natural rhythms and delights. Life was structured by the daily rising and setting of the sun, and by the change of seasons. Crops were planted and harvested; livestock was bred, its young delivered; sheep were sheared, some livestock slaughtered. Market days and fairs saw the produce and crafts of the town arrayed as people came to sell and shop—and be entertained by musicians, dancers, and troupes of actors. But even in Stratford, the lurking tensions and dangers could be daily sensed. A few months before Shakespeare was born, there had been a shocking "defacing" of images in the church, as workmen, not content merely to whitewash over the religious paintings decorating the interior as they were ordered, gouged large holes in those felt to be too "Catholic"; a few months after Shakespeare's birth, the register of the same church records another deadly outbreak of plague. The sleepy market town on the northern bank of the gently flowing river Avon was not immune from the menace of the world that surrounded it.

This was the world into which Shakespeare was born. England at his birth was still poor and backward, a fringe nation on the periphery of Europe. English itself was a minor language, hardly spoken outside of the country's borders. Religious tension was inescapable, as the old Catholic faith was trying determinedly to hold on, even as Protestantism was once again anxiously trying to establish itself as the national religion. The country knew itself vulnerable to serious threats both from without and from within. In 1562, the young Queen, upon whom so many people's hopes rested, almost fell victim to smallpox, and in 1569 a revolt of the Northern earls tried to remove her from power and restore Catholicism as the national religion. The following year, Pope

Pius V pronounced the excommunication of "Elizabeth, the pretended queen of England" and forbade Catholic subjects obedience to the monarch on pain of their own excommunication. "Now we are in an evil way and going to the devil," wrote one clergyman, "and have all nations in our necks."

It was a world of dearth, danger, and domestic unrest. Yet it would soon dramatically change, and Shakespeare's literary contribution would, for future generations, come to be seen as a significant measure of England's remarkable transformation. In the course of Shakespeare's life, England, hitherto an unsophisticated and underdeveloped backwater acting as a bit player in the momentous political dramas taking place on the European continent, became a confident, prosperous, global presence. But this new world was only accidentally, as it is often known today, "The Age of Shakespeare." To the degree that historical change rests in the hands of any individual, credit must be given to the Queen. This new world arguably was "The Age of Elizabeth," even if it was not the Elizabethan Golden Age, as it has often been portrayed.

The young Queen quickly imposed her personality upon the nation. She had talented councilors around her, all with strong ties to her of friendship or blood, but the direction of government was her own. She was strong willed and cautious, certain of her right to rule and convinced that stability was her greatest responsibility. The result may very well have been, as historians have often charged, that important issues facing England were never dealt with head-on and left to her successors to settle, but it meant also that she was able to keep her England unified and for the most part at peace.

Religion posed her greatest challenge, though it is important to keep in mind that in this period, as an official at Elizabeth's court said, "Religion and the commonwealth cannot be parted asunder." Faith then was not the largely voluntary commitment it is today, nor was there any idea of some separation of church and state. Religion was literally a matter of life and death, of salvation and damnation, and the Church was the Church of England. Obedience to it was not only a matter of conscience but also of law. It was the single issue on which the nation was most likely to be torn apart.

Elizabeth's great achievement was that she was successful in ensuring that the Church of England became formally a Protestant Church, but she did so without either driving most of her Catholic subjects to sedition or alienating the more radical Protestant community. The so-called "Elizabethan Settlement" forged a broad Christian community of what has been called prayer-book Protestantism, even as many of its practitioners retained, as a clergyman said, "still a smack and savor of popish principles." If there were forces on both sides who were uncomfortable with the Settlement—committed Protestants, who wanted to do away with all vestiges of the old faith, and convinced Catholics, who continued to swear their allegiance to Rome—the majority of the country, as she hoped, found ways to live comfortably both within the law and within their faith. In 1571, she wrote to the Duke of Anjou that the forms of worship she recommended would "not properly compel any man to alter his opinion in the great matters now in controversy in the Church." The official toleration of religious ambiguity, as well as the familiar experience of an official change of state religion accompanying the crowning of a new monarch, produced a world where the familiar labels of Protestant and Catholic failed to define the forms of faith that most English people practiced. But for Elizabeth, most matters of faith could be left to individuals, as long as the Church itself, and Elizabeth's position at its head, would remain unchallenged.

In international affairs, she was no less successful with her pragmatism and willingness to pursue limited goals. A complex mix of prudential concerns about religion, the economy, and national security drove her foreign policy. She did not have imperial ambitions; in the main, she wanted only to be sure there would be no invasion of England and to encourage English trade. In the event, both goals brought England into conflict with Spain, determining the increasingly anti-Catholic tendencies of English foreign policy and, almost accidentally, England's emergence as a world power. When Elizabeth came to the throne, England was in many ways a mere satellite nation to the Netherlands, which was part of the Hapsburg Empire that the Catholic Philip II (who had briefly and unhappily been married to her predecessor and half sister, Queen Mary) ruled from Spain; by the end of her reign England was Spain's most bitter rival.

The transformation of Spain from ally to enemy came in a series of small steps (or missteps), no one of which was intended to produce what in the end came to pass. A series of posturings and provocations on both sides led to the rupture. In 1568, things moved to their breaking point, as the English confiscated a large shipment of gold that the Spanish were sending to their troops in the Netherlands. The following year saw the revolt of the Catholic earls in Northern England, followed by the papal excommunication of the Queen in 1570, both of which were by many in England assumed to be at the initiative, or at very least with the tacit support, of Philip. In fact he was not involved, but England under Elizabeth would never again think of Spain as a loyal friend or reliable ally. Indeed, Spain quickly became its mortal enemy. Protestant Dutch rebels had been opposing the Spanish domination of the Netherlands since the early 1560s, but, other than periodic financial support, Elizabeth had done little to encourage them. But in 1585, she sent troops under the command of the Earl of Leicester to support the Dutch rebels against the Spanish. Philip decided then to launch a full-scale attack on England, with the aim of deposing Elizabeth and restoring the Catholic faith. An English assault on Cadiz in 1587 destroyed a number of Spanish ships, postponing Philip's plans, but in the summer of 1588 the mightiest navy in the world, Philip's grand armada, with 132 ships and 30,493 sailors and troops, sailed for England.

By all rights, it should have been a successful invasion, but a combination of questionable Spanish tactics and a fortunate shift of wind resulted in one of England's greatest victories. The English had twice failed to intercept the armada off the coast of Portugal, and the Spanish fleet made its way to England, almost catching the English ships resupplying in Plymouth. The English navy was on its heels, when conveniently the Spanish admiral decided to anchor in the English Channel off the French port of Calais to wait for additional troops coming from the Netherlands. The English attacked with fireships, sinking four Spanish galleons, and strong winds from the south prevented an effective counterattack from the Spanish. The Spanish fleet was pushed into the North Sea, where it regrouped and decided its safest course was to attempt the difficult voyage home around Scotland and Ireland, losing almost half its ships on the way. For many in England the improbable victory was a miracle, evidence of God's favor for Elizabeth and the Protestant nation. Though war with Spain would not end for another fifteen years, the victory over the armada turned England almost overnight into a major world power, buoyed by confidence that they were chosen by God and, more tangibly, by a navy that could compete for control of the seas.

From a backward and insignificant Hapsburg satellite, Elizabeth's England had become, almost by accident, the leader of Protestant Europe. But if the victory over the armada signaled England's new place in the world, it hardly marked the end of England's travails. The economy, which initially was fueled by the military buildup, in the early 1590s fell victim to inflation, heavy taxation to support the war with Spain, the inevitable wartime disruptions of trade, as well as crop failures and a general economic downturn in Europe. Ireland, over which England had been attempting to impose its rule since 1168, continued to be a source of trouble and great expense (in some years costing the crown nearly one fifth of its total revenues). Even when the most organized of the rebellions, begun in 1594 and led by Hugh O'Neill, Earl of Tyrone, formally ended in 1603, peace and stability had not been achieved.

But perhaps the greatest instability came from the uncertainty over the succession, an uncertainty that marked Elizabeth's reign from its beginning. Her near death from smallpox in 1562 reminded the nation that an unmarried queen could not insure the succession, and Elizabeth was under constant pressure to marry and produce an heir. She was always aware of and deeply resented the pressure, announcing as early as 1559: "this shall be for me sufficient that a marble stone shall declare that a queen, having reigned such a time, lived and died a virgin." If, however, it was for her "sufficient," it was not so for her advisors and for much of the nation, who hoped she would wed. Arguably Elizabeth was the wiser, knowing that her unmarried hand was a political advantage, allowing her to diffuse threats or create alliances with the seeming possibility of a match. But as with so much in her reign, the strategy bought temporary stability at the price of longer-term solutions.

By the mid 1590s, it was clear that she would die unmarried and without an heir, and various candidates were positioning themselves to succeed her. Enough anxiety was produced that all published debate about the succession was forbidden by law. There was no direct descendant of the English crown to claim rule, and all the claimants had to reach well back into their family history to find some legitimacy. The best genealogical claim belonged to King James VI of Scotland. His mother, Mary, Queen of Scots, was the granddaughter of James IV of Scotland and Margaret Tudor, sister to Elizabeth's father, Henry VIII. Though James had right on his side, he was, it must be remembered, a foreigner. Scotland shared the island with England but was a separate nation. Great Britain, the union of England and Scotland, would not exist formally until 1707, but with Elizabeth's death early in the morning of March 24, 1603, surprisingly uneventfully the thirty-seven-year-old James succeeded to the English throne. Two nations, one king: King James VI of Scotland, King James I of England.

Most of his English subjects initially greeted the announcement of their new monarch with delight, relieved that the crown had successfully been transferred without any major disruption and reassured that the new King was married with two living sons. However, quickly many became disenchanted with a foreign King who spoke English with a heavy accent, and dismayed even further by the influx of Scots in positions of power. Nonetheless, the new King's greatest political liability may well have been less a matter of nationality than of temperament: he had none of Elizabeth's skill and ease in publicly wooing her subjects. The Venetian ambassador wrote back to the doge that the new King was unwilling to "caress the people, nor make them that good cheer the late Queen did, whereby she won their loves."

He was aloof and largely uninterested in the daily activities of governing, but he was interested in political theory and strongly committed to the cause of peace. Although a steadfast Protestant, he lacked the reflexive anti-Catholicism of many of his subjects. In England, he achieved a broadly consensual community of Protestants. The so-called King James Bible, the famous translation published first in 1611, was the result of a widespread desire to have an English Bible that spoke to all the nation, transcending the religious divisions that had placed three different translations in the hands of his subjects. Internationally, he styled himself *Rex Pacificus* (the peace-loving king). In 1604, the Treaty of London brought Elizabeth's war with Spain formally to an end, and over the next decade he worked to bring about political marriages that might cement stable alliances. In 1613, he married his daughter to the leader of the German Protestants, while the following year he began discussions with Catholic Spain to marry his son to the Infanta Maria. After some ten years of negotiations, James's hopes for what was known as the Spanish match were finally abandoned, much to the delight of the nation, whose long-felt fear and hatred for Spain outweighed the subtle political logic behind the plan.

But if James sought stability and peace, and for the most part succeeded in his aims (at least until 1618, when the bitter religio-political conflicts on the European continent swirled well out of the King's control), he never really achieved concord and cohesion. He ruled over two kingdoms that did not know, like, or even want to understand one another, and his rule did little to bring them closer together. His England remained separate from his Scotland, even as he ruled over both. And even his England remained self divided, as in truth it always was under Elizabeth, ever more a nation of prosperity and influence but still one forged out of deep-rooted divisions of means, faiths, and allegiances that made the very nature of English identity a matter of confusion and concern. Arguably this is the very condition of great drama—sufficient peace and prosperity to support a theater industry and sufficient provocation in the troubling uncertainties about what the nation was and what fundamentally mattered to its people to inspire plays that would offer tentative solutions or at the very least make the troubling questions articulate and moving.

Nine years before James would die in 1625, Shakespeare died, having returned from London to the small market town in which he was born. If London, now a thriving modern metropolis of well over 200,000 people, had, like the nation itself, been transformed in the course of his life, the Warwickshire market town still was much the same. The house in which Shakespeare was born still stood, as did the church in which he was baptized and the school in which he learned to read and write. The river Avon still ran slowly along the town's southern limits. What had changed was that Shakespeare was now its most famous citizen, and, although it would take more than another 100 years to fully achieve this, he would in time become England's, for having turned the great ethical, social, and political issues of his own age into plays that would live forever.

William Shakespeare: A Chronology

1558	**November 17: Queen Elizabeth crowned**
1564	April 26: Shakespeare baptized, third child born to John Shakespeare and Mary Arden
1564	**May 27: Death of Jean Calvin in Geneva**
1565	John Shakespeare elected alderman in Stratford-upon-Avon
1568	**Publication of the Bishops' Bible**
1568	September 4: John Shakespeare elected Bailiff of Stratford-upon-Avon
1569	**Northern Rebellion**
1570	**Queen Elizabeth excommunicated by the Pope**
1572	**August 24: St. Bartholomew's Day Massacre in Paris**
1576	**The Theatre is built in Shoreditch**
1577–1580	**Sir Francis Drake sails around the world**
1582	November 27: Shakespeare and Anne Hathaway married (Shakespeare is 18)
1583	Queen's Men formed
1583	May 26: Shakespeare's daughter, Susanna, baptized
1584	**Failure of the Virginia Colony**

1585 February 2: Twins, Hamnet and Judith, baptized (Shakespeare is 20)

1586 Babington Plot to dethrone Elizabeth and replace her with Mary, Queen of Scots

1587 February 8: Execution of Mary, Queen of Scots

1587 Rose Theatre built

1588 August: Defeat of the Spanish armada (Shakespeare is 24)

1588 September 4: Death of Robert Dudley, Earl of Leicester

1590 First three books of Spenser's *Faerie Queene* published; Marlowe's *Tamburlaine* published

1592 March 3: *Henry VI, Part One* performed at the Rose Theatre (Shakespeare is 27)

1593 February–November: Theaters closed because of plague

1593 Publication of *Venus and Adonis*

1594 Publication of *Titus Andronicus*, first play by Shakespeare to appear in print (though anonymously)

1594 Lord Chamberlain's Men formed

1595 March 15: Payment made to Shakespeare, Will Kemp, and Richard Burbage for performances at court in December, 1594

1595 Swan Theatre built

1596 Books 4–6 of *The Faerie Queene* published

1596 August 11: Burial of Shakespeare's son, Hamnet (Shakespeare is 32)

1596–1599 Shakespeare living in St. Helen's, Bishopsgate, London

1596 October 20: Grant of Arms to John Shakespeare

| 1597 | May 4: Shakespeare purchases New Place, one of the two largest houses in Stratford (Shakespeare is 33) |

1598   Publication of *Love's Labor's Lost*, first extant play with Shakespeare's name on the title page

1598   Publication of Francis Meres's *Palladis Tamia*, citing Shakespeare as "the best for Comedy and Tragedy" among English writers

1599   Opening of the Globe Theatre

1601   February 7: Lord Chamberlain's Men paid 40 shillings to play *Richard II* by supporters of the Earl of Essex, the day before his abortive rebellion

1601   February 17: Execution of Robert Devereaux, Earl of Essex

1601   September 8: Burial of John Shakespeare

1602   May 1: Shakespeare buys 107 acres of farmland in Stratford

1603   March 24: Queen Elizabeth dies; James VI of Scotland succeeds as James I of England (Shakespeare is 39)

1603   May 19: Lord Chamberlain's Men reformed as the King's Men

1604   Shakespeare living with the Mountjoys, a French Huguenot family, in Cripplegate, London

1604   First edition of Marlowe's *Dr. Faustus* published (written c. 1589)

1604   March 15: Shakespeare named among "players" given scarlet cloth to wear at royal procession of King James

1604   Publication of authorized version of *Hamlet* (Shakespeare is 40)

1605   Gunpowder Plot

1605   June 5: Marriage of Susanna Shakespeare to John Hall

1608   Publication of *King Lear* (Shakespeare is 44)

1608–1609   Acquisition of indoor Blackfriars Theatre by King's Men

1609   *Sonnets* published

1611   King James Bible published (Shakespeare is 47)

1612   November 6: Death of Henry, eldest son of King James

1613   February 14: Marriage of King James's daughter Elizabeth to Frederick, the Elector Palatine

1613   March 10: Shakespeare, with some associates, buys gatehouse in Blackfriars, London

1613   June 29: Fire burns the Globe Theatre

1614   Rebuilt Globe reopens

1616   February 10: Marriage of Judith Shakespeare to Thomas Quiney

1616   March 25: Shakespeare's will signed

1616   April 23: Shakespeare dies (age 52)

1616   April 23: Cervantes dies in Madrid

1616   April 25: Shakespeare buried in Holy Trinity Church in Stratford-upon-Avon

1623   August 6: Death of Anne Shakespeare

1623   October: Prince Charles, King James's son, returns from Madrid, having failed to arrange his marriage to Maria Anna, Infanta of Spain

1623   First Folio published with 36 plays (18 never previously published)

Words, Words, Words: Understanding Shakespeare's Language
by David Scott Kastan

t is silly to pretend that it is easy to read Shakespeare. Reading Shakespeare isn't like picking up a copy of *USA Today* or *The New Yorker*, or even F. Scott Fitzgerald's *Great Gatsby* or Toni Morrison's *Beloved*. It is hard work, because the language is often unfamiliar to us and because it is more concentrated than we are used to. In the theater it is usually a bit easier. Actors can clarify meanings with gestures and actions, allowing us to get the general sense of what is going on, if not every nuance of the language that is spoken. "Action is eloquence," as Volumnia puts it in *Coriolanus*, "and the eyes of th' ignorant / More learnèd than the ears" (3.276–277). Yet the real greatness of Shakespeare rests not on "the general sense" of his plays but on the specificity and suggestiveness of the words in which they are written. It is through language that the plays' full dramatic power is realized, and it is that rich and robust language, often pushed by Shakespeare to the very limits of intelligibility, that we must learn to understand. But we can come to understand it (and enjoy it), and this essay is designed to help.

Even experienced readers and playgoers need help. They often find that his words are difficult to comprehend. Shakespeare sometimes uses words no longer current in English or with meanings that have changed. He regularly multiplies words where seemingly one might do as well or even better. He characteristically writes sentences that are syntactically complicated and imaginatively dense. And it isn't just we, removed by some 400 years from his world, who find him difficult to read; in his own time, his friends and fellow actors knew Shakespeare was hard. As two of them, John Hemings and Henry Condell, put it in their prefatory remarks to Shakespeare's First Folio in 1623, "read him, therefore, and again and again; and if then you do not like him, surely you are in some manifest danger not to understand him."

From the very beginning, then, it was obvious that the plays both deserve and demand not only careful reading but continued re-reading—and that not to read Shakespeare with all the attention a reader can bring to bear on the language is almost to guarantee that a reader will not "understand him" and remain among those who "do not like him." But Shakespeare's colleagues were nonetheless confident that the plays exerted an attraction strong enough to ensure and reward the concentration of their readers, confident, as they say, that in them "you will find enough, both to draw and hold you." The plays do exert a kind of magnetic pull, and have successfully drawn in and held readers for over 400 years.

Once we are drawn in, we confront a world of words that does not always immediately yield its delights; but it will—once we learn to see what is demanded of us. Words in Shakespeare do a lot, arguably more than anyone else has ever asked them to do. In part, it is because he needed his words to do many things at once. His stage had no sets and few props, so his words are all we have to enable us to imagine what his characters see. And they also allow us to see what the characters don't see, especially about themselves. The words are vivid and immediate, as well as complexly layered and psychologically suggestive. The difficulties they pose are not the "thee's" and "thou's" or "prithee's" and "doth's" that obviously mark the chronological distance between Shakespeare and us. When Gertrude says to Hamlet, "thou hast thy father much offended"

(3.4.8), we have no difficulty understanding her chiding, though we might miss that her use of the "thou" form of the pronoun expresses an intimacy that Hamlet pointedly refuses with his reply: "Mother, *you* have my father much offended" (3.4.9; italics mine).

Most deceptive are words that look the same as words we know but now mean something different. Words often change meanings over time. When Horatio and the soldiers try to stop Hamlet as he chases after the Ghost, Hamlet pushes past them and says, "I'll make a ghost of him that lets me" (1.4.85). It seems an odd thing to say. Why should he threaten someone who "lets" him do what he wants to do? But here "let" means "hinder," not, as it does today, "allow" (although the older meaning of the word still survives, for example, in tennis, where a "let serve" is one that is hindered by the net on its way across). There are many words that can, like this, mislead us: "his" sometimes means "its," "an" often means "if," "envy" means something more like "malice," "cousin" means more generally "kinsman," and there are others, though all are easily defined. The difficulty is that we may not stop to look thinking we already know what the word means, but in this edition a ° following the word alerts a reader that there is a gloss in the left margin, and quickly readers get used to these older meanings.

Then, of course, there is the intimidation factor—strange, polysyllabic, or Latinate words that not only are foreign to us but also must have sounded strange even to Shakespeare's audiences. When Macbeth wonders whether all the water in all the oceans of the world will be able to clean his bloody hands after the murder of Duncan, he concludes: "No; this my hand will rather / The multitudinous seas incarnadine, / Making the green one red" (2.2.64–66). Duncan's blood staining Macbeth's murderous hand is so offensive that, not merely does it resist being washed off in water, but it will "the multitudinous seas incarnadine": that is, turn the sea-green oceans blood-red. Notes will easily clarify the meaning of the two odd words, but it is worth observing that they would have been as odd to Shakespeare's readers as they are to us. The *Oxford English Dictionary (OED)* shows no use of "multitudinous" before this, and it records no use of "incarnadine" before 1591 (*Macbeth* was written about 1606). Both are new words, coined from the Latin, part of a process in Shakespeare's time where English adopted many Latinate words as a mark of its own emergence as an important vernacular language. Here they are used to express the magnitude of Macbeth's offense, a crime not only against the civil law but also against the cosmic order, and then the simple monosyllables of turning "the green one red" provide an immediate (and needed) paraphrase and register his own sickening awareness of the true hideousness of his deed.

As with "multitudinous" in *Macbeth*, Shakespeare is the source of a great many words in English. Sometimes he coined them himself, or, if he didn't invent them, he was the first person whose writing of them has survived. Some of these words have become part of our language, so common that it is hard to imagine they were not always part of it: for example, "assassination" (*Macbeth*, 1.7.2), "bedroom" (*A Midsummer Night's Dream*, 2.2.57), "countless" (*Titus Andronicus*, 5.3.59), "fashionable" (*Troilus and Cressida*, 3.3.165), "frugal" (*The Merry Wives of Windsor*, 2.1.28), "laughable" (*The Merchant of Venice*, 1.1.56), "lonely" (*Coriolanus*, 4.1.30), and "useful" (*King John*, 5.2.81). But other words that he originated were not as, to use yet another Shakespearean coinage, "successful" (*Titus Andronicus*, 1.1.66). Words like "crimeless" (*Henry VI, Part Two*, 2.4.63, meaning "innocent"), "facinorous" (*All's Well That Ends Well*, 2.3.30, meaning "extremely wicked"), and "recountment" (*As You Like It*, 4.3.141, meaning "narrative" or "account") have, without much resistance, slipped into oblivion. Clearly Shakespeare liked words, even unwieldy ones. His working vocabulary, about 18,000 words, is staggering, larger than almost any other English writer, and he seems to be the first person to use in print about 1,000 of these. Whether he coined the new words himself or was intrigued by the new words he heard in the streets of London doesn't really matter; the point is that he was remarkably alert to and engaged with a dynamic language that was expanding in response to England's own expanding contact with the world around it.

But it is neither new words nor old ones that are the source of the greatest difficulty of Shakespeare's language. The real difficulty (and the real delight) comes in trying to see how he uses the words, how he endows them with more than their denotative meanings. Why, for example, does Macbeth say that he hopes that the "sure and firm-set earth" (2.1.56) will not hear his steps as he goes forward to murder Duncan? Here "sure" and "firm-set" mean virtually the same thing: stable, secure, fixed. Why use two words? If this were a student paper, no doubt the teacher would circle one of them and write "redundant." But the redundancy is exactly what Shakespeare wants. One word would do if the purpose were to describe the solidity of the earth, but here the redundancy points to something different. It reveals something about Macbeth's mind, betraying through the doubling how deep is his awareness of the world of stable values that the terrible act he is about to commit must unsettle.

Shakespeare's words usually work this way: in part describing what the characters see and as often betraying what they feel. The example from *Macbeth* is a simple example of how this works. Shakespeare's words are carefully patterned. How one says something is every bit as important as what is said, and the conspicuous patterns that are created alert us to the fact that something more than the words' lexical sense has been put into play. Words can be coupled, as in the example above, or knit into even denser metaphorical constellations to reveal something about the speaker (which often the speaker does not know), as in Prince Hal's promise to his father that he will outdo the rebels' hero, Henry Percy (Hotspur):

> Percy is but my factor, good my lord,
> To engross up glorious deeds on my behalf.
> And I will call him to so strict account
> That he shall render every glory up,
> Yea, even the slightest worship of his time,
> Or I will tear the reckoning from his heart.
>
> *(Henry IV, Part One, 3.2.148–153)*

The Prince expresses his confidence that he will defeat Hotspur, but revealingly in a reiterated language of commercial exchange ("factor," "engross," "account," "render," "reckoning") that tells us something important both about the Prince and the ways in which he understands his world. In a play filled with references to coins and counterfeiting, the speech demonstrates not only that Hal has committed himself to the business at hand, repudiating his earlier, irresponsible tavern self, but also that he knows it is a business rather than a glorious world of chivalric achievement; he inhabits a world in which value (political as well as economic) is not intrinsic but determined by what people are willing to invest, and he proves himself a master of producing desire for what he has to offer.

Or sometimes it is not the network of imagery but the very syntax that speaks, as when Claudius announces his marriage to Hamlet's mother:

> Therefore our sometime sister, now our Queen,
> Th' imperial jointress to this warlike state,
> Have we—as 'twere with a defeated joy,
> With an auspicious and a dropping eye,
> With mirth in funeral and with dole in marriage,
> In equal scale weighing delight and dole—
> Taken to wife.   *(Hamlet, 1.2.8–14)*

All he really wants to say here is that he has married Gertrude, his former sister-in-law: "Therefore our sometime sister . . . Have we . . . Taken to wife." But the straightforward sentence gets interrupted and complicated, revealing his own discomfort with the announcement. His elaborations and intensifications of Gertrude's role ("sometime sister," "Queen," "imperial jointress"), the self-conscious rhetorical balancing of the middle three lines (indeed "in equal scale weighing delight and dole"), all declare by the all-too obvious artifice how desperate he is to hide the awkward facts behind a veneer of normalcy and propriety. The very unnaturalness of the sentence is what alerts us that we are meant to understand more than the simple relation of fact.

Why doesn't Shakespeare just say what he means? Well, he does—exactly what he means. In the example from *Hamlet* just above, Shakespeare shows us something about Claudius that Claudius doesn't know himself. Always Shakespeare's words will offer us an immediate sense of what is happening, allowing us to follow the action, but they also offer us a counterplot, pointing us to what might be behind the action, confirming or contradicting what the characters say. It is a language that shimmers with promise and possibility, opening the characters' hearts and minds to our view—and all we have to do is learn to pay attention to what is there before us.

Shakespeare's Verse

Another distinctive feature of Shakespeare's dramatic language is that much of it is in verse. Almost all of the plays mix poetry and prose, but the poetry dominates. *The Merry Wives of Windsor* has the lowest percentage (only about 13 percent verse), while *Richard II* and *King John* are written entirely in verse (the only examples, although *Henry VI, Part One* and *Part Three* have only a very few prose lines). In most of the plays, about 70 percent of the lines are written in verse.

Shakespeare's characteristic verse line is a non-rhyming iambic pentameter ("blank verse"), ten syllables with every second one stressed. In *A Midsummer Night's Dream*, Titania comes to her senses after a magic potion has led her to fall in love with an ass-headed Bottom: "Methought I was enamored of an ass" (4.1.76). Similarly, in *Romeo and Juliet*, Romeo gazes up at Juliet's window: "But soft, what light through yonder window breaks" (2.2.2). In both these examples, the line has ten syllables organized into five regular beats (each beat consisting of the stress on the second syllable of a pair, as in "But soft," the da-dum rhythm forming an "iamb"). Still, we don't hear these lines as jingles; they seem natural enough, in large part because this dominant pattern is varied in the surrounding lines.

The play of stresses indeed becomes another key to meaning, as Shakespeare alerts us to what is important. In *Measure for Measure*, Lucio urges Isabella to plead for her brother's life: "Oh, to him, to him, wench! He will relent" (2.2.129). The iambic norm (unstressed-stressed) tells us (and an actor) that the emphasis at the beginning of the line is on "to" not "him"—it is the action not the object that is being emphasized—and at the end of the line the stress falls on "will." Alternatively, the line can play against the established norm. In *Hamlet*, Claudius corrects Polonius's idea of what is bothering the Prince: "Love? His affections do not that way tend" (3.1.161). The iambic norm forces the emphasis onto "that" ("do not *that* way tend"), while the syntax forces an unexpected stress on the opening word, "Love." In the famous line, "The course of true love never did run smooth" (*A Midsummer Night's Dream*, 1.1.134), the iambic expectation is varied in both the middle and at the end of the line. Both "love" and the first syllable of "never" are stressed, as are both syllables at the end—"run smooth"—which creates a metrical foot in which both syllables are stressed (called a "spondee"). The point to notice is that the "da-dum, da-dum, da-dum, da-dum, da-dum" line is not inevitable; it merely sets an expectation against which many variations can be heard.

In fact, even the ten-syllable norm can be varied. Shakespeare sometimes writes lines with fewer or more syllables. Often there is an extra, unstressed syllable at the end of a line (a so-called "feminine ending"); sometimes there are verse lines with only nine. In *Henry IV, Part One*, King Henry replies incredulously to the rebel Worcester's claim that he hadn't "sought" the confrontation with the King: "You have not sought it. How comes it then?" (5.1.27). There are only nine syllables here (some earlier editors, seeking to "correct" the verse, added the word "sir" after the first question to regularize the line). But the pause where one expects a stressed syllable is dramatically effective, allowing the King's anger to be powerfully present in the silence.

As even these few examples show, Shakespeare's verse is unusually flexible, allowing a range of rhythmical effects. It should not be understood as a set of strict rules but as a flexible set of practices rooted in dramatic necessity. It is designed to highlight ideas and emotions, and it is based less upon rigid syllable counts than on an arrangement of stresses within an understood temporal norm, as one might expect from a poetry written to be heard in the theater rather than read on the page.

Here Follows Prose

Although the plays are dominated by verse, prose plays a significant role. Shakespeare's prose has its own rhythms, but it lacks the formal patterning of verse, and so is printed without line breaks and without the capitals that mark the beginning of a verse line. Like many of his fellow dramatists, Shakespeare tended to use prose for comic scenes, the shift from verse serving, especially in his early plays, as a social marker. Upper-class characters speak in verse; lower-class characters speak in prose. Thus, in *A Midsummer Night's Dream*, the Athenians of the court, as well as the fairies, all speak in verse, but the "rude mechanicals," Bottom and his artisan friends, all speak in prose, except for the comic verse they speak in their performance of "Pyramis and Thisbe."

As Shakespeare grew in experience, he became more flexible about the shifts from verse to prose, letting it, among other things, mark genre rather than class and measure various kinds of intensity. Prose becomes in the main the medium of comedy. The great comedies, like *Much Ado About Nothing*, *Twelfth Night*, and *As You Like It*, are all more than 50 percent prose. But even in comedy, shifts between verse and prose may be used to measure subtle emotional changes. In Act One, scene three of *The Merchant of Venice*, Shylock and Bassanio begin the scene speaking of matters of business in prose, but when Antonio enters and the deep conflict between the Christian and the Jew becomes evident, the scene shifts to verse. But prose may itself serve in moments of emotional intensity. Shylock's famous speech at 3.1.51–64, "Hath not a Jew eyes . . ." is all in prose, as is Hamlet's expression of disgust at the world ("I have of late— but wherefore I know not—lost all my mirth . . .") at 2.2.259–260. Shakespeare comes to use prose to vary the tone of a scene, as the shift from verse subtly alerts an audience or a reader to some new emotional register.

Prose becomes, as Shakespeare's art matures, not inevitably the mark of the lower classes but the mark of a salutary daily-ness. It is appropriately the medium in which letters are written, and it is the medium of a common sense that will at least challenge the potential self-deceptions of grandiloquent speech. When Rosalind mocks the excesses and artifice of Orlando's wooing in Act Four, scene one of *As You Like It*, it is in prose that she seeks something genuine in the expression of love:

> The poor world is almost six thousand years old, and in all this time there was not any man died in his own person, *videlicit* [i.e., namely], in a love cause. . . . Men have died from time to time, and worms have eaten them, but not for love.

Here the prose becomes the sound of common sense, an effective foil to the affectation of pinning poems to trees and thinking that it is real love.

It is not that prose is artless; Shakespeare's prose is no less self-conscious than his verse. The artfulness of his prose is different, of course. The seeming ordinariness of his prose is no less an effect of his artistry than is the more obvious patterning of his verse. Prose is no less serious, compressed, or indeed figurative. As with his verse, Shakespeare's prose performs numerous tasks and displays various, subtle formal qualities; and recognizing the possibilities of what it can achieve is still another way of seeing what Shakespeare puts right before us to show us what he has hidden.

Further Reading

N. F. Blake, *Shakespeare's Language: An Introduction* (New York: St. Martin's Press, 1983).

Jonathan Hope, *Shakespeare's Grammar* (London: Thomson, 2003).

Sister Miriam Joseph, *Shakespeare's Use of the Arts of Language* (New York: Columbia University Press, 1947).

M. M. Mahood, *Shakespeare's Wordplay* (London: Methuen, 1957).

Russ McDonald, *Shakespeare and the Arts of Language* (Oxford: Oxford University Press, 2001).

Brian Vickers, *The Artistry of Shakespeare's Prose* (London: Methuen, 1968).

George T. Wright, *Shakespeare's Metrical Art* (Berkeley: University of California Press, 1991).

Key to the Play Text

Symbols

°   Indicates an explanation or definition in the left-hand margin.

¹   Indicates a gloss on the page facing the play text.

[ ]   Indicates something added or changed by the editors (i.e., not in the early printed text that this edition of the play is based on).

Terms

F, Folio, or *First Folio*   The first collected edition of Shakespeare's plays, published in 1623. This edition is based on the text printed in the Folio.

Q, Quarto   The usual format in which the individual plays were first published. An unauthorized quarto version was published in 1600, with reprints in 1602 and 1619.

Henry V

William Shakespeare

List of Roles

Chorus

King Henry the Fifth
Duke of Gloucester
Duke of Bedford   } the King's brothers
Duke of Clarence
Duke of Exeter
Duke of York   the King's uncle
Earl of Salisbury   the King's cousin
Earl of Westmorland
Earl of Warwick
Earl of Huntingdon
Archbishop of Canturbury
Bishop of Ely
Richard, Earl of Cambridge } conspirators against the King
Henry Lord Scroop
Sir Thomas Grey
Sir Thomas Erpingham
Captain Fluellen
Captain Gower   } officers in the King's army
Captain Jamy
Captain MacMorris
John Bates
Alexander Court   } soldiers in the King's army
Michael Williams
Herald
Bardolph
Nym   } former friends of Falstaff, now soldiers
Pistol
Hostess   formerly Mistress Quickly, now married to Pistol
Boy   Falstaff's former page

King of France (Charles the Sixth)
Queen Isabel   his wife
Katharine   their daughter
Alice   her lady-in-waiting
Lewis, the Dauphin   son of Charles and Isabel, and heir to the throne
Duke of Burgundy
Duke of Orléans
Duke of Britaine
Duke of Berri   French noblemen
Duke of Bourbon
Constable
Grandpré
Rambures
Governor of Harfleur
Montjoy   a French herald
Ambassadors
French Soldier
Messenger
Lords, captains, soldiers, prisoners, citizens, messengers, and attendants

1 *muse of fire*

   Inspiration as brilliant as fire

2 *A kingdom for a stage*

   I.e., if only we had an actual kingdom instead of this stage

3 *like himself*

   I.e., depicted in a way that matches
   his greatness

4 *Assume the port of Mars*

   Appear with the bearing of Mars,
   the Roman god of war

5 *Crouch for employment*

   Stand in anticipation, waiting to
   do service

6 *flat unraisèd spirits*

   I.e., dull, uninspired actors (with
   unraisèd spirits punning on the rais-
   ing, or conjuring, of spirits)

7 *this cockpit*

   I.e., this playhouse; literally, a small
   circular arena for cockfighting

8 *this wooden O*

   The theater itself, here perhaps the
   Globe, built in 1599, the same year
   that *Henry V* was written. Elizabethan
   public theaters were round or nearly
   round in shape and built of timber,
   with two or three tiers of covered

galleries surrounding an open yard
into which the stage projected.
(See pp. 344–345.)

9 *the very casques*

   The actual helmets (worn during
   the battle)

10 *Agincourt*

    Battlefield where Henry defeated
    the French in 1415

11 *crooked figure may / Attest in little place a
    million*

    A zero (*crooked* means "curved"
    or "rounded") added at the end
    (*in little place*) turns 100,000 into
    1,000,000.

12 *ciphers to this great account*

    (1) zeroes in this large sum; (2)
    people of no importance in this
    important narrative

13 *imaginary forces*

    Imaginative powers

14 *The perilous narrow ocean*

    I.e., The English Channel, which
    separates the cliffs (*fronts*) at Dover
    and Calais

Act 1, Prologue

Enter [**Chorus**].

Chorus

Oh, for a muse of fire [1] that would ascend

imagination; creativity The brightest heaven of invention,°

A kingdom for a stage, [2] princes to act,

majestic And monarchs to behold the swelling° scene!

Then should the warlike Harry, like himself, [3]   5

Assume the port of Mars, [4] and at his heels,

Leashed in like hounds, should famine, sword, and
    fire

gentlemen and -women Crouch for employment. [5] But pardon, gentles° all,

The flat unraisèd spirits [6] that hath dared

stage; platform On this unworthy scaffold° to bring forth   10

So great an object. Can this cockpit [7] hold

vast The vasty° fields of France? Or may we cram

Within this wooden O [8] the very casques [9]

That did affright the air at Agincourt? [10]

Oh, pardon, since a crooked figure may   15

Attest in little place a million, [11]

And let us, ciphers to this great account, [12]

On your imaginary forces [13] work.

belt; enclosure Suppose within the girdle° of these walls

Are now confined two mighty monarchies,   20

frontiers Whose high uprearèd and abutting fronts°

The perilous narrow ocean [14] parts asunder.

Fill Piece° out our imperfections with your thoughts:

Into a thousand parts divide one man

armies And make imaginary puissance.°   25

Think, when we talk of horses, that you see them

Printing their proud hoofs i' th' receiving earth,

adorn; outfit For 'tis your thoughts that now must deck° our kings,

1   *for the which supply*

     I.e., to support you in these tasks

2   *Admit me Chorus to this history*

     Allow me to serve as a commenta-
     tor on the story. Although none of
     the speeches of the Chorus appears
     in the Quarto, the Folio prints them
     before each new act, a feature
     adapted from classical drama in
     which the chorus generally repre-
     sents the voice of the community
     or some part of the community
     (though should not there or here
     be taken as either the voice of the
     author or even as a thoroughly reli-
     able commentator on the action).

Carry them here and there, jumping o'er times,
Turning th' accomplishment of many years   30
Into an hourglass—for the which supply,[1]
Admit me Chorus to this history,[2]
Who, Prologue-like, your humble patience pray,
Gently to hear, kindly to judge, our play.   *He exits.*

1   Act 1, Scene 1

This scene is omitted in the Quarto. On stage it is often cut or significantly condensed. Nonetheless, the scene raises important questions about the ethical and legal validity of the war in France.

2   *That self bill*

That same piece of legislation. The *bill* in question would give the King possession of all *temporal lands* (lands used for non-spiritual ends) that had been bequeathed to the Church, thus threatening the Church's political and economic power.

3   *Was like, and had indeed against us passed*

Was likely to be—and would indeed have been—passed against us

4   *scambling*

Contentious; turbulent. Canterbury refers to the civil uprisings that occurred during the reign of Henry V's father, Henry IV (recounted in Shakespeare's *Henry IV, Parts One* and *Two*).

5   *farther question*

Further debate

6   *maintain*

Pay the costs of supporting

7   *esquires*

Gentlemen immediately below the rank of knight

8   *past corporal toil*

Unable to do physical work

Act 1, Scene 1[1]

*Enter the two bishops, [the Archbishop] of **Canterbury** and [the Bishop of] **Ely**.*

Canterbury
My lord, I'll tell you: that self bill[2] is urged
Which in th' eleventh year of the last King's reign
Was like, and had indeed against us passed,[3]
But that the scambling[4] and unquiet time
Did push it out of farther question.[5]   5

Ely
But how, my lord, shall we resist it now?

Canterbury
It must be thought on. If it pass against us,
We lose the better half of our possession,
Because For° all the temporal lands which men devout
will (legal document) By testament° have given to the Church   10
Would they strip from us, being valued thus:
As much as would maintain,[6] to the King's honor,
No fewer than Full° fifteen earls and fifteen hundred knights,
Six thousand and two hundred good esquires,[7]
lepers And, to relief of lazars° and weak age   15
impoverished Of indigent° faint souls past corporal toil,[8]
poorhouses A hundred almshouses° right well supplied,
besides; in addition And to the coffers of the King beside°
A thousand pounds by th' year. Thus runs the bill.

Ely
This would drink deep.

Canterbury
                                    'Twould drink the cup and all.   20

Ely
But what prevention?

1   *fair regard*

(1) good intentions (toward the Church); (2) well respected

2   *offending Adam*

(1) original sin; (2) bad behavior (i.e., his earlier *wildness*). The phrase alludes to the story in Genesis of Adam and Eve, who were expelled from Eden for disobeying God's commandment not to eat from the tree of knowledge.

3   *heady currance*

Strong current; flow

4   *Hydra-headed*

Many-headed. In Greek mythology, Hercules was sent to kill the Hydra, a nine-headed monster that sprouted two heads to replace each one Hercules managed to lop off.

5   *his seat*

Its power

6   *reason in divinity*

Discuss theology

7   *all in all*

Entirely

8   *rendered you in music*

I.e., described to you eloquently

9   *cause of policy*

Political problem

10 *The Gordian knot of it he will unloose, / Familiar as his garter*

Gordius of Phrygia tied a knot of incredible complexity, about which it was prophesied that whoever untied it would rule Asia; Alexander the Great cut the knot with his sword and went on to conquer Asia. Canterbury imagines Henry outdoing Alexander by *unloosing* the knot as easily as if it were his garter; that is, Henry is able to resolve difficult political issues by understanding them, not by forcing them. Alexander is at several points in the play a kind of alter ego for Henry: compare also Fluellen's conversation with Gower, 4.7.11–51.

Canterbury

virtue; God's favor The King is full of grace° and fair regard.[1]

Ely

And a true lover of the holy Church.

Canterbury

The courses of his youth promised it not.

The breath no sooner left his father's body   25

suppressed; deadened But that his wildness, mortified° in him,

Seemed to die too; yea, at that very moment

Self-awareness Consideration° like an angel came

And whipped th' offending Adam[2] out of him,

Leaving his body as a paradise   30

T' envelop and contain celestial spirits.

Never was such a sudden scholar made;

Never came reformation in a flood

cleaning With such a heady currance,[3] scouring° faults,

Nor never Hydra-headed[4] willfulness   35

So soon did lose his seat,[5] and all at once,

As in this King.

Ely

We are blessed in the change.

Canterbury

If you heard Hear° him but reason in divinity,[6]

And, all-admiring, with an inward wish

church official You would desire the King were made a prelate.°   40

Hear him debate of commonwealth affairs,

You would say it hath been all in all[7] his study.

Listen to List° his discourse of war, and you shall hear

A fearful battle rendered you in music.[8]

Turn him to any cause of policy,[9]   45

The Gordian knot of it he will unloose,

so that Familiar as his garter,[10] that,° when he speaks,

1   *chartered libertine*

Someone licensed to move about freely

2   *the mute wonder lurketh in men's ears /*
    To steal his sweet and honeyed sentences

I.e., men fall silent to hear his well-phrased maxims. (*Wonder* is personified: it sits, silently, *in men's ears* and awaits Henry's wisdom.)

3   *So that the art and practic part of life /*
    Must be the mistress to this theoric

I.e., and we must assume that his practical life experiences have taught him his theoretical sophistication (as expressed in his maxims). *Mistress* can mean either "patron" or "creator."

4   *courses vain*

Frivolous behavior

5   *riots*

Reveling; heavy drinking

6   *sequestration / From open haunts and popularity*

Avoidance of public places and common people. (*Popularity* also suggests "pursuit of public favor.")

7   *crescive in his faculty*

Prone to growth by its nature

8   *miracles are ceased*

Protestant doctrine held that the age of miracles ended with the death of the last of the Apostles. Here, Canterbury uses the phrase almost proverbially in the service of an avowedly secular political reasoning. Henry, on the other hand, consistently refers all events to God, interpreting them as signs of divine favor. The play confronts the claims of political reason with the claims of the divine: at stake, at some level, is the nature of human political life, as the space of rational calculation or of providential order.

9   *we must needs admit the means / How*

We must concede the natural causes whereby

The air, a chartered libertine,[1] is still,
And the mute wonder lurketh in men's ears
To steal his sweet and honeyed sentences;[2]   50
So that the art and practic part of life
Must be the mistress to this theoric [3]—

have learned   Which is a wonder how his Grace should glean° it,
inclination   Since his addiction° was to courses vain,[4]
companions / illiterate   His companies° unlettered,° rude, and shallow,   55
amusements   His hours filled up with riots,[5] banquets, sports,°
was seen   And never noted° in him any study,
                         Any retirement, any sequestration
                         From open haunts and popularity.[6]

Ely

                         The strawberry grows underneath the nettle,   60
                         And wholesome berries thrive and ripen best
lesser; more vulgar   Neighbored by fruit of baser° quality;
                         And so the Prince obscured his contemplation
i.e., contemplation   Under the veil of wildness, which,° no doubt,
                         Grew like the summer grass, fastest by night,   65
                         Unseen, yet crescive in his faculty.[7]

Canterbury

                         It must be so, for miracles are ceased,[8]
                         And therefore we must needs admit the means
                         How[9] things are perfected.

Ely

                                                     But, my good lord,
reducing the severity   How now for mitigation° of this bill   70
House of Commons   Urged by the Commons?° Doth his Majesty
                          Incline to it, or no?

Canterbury

impartial   He seems indifferent,°
                         Or rather swaying more upon our part

1   *th' exhibiters*

     Those who are sponsoring the bill

2   *Upon*

     (1) on behalf of; (2) on the occasion of

3   *spiritual convocation*

     Formal gathering of the clergy

4   *causes now in hand*

     Matters now pressing

5   *opened to his Grace at large*

     Discussed in full with the King

6   *The severals and unhidden passages*

     **The particulars and inarguable
     claims**

7   *to know his embassy*

     **To learn what message the ambas-
     sador has brought**

Than cherishing th' exhibiters [1] against us;

For I have made an offer to his Majesty,   75

Upon [2] our spiritual convocation [3]

And in regard of causes now in hand, [4]

Which I have opened to his Grace at large, [5]

regarding As touching° France, to give a greater sum

Than ever at one time the clergy yet   80

with Did to his predecessors part withal.°

Ely

How did this offer seem received, my lord?

Canterbury

With good acceptance of his Majesty,

Except Save° that there was not time enough to hear,

gladly As I perceived his Grace would fain° have done,   85

The severals and unhidden passages [6]

Of his true titles to some certain dukedoms,

And generally to the crown and seat of France,

i.e., Edward III Derived from Edward,° his great-grandfather.

Ely

What was th' impediment that broke this off?   90

Canterbury

The French ambassador upon that instant

Craved audience—and the hour I think is come

To give him hearing. Is it four o'clock?

Ely

It is.

Canterbury

Then go we in to know his embassy, [7]   95

Which I could with a ready guess declare

Before the Frenchman speak a word of it.

Ely

I'll wait upon you, and I long to hear it.   *They exit.*

1   *in presence*

     I.e., at court

2   *my cousin*

     Henry was distantly related to
     Westmorland through marriage.

3   *law Salic*

     Canterbury describes the law, which
     prevented inheritance through the
     female, beginning at 1.2.36.

Act 1, Scene 2

Enter the **King***, Humphrey [Duke of* **Gloucester***],* **Bedford***,* **Clarence***,* **Warwick***,* **Westmorland***, and* **Exeter** *[with attendants]*.

King Henry
Where is my gracious lord of Canterbury?
Exeter
Not here in presence.[1]
King Henry
                  Send for him, good uncle.
Westmorland
Shall we call in th' ambassador, my liege?
King Henry
freed from doubt   Not yet, my cousin.[2] We would be resolved,°
Before we hear him, of some things of weight   5
tax; burden   That task° our thoughts concerning us and France.

Enter two bishops [the Archbishop of **Canterbury** *and the Bishop of* **Ely***]*.

Canterbury
God and his angels guard your sacred throne
honor; occupy   And make you long become° it!
King Henry
                     Sure we thank you.
My learnèd lord, we pray you to proceed
And justly and religiously unfold   10
Why the law Salic[3] that they have in France
Either   Or° should or should not bar us in our claim.
And God forbid, my dear and faithful lord,
That you should fashion, wrest, or bow your reading,

1   *Or nicely charge your understanding soul /*
    With opening titles miscreate, whose
    right / Suits not in native colors with
    the truth

    I.e., or, through overly subtle argu-
    ments, burden your soul—which
    understands truth and falsity—
    with invalid assertions, the claims
    of which fail to match the truth

2   *how you impawn our person*
    Of what you commit me to

3   *brief mortality*
    I.e., human life

4   "In terram Salicam mulieres ne
    succedant": / "*No woman shall succeed*
    in Salic land."

    Henry's claim to the throne of
    France derives from his great-great-
    grandmother Isabella, daughter of
    Philip IV of France. Canterbury
    says first that France does not lie
    within Salic land at all; then he
    says that the French monarchs
    themselves have not faithfully
    followed the injunction against
    female inheritance. For these
    reasons, Canterbury argues, Henry
    would be justified in raising an
    army and attempting to claim the
    French throne. (See Longer Note
    on page 331.)

5   *female bar*
    Obstacle to inheriting through the
    matrilineal line

Or nicely charge your understanding soul   15
With opening titles miscreate, whose right
natural   Suits not in native° colors with the truth, [1]
For God doth know how many now in health
putting to the test   Shall drop their blood in approbation°
prompt; provoke   Of what your reverence shall incite° us to.   20
Therefore take heed how you impawn our person, [2]
How you awake our sleeping sword of war.
We charge you, in the name of God, take heed,
For never two such kingdoms did contend
Without much fall of blood, whose guiltless drops   25
grievous   Are every one a woe, a sore° complaint
'Gainst him whose wrongs gives edge unto the swords
That makes such waste in brief mortality. [3]
solemn charge   Under this conjuration,° speak, my lord,
For we will hear, note, and believe in heart   30
That what you speak is in your conscience washed
As pure as sin with baptism.

Canterbury

Then hear me, gracious sovereign, and you peers,
That owe yourselves, your lives, and services
To this imperial throne. There is no bar   35
To make against your Highness' claim to France
(a legendary king)   But this, which they produce from Pharamond:°
"*In terram Salicam mulieres ne succedant*":
"No woman shall succeed in Salic land." [4]
interpret   Which Salic land the French unjustly gloze°   40
To be the realm of France, and Pharamond
The founder of this law and female bar. [5]
Yet their own authors faithfully affirm
That the land Salic is in Germany,
rivers   Between the floods° of Saale and of Elbe,   45

1   *Charles the Great*

    **Charlemagne (742–814), a power-
    ful King of the Franks (an early
    medieval confederation of peoples
    living in what is modern Germany
    and France) who conquered and
    consolidated western Europe**

2   *dishonest manners*

    Unchaste behavior

3   *heir general*

    Lawful inheritor

4   *fine*

    **Refine, purify. This is the reading of
    Q.; the Folio has "find," but "find . . .
    with" makes little sense here and
    "e" and "d" misreadings are com-
    mon.**

5   *Conveyed himself as*

    Claimed he was

6   *Charlemagne*

    **Actually Charles II (the Bold); an
    error Shakespeare copied from his
    source, Raphael Holinshed's 1587
    *Chronicles of England, Scotland and
    Ireland*.**

7   *the Tenth*

    **Should be the Ninth; again, an
    error Shakespeare copied from his
    source**

Where Charles the Great,[1] having subdued the Saxons,
There left behind and settled certain French,
Who, holding in disdain the German women
For some dishonest manners [2] of their life,
Established then this law: to wit, no female   50
inheritor Should be inheritrix° in Salic land—
Which Salic, as I said, 'twixt Elbe and Saale,
Is at this day in Germany called Meissen.
Then doth it well appear the Salic law
Was not devisèd for the realm of France,   55
Nor did the French possess the Salic land
Until four hundred one-and-twenty years
the death After defunction° of King Pharamond,
Frivolously Idly° supposed the founder of this law,
Who died within the year of our redemption   60
Four hundred twenty-six; and Charles the Great
Subdued the Saxons and did seat the French
Beyond the River Saale in the year
Eight hundred five. Besides, their writers say,
who King Pepin, which° deposèd Childeric,   65
Did, as heir general,[3] being descended
Of Blithild, which was daughter to King Clothair,
Make claim and title to the crown of France.
Hugh Capet also, who usurped the crown
Of Charles the Duke of Lorraine, sole heir male   70
Of the true line and stock of Charles the Great,
To fine [4] his title with some shows of truth,
Though, in pure truth, it was corrupt and naught,
Conveyed himself as [5] th' heir to th' Lady Lingard,
Daughter to Charlemagne,[6] who was the son   75
To Lewis the Emperor, and Lewis the son
Of Charles the Great. Also King Lewis the Tenth,[7]
Who was sole heir to the usurper Capet,

1   *lineal of*

    Descended directly from

2   *Lewis his*

    Lewis's

3   *Howbeit*

    I.e., no matter how much

4   *to hide them in a net*

    To conceal themselves in a tangle
    (of complex arguments)

5   *amply to embare*

    Openly to expose

6   *Book of Numbers*

    The next two lines paraphrase
    Numbers 27:8.

7   *great-grandsire's tomb, / From whom you
    claim*

    Edward III was Henry's great-
    grandfather and the son of Isabella,
    daughter of King Philip IV of France,
    from whom the claim to the French
    throne derives.

8   *a tragedy*

    I.e., the 1346 battle at Crécy, a
    significant English victory in the
    Hundred Years War against France.

Could not keep quiet in his conscience,
Wearing the crown of France, till satisfied   80
That fair Queen Isabel, his grandmother,
Was lineal of[1] the Lady Ermengard,
Daughter to Charles the foresaid Duke of Lorraine,
By the which marriage the line of Charles the Great
Was reunited to the crown of France.   85
So that, as clear as is the summer's sun,
King Pepin's title and Hugh Capet's claim,
are plainly seen King Lewis his[2] satisfaction, all appear°
To hold in right and title of the female;
So do the kings of France unto this day,   90
Howbeit[3] they would hold up this Salic law
To bar your Highness claiming from the female,
And rather choose to hide them in a net[4]
Than amply to embare[5] their crooked titles
Usurped from you and your progenitors.   95

King Henry

May I with right and conscience make this claim?

Canterbury

The sin upon my head, dread sovereign!
For in the Book of Numbers[6] is it writ,
When the man dies, let the inheritance
Descend unto the daughter. Gracious lord,   100
unfurl Stand for your own, unwind° your bloody flag,
Look back into your mighty ancestors.
Go, my dread lord, to your great-grandsire's tomb,
From whom you claim.[7] Invoke his warlike spirit,
And your great-uncle's, Edward the Black Prince,   105
Who on the French ground played a tragedy,[8]
Making defeat on the full power of France,
i.e., Edward III Whiles his most mighty father° on a hill
Stood smiling to behold his lion's whelp

1   *Forage in*

     Glut himself upon

2   *cold for action*

     Cold **(or stiff) because of inaction**

3   *renownèd them*

     Brought them renown

4   *thrice-puissant*

     **(1) strongest; most powerful; (2)
     made triply strong by the three
     reasons just given**

5   *very May morn*

     Full bloom; prime

6   *So hath your Highness*

     **And indeed your Highness does
     have these things.**

Forage in ¹ blood of French nobility.   110

engage   O noble English, that could entertain°

power   With half their forces the full pride° of France

And let another half stand laughing by,

All out of work and cold for action.²

Ely

Awake remembrance of these valiant dead,   115

powerful And with your puissant° arm renew their feats!

You are their heir; you sit upon their throne.

The blood and courage that renownèd them ³

Runs in your veins, and my thrice-puissant⁴ liege

Is in the very May morn ⁵ of his youth,   120

Ripe for exploits and mighty enterprises.

Exeter

Your brother kings and monarchs of the Earth

Do all expect that you should rouse yourself

As did the former lions of your blood.

Westmorland

They know your Grace hath cause and means and
    might;   125

So hath your Highness.⁶ Never king of England

Had nobles richer and more loyal subjects,

Whose hearts have left their bodies here in England

encamped in tents And lie pavilioned° in the fields of France.

Canterbury

Oh, let their bodies follow, my dear liege,   130

With blood and sword and fire to win your right!

clergy   In aid whereof we of the spiritualty°

Will raise your Highness such a mighty sum

As never did the clergy at one time

Bring in to any of your ancestors.   135

King Henry

We must not only arm t' invade the French

1   *lay down our proportions*

     I.e., estimate the troops and resources we need

2   *the Scot*

     The Scots (see lines 144–154). In 3.2, a Scot named Jamy appears as one of Henry's captains. In 1599, when the play was first performed, James VI of Scotland was a likely successor to Queen Elizabeth; he did in fact succeed her when she died four years later. It was forbidden to speak openly of the succession in the last years of Elizabeth's reign, but Shakespeare may well have been thinking about the future relationship between England and Scotland, as nations living under a single king but with a long history of violent conflict.

3   *With all advantages*

     At any opportunity

4   *coursing snatchers*

     Horse-riding thieves

5   *main intendment*

     Primary aim

6   *Who hath been still a giddy neighbor*

     Who has been always an unreliable neighbor

7   *Galling the gleanèd land with hot assays*

     Vexing the stripped (i.e., empty of defenders) land with ferocious assaults

8   *She hath been then more feared than harmed*

     England, in that case, has been more frightened than actually hurt.

9   *For hear her but exampled by herself*

     I.e., listen to the way in which England's own history supplies examples.

10   *King of Scots, whom she did send to France*

     David II, captured in 1346. He was jailed in England afterward; the account of his joining Edward III in France is historically inaccurate.

11   *sumless treasuries*

     Immeasurable treasures

But lay down our proportions [1] to defend

inroads; raids   Against the Scot, [2] who will make road° upon us

With all advantages. [3]

Canterbury

border areas   They of those marches,° gracious sovereign,   140

Shall be a wall sufficient to defend

i.e., Scots   Our inland from the pilfering borderers. °

King Henry

We do not mean the coursing snatchers [4] only

But fear the main intendment [5] of the Scot,

Who hath been still a giddy neighbor [6] to us;   145

For you shall read that my great-grandfather

Never went with his forces into France

unprotected   But that the Scot on his unfurnished° kingdom

Came pouring, like the tide into a breach,

brimming   With ample and brim° fullness of his force,   150

Galling the gleanèd land with hot assays, [7]

Girding with grievous siege castles and towns,

That England, being empty of defense,

behavior of its neighbor   Hath shook and trembled at th' ill neighborhood.°

Canterbury

She hath been then more feared than harmed, [8] my

liege,   155

For hear her but exampled by herself: [9]

knights; nobles   When all her chivalry° hath been in France

And she a mourning widow of her nobles,

She hath herself not only well defended

But taken and impounded as a stray   160

The King of Scots, whom she did send to France [10]

To fill King Edward's fame with prisoner kings

history   And make her chronicle° as rich with praise

As is the ooze and bottom of the sea

wreckage   With sunken wrack° and sumless treasuries. [11]   165

1 Westmorland

The Folio assigns this speech to Ely, but he is here to support Canterbury. The corresponding speech in Holinshed belongs to Westmorland, and while the Quarto assigns it to "A Lord," this seems a reasonable identification for the speaker.

2 *in prey*

Engaged in hunting

3 *'tame and havoc*

Attame (break into) and destroy

4 *a crushed necessity*

A forced conclusion (rather than a necessary one)

5 *though high, and low, and lower, / Put into parts, doth keep in one consent*

Although divided into three classes in society, each with separate functions, is able to function harmoniously. The image is of musical harmony formed from disparate vocal lines and pitches.

6 *close*

(1) union; concord; (2) musical cadence (which moves to a harmonic close)

7 *butt*

Target (from archery)

8 *a king*

During Shakespeare's time, bee-hives were usually thought to be organized around a male insect. The first English account of the actual ordering of the hive around a queen bee was published in 1609.

9 *Make boot upon*

Plunder

Westmorland [1]
But there's a saying very old and true:
>   "If that you will France win,
>   Then with Scotland first begin."
For once the eagle England being in prey, [2]
To her unguarded nest the weasel Scot   170
Comes sneaking, and so sucks her princely eggs,
Playing the mouse in absence of the cat,
To 'tame and havoc [3] more than she can eat.

Exeter
It follows then the cat must stay at home;
Yet that is but a crushed necessity, [4]   175
Since we have locks to safeguard necessaries
ingenious   And pretty° traps to catch the petty thieves.
While that the armèd hand doth fight abroad,
well-advised; prudent   Th' advisèd° head defends itself at home,
For government, though high, and low, and lower,   180
Put into parts, doth keep in one consent, [5]
Agreeing   Congreeing° in a full and natural close, [6]
Like music.

Canterbury
                      Therefore doth Heaven divide
various   The state of man in divers° functions,
Setting endeavor in continual motion,   185
i.e., which endeavor   To which° is fixèd, as an aim or butt, [7]
Obedience; for so work the honeybees,
Creatures that by a rule in nature teach
The act of order to a peopled kingdom.
various ranks   They have a king [8] and officers of sorts,°   190
i.e., punish wrongdoers   Where some, like magistrates, correct° at home;
Others, like merchants, venture trade abroad;
Others, like soldiers, armèd in their stings,
Make boot upon [9] the summer's velvet buds,

1 *mechanic porters*

   Hard-working janitors

2 *pale*

   Possibly because of its association
   with death or perhaps because the
   face seems pale showing through
   the black hood

3 *many things, having full reference / To
   one consent, may work contrariously*

   Many things, together committed
   to a common purpose, may work
   in diverse ways. This image of a
   multiplicity of actions united in the
   one consent of the king (206), while
   it finds its inspiration in Exeter's
   preceding speech, may reverse its
   meaning: Exeter imagines a society
   that, although divided by degree,
   nevertheless keeps *one consent*, that
   is, one harmony (181–183). But in
   harmony, the various parts work
   together equally: this is what Exeter's *consent* means, from the Latin
   word *concinere*, "to sing together."
   Canterbury's *one consent*, on the
   other hand, seems to designate
   the single will of King Henry, who
   sets all these multiple actions in
   motion.

4 *loosèd several ways*

   Released from different locations

5 *close in the dial's center*

   Meet at the sundial's center

6 *worried*

   Savaged; shaken in the jaws of a dog
   (but also with the familiar sense
   "made anxious"). See also 2.2.81.

7 *The name of hardiness and policy*

   Its reputation for courage and
   statesmanship

8 *the Dauphin*

   French king's eldest son and heir
   apparent

9 *bend it to our awe*

   I.e., force it to submit to our power

booty; treasure	Which pillage° they with merry march bring home
	To the tent royal of their emperor,
royal duty	Who, busied in his majesty,° surveys
builders	The singing masons° building roofs of gold,
	The civil citizens kneading up the honey,
	The poor mechanic porters¹ crowding in
	Their heavy burdens at his narrow gate,
solemn-looking	The sad-eyed° justice with his surly hum
executioners	Delivering o'er to executors° pale²
	The lazy yawning drone. I this infer:
	That many things, having full reference
	To one consent, may work contrariously.³
	As many arrows loosèd several ways⁴
	Come to one mark, as many ways meet in one town,
	As many fresh streams meet in one salt sea,
	As many lines close in the dial's center,⁵
	So may a thousand actions once afoot
	End in one purpose and be all well borne
	Without defeat. Therefore to France, my liege.
fortunate	Divide your happy° England into four,
	Whereof take you one quarter into France,
Gaul, i.e., France	And you withal shall make all Gallia° shake.
	If we with thrice such powers left at home
	Cannot defend our own doors from the dog,
	Let us be worried⁶ and our nation lose
	The name of hardiness and policy.⁷

King Henry
Call in the messengers sent from the Dauphin.⁸
[Some attendants exit.]
Now are we well resolved, and by God's help
And yours, the noble sinews of our power,
France being ours, we'll bend it to our awe⁹

Either Or break it all to pieces. Or° there we'll sit,

195
200
205
210
215
220
225

1   *Tombless, with no remembrance over*
    them
    I.e., without a marker or monu-
    ment, and without an epitaph

2   *with full mouth*
    Loudly

3   *Turkish mute*
    A Turkish slave whose tongue has
    been cut out (to keep him from
    talking about what he has heard,
    seen, or done). Here, the Turkish
    mute embodies the silence of a
    forgotten grave, the antithesis of
    the *full voice* **of history.**

4   *Not worshipped with a waxen epitaph*
    I.e., without even an inscription in
    wax (which can easily be erased)

5   *in charge*
    Been commanded to say

6   *sparingly show you far off*
    I.e., discreetly and obliquely relate
    to you

sovereignty   Ruling in large and ample empery°

O'er France and all her almost kingly dukedoms,

i.e., grave   Or lay these bones in an unworthy urn,°

Tombless, with no remembrance over them.[1]

Either our history shall with full mouth [2]   230

Speak freely of our acts or else our grave,

Like Turkish mute,[3] shall have a tongueless mouth,

Not worshipped with a waxen epitaph.[4]

Enter **Ambassadors** *of France.*

Now are we well prepared to know the pleasure

Of our fair cousin Dauphin, for we hear   235

Your greeting is from him, not from the King.

First Ambassador

May 't please your Majesty to give us leave

Freely to render what we have in charge,[5]

Or shall we sparingly show you far off [6]

message   The Dauphin's meaning and our embassy? °   240

King Henry

We are no tyrant but a Christian king,

virtue   Unto whose grace° our passion is as subject

As is our wretches fettered in our prisons.

Therefore with frank and with uncurbèd plainness

Tell us the Dauphin's mind.

First Ambassador

few words   Thus, then, in few: °   245

Your Highness, lately sending into France,

Did claim some certain dukedoms, in the right

Of your great predecessor, King Edward the Third.

In answer of which claim, the Prince our master

have a taste of   Says that you savor° too much of your youth   250

nothing   And bids you be advised there's naught° in France

1   *When we have matched our rackets to these balls*

    (1) struck the balls with a tennis racket; (2) responded to this provocation with a loud armed attack. Henry continues the metaphor in the following lines (e.g., *set, strike, match,* and *courts*).

2   *Shall strike his father's crown into the hazard*

    That will (1) put the King of France's wager (on the Dauphin to win the match) in jeopardy; a *crown* was a coin (2) put the French King's royal crown in danger (of being lost to Henry). An opening in the indoor tennis courts of Shakespeare's time was called a hazard; balls struck into the *hazard* scored a point.

3   *the courts of France will be disturbed / With chases*

    (1) the tennis courts of France will be disrupted by many winning shots; (2) the royal courts of France will be overrun by pursuing English armies. In Elizabethan tennis, a *chase* was a shot left unreturned; the location of the shot's second bounce determined the points scored.

4   *comes o'er us with*

    Sneers at me by invoking

5   *hence*

    i.e., away from the court

6   *my state*

    (1) my dignity; (2) that which I claim and rule as king; (3) my throne

7   *rouse me in*

    (1) raise myself into; (2) arouse (waken) myself concerning

8   *a man for working days*

    I.e., a common laborer

(type of spirited dance)   That can be with a nimble galliard° won;

You cannot revel into dukedoms there.

more fitting   He therefore sends you, meeter° for your spirit,

box   This tun° of treasure, and in lieu of this   255

Desires you let the dukedoms that you claim

Hear no more of you. This the Dauphin speaks.

King Henry

What treasure, uncle?

[*A casket is presented;* **Exeter** *examines its contents.*]

Exeter

Tennis balls, my liege.

King Henry

jocular   We are glad the Dauphin is so pleasant° with us.

His present and your pains we thank you for.   260

When we have matched our rackets to these balls,[1]

We will, in France, by God's grace, play a set

Shall strike his father's crown into the hazard.[2]

opponent   Tell him he hath made a match with such a wrangler°

That all the courts of France will be disturbed   265

With chases.[3] And we understand him well,

How he comes o'er us with[4] our wilder days,

Not measuring what use we made of them.

throne   We never valued this poor seat° of England,

And therefore, living hence,[5] did give ourself   270

To barbarous license—as 'tis ever common

That men are merriest when they are from home.

But tell the Dauphin I will keep my state,[6]

i.e., unfurl   Be like a king and show° my sail of greatness

When I do rouse me in[7] my throne of France.   275

royal trappings   For that I have laid by my majesty°

And plodded like a man for working days,[8]

But I will rise there with so full a glory

1 *stand sore chargèd*

   Be grievously blamed

2 *Shall this his mock mock out of*

   **Will by this, the Dauphin's taunt, be
   robbed of**

3 *venge me*

   Avenge myself

4 *omit no happy hour*

   **I.e., do not overlook any favorable
   occasion**

5 *Save those to God, that run before our
   business*

   **Excluding those thoughts of God,
   which are more important than our
   (military) preparations**

6 *proportions*

   **Troops and equipment (see line 137
   and note)**

That I will dazzle all the eyes of France,
Yea, strike the Dauphin blind to look on us.   280
And tell the pleasant Prince this mock of his
cannonballs   Hath turned his balls to gunstones,° and his soul
destructive   Shall stand sore chargèd[1] for the wasteful° vengeance
i.e., widows-to-be   That shall fly with them; for many a thousand widows°
Shall this his mock mock out of[2] their dear husbands,   285
Mock mothers from their sons, mock castles down,
unbegotten   And some are yet ungotten° and unborn
That shall have cause to curse the Dauphin's scorn.
But this lies all within the will of God,
To whom I do appeal, and in whose name   290
Tell you the Dauphin I am coming on
To venge me[3] as I may and to put forth
My rightful hand in a well-hallowed cause.
So get you hence in peace, and tell the Dauphin
His jest will savor but of shallow wit   295
When thousands weep more than did laugh at it.
—Convey them with safe conduct.—Fare you well.
                                        Ambassadors *exit.*

Exeter
This was a merry message.

King Henry
We hope to make the sender blush at it;
Therefore, my lords, omit no happy hour[4]   300
That may give furth'rance to our expedition,
For we have now no thought in us but France,
Save those to God, that run before our business.[5]
Therefore let our proportions[6] for these wars
Be soon collected, and all things thought upon   305
That may with reasonable swiftness add

1   *God before*

     With God leading us; God willing

2   *on foot be brought*

     Get started

More feathers to our wings, for, God before,[1]
We'll chide this Dauphin at his father's door.
tax; direct Therefore let every man now task° his thought
That this fair action may on foot be brought.[2]   310

                                        They exit.

1   *silken dalliance in the wardrobe lies*

Silken dalliance means both "easy, leisurely pursuits" and "luxurious clothing," neither of which are appropriate now.

2   *honor's thought / Reigns solely in the breast of every man*

I.e., every man thinks only of honor

3   *mirror*

Model; best example. A *mirror* in this sense is an exemplar or a pattern for imitation.

4   *Mercurys*

A reference to the speed with which they acted. In Roman mythology, Mercury was the messenger to the gods as well as the god of commerce and thievery; he was usually portrayed wearing sandals with wings.

5   *hides a sword from hilts unto the point / With crowns imperial, crowns and coronets*

Encircles the blade of his sword, from the crosspiece to the tip, with emperors' crowns, regal crowns, and smaller crowns (as symbols of conquests)

6   *intelligence*

Information gathering; espionage

7   *pale policy*

Ineffectual plots

8   *model to thy inward greatness*

The external form that encloses your inner excellence

9   *that honor would thee do*

(1) that desire for honor would urge you to do; (2) that would do you honor

10 *grace of kings*

I.e., king who best honors the title of "king"

Act 2, Prologue

Flourish. Enter **Chorus**.

Chorus

Now all the youth of England are on fire,
And silken dalliance in the wardrobe lies.[1]
Now thrive the armorers, and honor's thought
Reigns solely in the breast of every man.[2]
They sell the pasture now to buy the horse,   5
Following the mirror[3] of all Christian kings,
With wingèd heels, as English Mercurys.[4]
For now sits Expectation in the air

crossguard And hides a sword from hilts° unto the point
With crowns imperial, crowns and coronets,[5]   10
Promised to Harry and his followers.
The French, advised by good intelligence[6]

planned invasion Of this most dreadful preparation,°
Shake in their fear and with pale policy[7]
Seek to divert the English purposes.   15
O England, model to thy inward greatness,[8]
Like little body with a mighty heart,
What mightst thou do, that honor would thee do,[9]
Were all thy children kind and natural?

the King of France But see, thy fault France° hath in thee found out,   20

false; empty A nest of hollow° bosoms, which he fills

gold coins With treacherous crowns;° and three corrupted men,
One, Richard, Earl of Cambridge, and the second,
Henry, Lord Scroop of Masham, and the third,
Sir Thomas Grey, knight, of Northumberland,   25

gold Have, for the gilt° of France—O guilt indeed!—

frightened Confirmed conspiracy with fearful° France,
And by their hands this grace of kings[10] must die,
If Hell and treason hold their promises,

1 *we'll digest / Th' abuse of distance, force*
a play

I.e., we'll smooth over the jarring
shifts of location, and stuff our play
full (of events). *Henry V* sets its action in several different places, thus
violating the classical rules of dramatic unity (which entail, among
other conditions, that all action in a
play occur in a single locale).

2 *charming the narrow seas*

I.e., putting spells on the English
Channel

3 *We'll not offend one stomach*

We won't (1) make anyone seasick;
(2) displease anyone.

4 *But, till the King come forth, and not till*
then, / Unto Southampton do we shift our
scene.

We will not move the play's action
from London to Southampton
(a port city on the south coast of
England) until the King appears.
The awkwardness of this postpone-
ment, and the fact that it is made in
a second couplet, apparently added
to a speech seemingly complete,
has led some editors to speculate
that Shakespeare belatedly added
2.1 and then adjusted this speech
correspondingly.

Before   Ere° he take ship for France, and in Southampton.   30
           Linger your patience on, and we'll digest
           Th' abuse of distance, force a play.[1]
           The sum is paid, the traitors are agreed,
           The King is set from London, and the scene
           Is now transported, gentles, to Southampton.   35
           There is the playhouse now, there must you sit,
safely   And thence to France shall we convey you safe°
           And bring you back, charming the narrow seas[2]
passage To give you gentle pass,° for, if we may,
           We'll not offend one stomach[3] with our play.   40
           But, till the King come forth, and not till then,
           Unto Southampton do we shift our scene.[4]   *He exits.*

1   *Nym*

Echoes the verb *nim*, "to steal."

2   *I will wink and hold out mine iron*

I will shut my eyes and hold out my sword.

3   *It will toast cheese*

I.e., it's a good skewer for heating cheese over a fire.

4   *will endure cold*

I.e., does not mind being unsheathed

5   *there's an end*

I.e., that's that.

6   *to France*

I.e., when we leave for France

7   *my rest*

My final resolve. Literally, "my reserved stake" (a term taken from primero, a card game; when the *rest* is lost, the game is over)

8   *Nell Quickly*

The Hostess of *Henry IV, Part One* and *Part Two*, who also appears in *The Merry Wives of Windsor*. Her first name is used here for the first time (*Nell* is a diminutive of Helen). By 5.1.76, however, Shakespeare seems to have forgotten it and refers to her as *Doll*.

Act 2, Scene 1

*Enter Corporal **Nym** and Lieutenant **Bardolph**.*

Bardolph

Well met, Corporal Nym.[1]

Nym

Good morrow, Lieutenant Bardolph.

Bardolph

Ensign; Flag bearer   What, are Ancient° Pistol and you friends yet?

Nym

For my part, I care not. I say little, but when time shall
serve, there shall be smiles—but that shall be as it   5
may. I dare not fight, but I will wink and hold out
i.e., so what   mine iron.[2] It is a simple one, but what° though? It
will toast cheese,[3] and it will endure cold[4] as another
man's sword will—and there's an end.[5]

Bardolph

I will bestow a breakfast to make you friends, and   10
we'll be all three sworn brothers to France.[6] Let 't be
so, good Corporal Nym.

Nym

Faith, I will live so long as I may, that's the certain of
it; and when I cannot live any longer, I will do as I may.
last resort; refuge   That is my rest;[7] that is the rendezvous° of it.   15

Bardolph

i.e., Pistol   It is certain, Corporal, that he° is married to Nell
Quickly,[8] and certainly she did you wrong, for you
betrothed   were troth-plight° to her.

Nym

I cannot tell. Things must be as they may. Men may
sleep, and they may have their throats about them at   20
that time, and some say knives have edges. It must be
as it may. Though patience be a tired mare, yet she will

85

1 *Though patience be a tired mare, yet she will plod. There must be conclusions.*

Nym alludes elliptically to his intended revenge on Pistol: he will remain patient, no matter how tiresome and how long it takes to avenge himself, but there will come a reckoning (*conclusions*) at some time.

2 *Pistol*

Pistols of Shakespeare's time were both loud and inaccurate.

3 *host*

(1) referring to Pistol's new status as husband of Hostess Quickly (i.e., the male counterpart to *hostess*); (2) inn or tavern keeper; (3) pimp

4 *Nor shall my Nell keep lodgers.*

I.e., Nell doesn't need to take in lodgers at the inn because I have money enough to support us.

5 *by the prick of their needles*

I.e., as seamstresses (with the obscene meaning of *prick* unintended by the Hostess)

6 *welladay, Lady*

I.e., alas, by our Lady; it is an expression of dismay, with *Lady* (i.e., Mary, mother of Jesus) being a mild oath.

7 *if he be not drawn*

If his sword is not out

8 *willful adultery*

The Hostess's tendency to misspeak makes the intended meaning of *willful adultery* unclear: it may be her mistake for "willful (i.e., deliberate) battery."

9 *Offer nothing*

Make no attempt to fight

10 *Iceland dog*

A shaggy breed of lapdog

11 *Will you shog off? I would have you solus.*

Will you walk away? I would like to have you alone. *Will you shog off?* may be addressed to the Hostess as a sharp "Go away!" but is more likely an invitation to Pistol to withdraw and fight.

plod. There must be conclusions.[1] Well, I cannot tell.

Enter **Pistol** *and* [**Hostess**] *Quickly.*

Bardolph

Here comes Ancient Pistol[2] and his wife. Good Corpo-
ral, be patient° here.   25

calm; mild

Nym

How now, mine host[3] Pistol?

Pistol

Base tike,° call'st thou me "host"? Now, by this hand,
I swear, I scorn the term! Nor shall my Nell keep
lodgers.[4]

cur; mutt

Hostess

No, by my troth, not long; for we cannot lodge and   30
board a dozen or fourteen gentlewomen that live
honestly° by the prick of their needles,[5] but it will be
thought we keep a bawdy-house° straight.

respectably; chastely
brothel

                              [**Nym** *and* **Pistol** *draw swords.*]
O welladay, Lady,[6] if he be not drawn![7] Now we shall
see willful adultery[8] and murder committed.   35

Bardolph

Good Lieutenant! Good Corporal! Offer nothing[9] here.

Nym

Pish!

Pistol

Pish for thee, Iceland dog,[10] thou prick-eared cur of
Iceland!

Hostess

Good Corporal Nym, show thy valor and put up° your   40
sword.   [*They sheathe their swords.*]

away

Nym

Will you shog off? I would have you *solus.*[11]

1   *The* solus *in thy teeth*

I.e., I throw your insult back at you (mistaking the Latin *solus* for an insult).

2   *pardie*

Indeed (a corruption of the French *par Dieu*, "by God")

3   *Pistol's cock is up*

I.e., Pistol's anger is roused. Pistol puns on his own name: his hammer is *cocked* and ready to fall on the charge (which will result in the *flashing fire* of the gunshot). He likely does not intend the obscene pun.

4   *conjure*

Exorcise. Nym equates Pistol's overblown language to a ritual exorcism and claims he is not afraid of it.

5   *If you grow foul with me, Pistol, I will scour you with my rapier*

(1) if you are abusive toward me, Pistol, I'll run my sword through you; (2) if you clog your barrel (as a result of misfiring), you pistol, I'll use my rapier (as a scouring rod or ramrod) to clean you out.

6   *in fair terms*

In plain language (as in line 65 and, as slightly varied, in line 55)

7   *walk off*

I.e., withdraw (in order to fight)

8   *that's the humor of it*

I.e., that's how it is.

9   *exhale*

(1) draw (your sword); (2) breathe (your last)

10 *I'll run him up to the hilts*

I.e., I'll stab him so deeply that only the handle of my sword will show.

11 *forefoot*

I.e., hand (no doubt suggested by his various references to Nym as a dog)

Pistol

terrible; wretched   *Solus*, egregious° dog? O viper vile!

The *solus* in thy most marvelous face!

The *solus* in thy teeth,[1] and in thy throat,   45

stomach   And in thy hateful lungs, yea, in thy maw,° pardie,[2]

And, which is worse, within thy nasty mouth!

I do retort the *solus* in thy bowels;

strike; take fire   For I can take,° and Pistol's cock is up,[3]

And flashing fire will follow.   50

Nym

(a devil's name)   I am not Barbason;° you cannot conjure[4] me. I have

inclination / moderately   an humor° to knock you indifferently° well. If you

grow foul with me, Pistol, I will scour you with my

rapier,[5] as I may, in fair terms.[6] If you would walk off,[7]

I would prick your guts a little, in good terms, as I   55

may, and that's the humor of it.[8]

Pistol

man   O braggart vile and damnèd furious wight!°

The grave doth gape, and doting death is near.

Therefore exhale![9]   [*They draw their swords.*]

Bardolph

Hear me; hear me what I say. He that strikes the first   60

stroke, I'll run him up to the hilts,[10] as I am a soldier.

[*He draws.*]

Pistol

great   An oath of mickle° might, and fury shall abate.

[*They sheathe their swords.*]

hand   [*to **Nym**] Give me thy fist;° thy forefoot[11] to me give.

valiant   Thy spirits are most tall.°

Nym

I will cut thy throat, one time or other, in fair terms.   65

That is the humor of it.

1   Couple à gorge!

    A corruption of the French *Couper la gorge* (cut the throat)

2   *hound of Crete*

    Another insult, paralleling the earlier *cur of Iceland* (lines 38–39), perhaps referring to another shaggy breed of dog

3   *powd'ring tub of infamy*

    I.e., sweating tub used to treat venereal disease

4   *lazar kite of Cressid's kind*

    I.e., disease-ridden, scavenging prostitute. *Lazar*, or "leper," echoes the belief in Shakespeare's time that leprosy was a venereal disease. A *kite* is a type of scavaging bird. *Cressid* is derived from the story of Cressida, Troilus's unfaithful Trojan lover, who in some versions is afflicted with leprosy for her betrayal.

5   *quondam*

    Former (Latin); *Quickly* is the Hostess's maiden name.

6   *For the only she*

    I.e., as the sole woman (for me)

7   pauca

    From the Latin *pauca verba*, "few words"

8   *Go to.*

    An expression of irritation

9   *my master*

    Sir John Falstaff, Henry's companion in the tavern plot of the *Henry IV* plays; the boy is presumably the page given to Falstaff by Henry: see *Henry IV, Part Two*, 1.2.11–13. At the end of *Henry IV, Part Two*, Shakespeare had promised to continue the story, *with Sir John in it*, but in *Henry V*, this promise is clearly not fulfilled.

10 *thy face*

    Bardolph's face is red and inflamed (with drink and boils, as described at 3.6.99–103).

11 *he'll yield the crow a pudding*

    His dead body will supply the crows with a meal. The line may refer to either the Boy or Falstaff; if the former, the phrase suggests that the Boy's sharp wit will eventually get him executed, with his body left for birds. If, as is more likely, it refers to Falstaff, the reference is to the fine meal his large body will provide.

12 *his*

    I.e., Falstaff's; a reference to Henry's rejection of Falstaff at the end of *Henry IV, Part Two*

Pistol

Couple à gorge! [1]

That is the word. I defy thee again.

O hound of Crete,[2] think'st thou my spouse to get?

charity hospital   No, to the spital° go,   70

And from the powd'ring tub of infamy [3]

Fetch forth the lazar kite of Cressid's kind,[4]

marry   Doll Tearsheet she by name, and her espouse.°

I have, and I will hold, the quondam [5] Quickly

For the only she; [6] and, *pauca*, [7] there's enough.   75

Go to.[8]

Enter the **Boy**.

Boy

Mine host Pistol, you must come to my master,[9] and you,

hostess. He is very sick and would to bed. Good

Bardolph, put thy face [10] between his sheets and do

the office of a warming pan. Faith, he's very ill.   80

Bardolph

Away, you rogue!

Hostess

By my troth, he'll yield the crow a pudding [11] one of

these days. The King has killed his [12] heart. Good

immediately   husband, come home presently.°   *She exits [with **Boy**].*

Bardolph

Come; shall I make you two friends? We must to France   85

together. Why the devil should we keep knives to cut

one another's throats?

Pistol

Let floods o'erswell and fiends for food howl on!

Nym

You'll pay me the eight shillings I won of you at betting?

1   *As manhood shall compound.*

    As valor will decide (i.e., let the bet-
    ter man win).

2   *Push home.*

    I.e., Thrust or stab vigorously (an
    invitation to fight).

3   *Sword is an oath*

    Punning on *sword* as *'s word* ("by
    God's word"), a mild oath. Pistol
    may also be noting that a soldier's
    vow on his sword is a serious oath.

4   *put up*

    Sheathe, put away (your sword)

5   *A noble shalt thou have, and present pay*

    I.e., you'll get six shillings eight
    pence (*a noble*), and I'll pay you
    immediately. Possibly a line is
    missing before this, in which Nym
    repeats his desire for the gambling
    debt to be repaid (see line 89).

6   *For I shall sutler be / Unto the camp*

    I.e., I will be a seller of provisions
    to the English army. Sutlers were
    commissioned to sell food and
    drink to the soldiers on campaign;
    they were notorious for their greed
    and for profiting from the hard
    conditions of war. Thomas Nashe's
    The Unfortunate Traveler begins with
    a trick played on such a man, who
    is convinced by the main character
    that he has been accused as a spy

by those who envy his wealth, and
that the only way to evade danger
is to give away all the liquor he has.
In the late Elizabethan period,
accusations about corruption in
and around the army were widespread. Shakespeare draws on
other aspects of this in the *Henry
IV* plays, in the scenes in which
Falstaff recruits his soldiers.

Pistol

Base is the slave that pays.   90

Nym

That now I will have. That's the humor of it.

Pistol

As manhood shall compound.[1] Push home.[2]

                                                            [*They*] *draw.*

Bardolph

[*Drawing*] By this sword, he that makes the first thrust,
I'll kill him! By this sword, I will.

Pistol

Sword is an oath,[3] and oaths must have their course.   95

                                                    [*He sheathes his sword.*]

Bardolph

if   Corporal Nym, an° thou wilt be friends, be friends;
an thou wilt not, why, then, be enemies with me too.
Prithee, put up.[4]

Pistol

A noble shalt thou have, and present pay;[5]
And liquor likewise will I give to thee,   100

unite (us)   And friendship shall combine,° and brotherhood.
I'll live by Nym, and Nym shall live by me.
Is not this just? For I shall sutler be
Unto the camp,[6] and profits will accrue.
Give me thy hand.   [**Nym** *sheathes his sword.*]   105

Nym

I shall have my noble?   [**Bardolph** *sheathes his sword.*]

Pistol

In cash, most justly paid.

Nym

Well, then, that's the humor of 't.

                    Enter **Hostess**.

1   *As ever you come of women*

    If you were born of women (i.e., if
    you have any natural compassion)

2   *he is so shaked of a burning quotidian*
    tertian

    I.e., he is shaking so much from a
    fever. A *quotidian* is a fever that
    returns every day, a *tertian* every
    other day; the Hostess likely
    conflates them in her agitation.

3   *run bad humors on the knight*

    Vented his bad temper on the
    knight (Falstaff)

4   *corroborate*

    Strengthened. *Corroborate* is Pistol's
    mistake for "corrupted" or some
    other word equivalent to *fracted*.

5   *he passes some humors and careers*

    The King indulges his moods and
    impulses. *Careers* is a term from
    horsemanship, referring to short
    gallops.

Hostess

As ever you come of women,[1] come in quickly to
Sir John. Ah, poor heart, he is so shaked of a burn-   110
ing quotidian tertian[2] that it is most lamentable to
behold. Sweet men, come to him.

Nym

The King hath run bad humors on the knight,[3] that's

simple truth   the even° of it.

Pistol

Nym, thou hast spoke the right.   115

fractured; broken   His heart is fracted° and corroborate.[4]

Nym

The King is a good king, but it must be as it may; he
passes some humors and careers.[5]

Pistol

offer condolences to   Let us condole° the knight, for, lambkins, we will live.

[They exit.]

1   *by and by*

     Soon

2   *smooth and even*

     Affably and calmly

3   *the man that was his bedfellow*

     Most likely referring to Scroop.
     Bedfellow **signifies here a favored**
     companion; during Shakespeare's
     time the sharing of a bed between
     friends was not an uncommon
     practice.

4   *dulled and cloyed*

     Satisfied and indulged

5   *a foreign purse*

     I.e., French money

6   *Now sits the wind fair*

     I.e., the wind is blowing favorably

7   *Doing the execution and the act*

     Performing the act of destruction

8   *in head*

     Into an army

Act 2, Scene 2

Enter **Exeter**, **Bedford**, *and* **Westmorland**.

Bedford
'Fore God, his Grace is bold to trust these traitors.

Exeter
They shall be apprehended by and by.[1]

Westmorland
How smooth and even[2] they do bear themselves,
As if allegiance in their bosoms sat,
Crownèd with faith and constant loyalty.   5

Bedford
information The King hath note° of all that they intend,
By interception which they dream not of.

Exeter
Nay, but the man that was his bedfellow,[3]
Whom he hath dulled and cloyed[4] with gracious favors—
That he should, for a foreign purse,[5] so sell   10
His sovereign's life to death and treachery!

> *Sound trumpets. Enter the* **King**, **Scroop**,
> **Cambridge**, *and* **Grey** [*and attendants*].

King Henry
Now sits the wind fair,[6] and we will aboard.
My Lord of Cambridge, and my kind Lord of Masham,
And you, my gentle knight, give me your thoughts.
armed forces Think you not that the powers° we bear with us   15
Will cut their passage through the force of France,
Doing the execution and the act[7]
For which we have in head[8] assembled them?

Scroop
No doubt, my liege, if each man do his best.

1   *We carry not a heart with us from hence /*
    That grows not in a fair consent with ours

    **I.e., all those who leave England to
    fight with us are in total sympathy
    with our goals.**

2   *Nor leave not one behind that doth not*
    wish / Success and conquest to attend
    on us

    **Nor (do we) leave anyone behind
    who does not want us to have
    success and victory. I.e., Henry
    is confident that the invasion is
    widely popular in England.**

3   *shall forget the office of our hand / Sooner*
    than quittance of desert and merit /
    According to the weight and worthiness

    **I.e., I'll forget how to use my hand
    before I'll forget appropriately to
    reward worthy behavior.**

4   *Enlarge the man committed*

    Free the man jailed

5   *on his more advice*

    **I.e., as a result of the man's subse-
    quent reflection (that he was wrong
    to criticize the King)**

King Henry

I doubt not that, since we are well persuaded   20
We carry not a heart with us from hence
That grows not in a fair consent with ours,[1]
Nor leave not one behind that doth not wish
Success and conquest to attend on us.[2]

Cambridge

Never was monarch better feared and loved   25
Than is your Majesty. There's not, I think, a subject
That sits in heart-grief and uneasiness
Under the sweet shade of your government.

Grey

True. Those that were your father's enemies

bitterness; resentment   Have steeped their galls° in honey, and do serve you   30
created   With hearts create° of duty and of zeal.

King Henry

We therefore have great cause of thankfulness
And shall forget the office of our hand
Sooner than quittance of desert and merit
According to the weight and worthiness.[3]   35

Scroop

So service shall with steelèd sinews toil,
i.e., hope of reward   And labor shall refresh itself with hope,°
To do your Grace incessant services.

King Henry

We judge no less. Uncle of Exeter,
Enlarge the man committed[4] yesterday   40
spoke ill; criticized   That railed° against our person. We consider
It was excess of wine that set him on,
And on his more advice[5] we pardon him.

Scroop

confidence   That's mercy, but too much security.°
Let him be punished, sovereign, lest example   45

1   *his sufferance*

     I.e., your tolerance of his abuse

2   *heavy orisons*

     Compelling petitions

3   *proceeding on distemper*

     **That happen because of a tem-
     porarily imbalanced mental or
     emotional state (as the result of
     being drunk)**

4   *winked at*

     Overlooked

5   *how shall we stretch our eye / When
     capital crimes, chewed, swallowed, and
     digested, / Appear before us?*

     **How will we judge the serious
     crimes, which are premeditated,
     when they are brought before us?**

6   *yet enlarge*

     Nonetheless release

7   *the late commissioners*

     **I.e., those who have been recently
     appointed to offices**

8   *it*

     **I.e., the letter of appointment to
     the commissioner's post**

Breed, by his sufferance,[1] more of such a kind.

King Henry

Oh, let us yet be merciful.

Cambridge

So may your Highness, and yet punish too.

Grey

Sir, you show great mercy if you give him life

punishment After the taste of much correction.° 50

King Henry

Alas, your too much love and care of me

Are heavy orisons[2] 'gainst this poor wretch.

If little faults proceeding on distemper[3]

Shall not be winked at,[4] how shall we stretch our eye

When capital crimes, chewed, swallowed, and digested, 55

Appear before us?[5] We'll yet enlarge[6] that man,

Though Cambridge, Scroop, and Grey, in their dear care

And tender preservation of our person,

Would have him punished. And now to our French

affairs causes:°

Who are the late commissioners?[7]

Cambridge

I one, my lord. 60

Your Highness bade me ask for it[8] today.

Scroop

So did you me, my liege.

Grey

And I, my royal sovereign.

King Henry

[*giving them papers*] Then, Richard Earl of Cambridge,
      there is yours.

There yours, Lord Scroop of Masham; and sir knight, 65

Grey of Northumberland, this same is yours.

1   *paper*

    I.e., as pale as paper

2   *have so cowarded and chased your blood /*
    Out of appearance

    Has frightened you so badly (liter-
    ally, "has made such a coward of
    your blood that it has chased it out
    of sight")

3   *quick in us but late*

    Alive in us just recently

4   *light crowns*

    I.e., coins of little weight or value

Read them and know I know your worthiness.
My Lord of Westmorland and uncle Exeter,
We will aboard tonight.—Why, how now, gentlemen?
What see you in those papers that you lose   70
color   So much complexion?°—Look ye how they change.
Their cheeks are paper.¹—Why, what read you there
That have so cowarded and chased your blood
Out of appearance?²

Cambridge
                                        I do confess my fault
And do submit me to your Highness' mercy.   75

Grey, **Scroop**
To which we all appeal.

King Henry
The mercy that was quick in us but late³
By your own counsel is suppressed and killed.
You must not dare, for shame, to talk of mercy,
For your own reasons turn into your bosoms,   80
shaking; tearing   As dogs upon their masters, worrying° you.
—See you, my princes and my noble peers,
These English monsters! My Lord of Cambridge here:
ready / agree   You know how apt° our love was to accord°
privileges   To furnish him with all appurtenants°   85
Belonging to his honor; and this man
easily; with readiness   Hath for a few light crowns⁴ lightly° conspired
plots   And sworn unto the practices° of France
To kill us here in Hampton. To the which
i.e., Grey   This knight,° no less for bounty bound to us   90
Than Cambridge is, hath likewise sworn.—But, oh,
What shall I say to thee, Lord Scroop, thou cruel,
Ingrateful, savage, and inhuman creature?
Thou that didst bear the key of all my counsels,
That knew'st the very bottom of my soul,   95

1 *coined me into gold*

   Used me to get as much money as you wanted

2 *practiced on me for thy use*

   Plotted against me for your own profit

3 *stands off as gross / As black and white*

   Is as obvious as black on white

4 *ever kept together*

   Have always conspired together

5 *yoke-devils*

   I.e., devils working together, like two yoked oxen

6 *Working so grossly in a natural cause / That admiration did not whoop at them*

   I.e., laboring together toward a purpose so obviously well suited (*natural*) to their evil nature that they provoked no outburst of surprise

7 *But thou, 'gainst all proportion, didst bring in / Wonder*

   But you, acting so unnaturally, do provoke surprise

8 *devils that suggest by treasons*

   I.e., devils who tempt people to commit treason

9 *Do botch and bungle up damnation / With patches, colors, and with forms being fetched / From glistering semblances of piety*

   Awkwardly hide their damnable acts with (disguises made from) scraps and showy fragments, (which those devils) have appropriated from glittering images of virtue. *Colors* is meant both literally and as "pretexts" or "reasons."

10 *he that tempered thee bade thee stand up*

   I.e., the devil who shaped you told you to rebel.

11 *Unless to dub thee with the name of traitor*

   I.e., other than to be given the title "traitor." An ironic allusion to the royal knighting ceremony, in which a king would *dub* a knight (i.e., grant him his title) by touching his shoulder with a sword.

12 *lion gait*

   An echo of 1 Peter 5:8: "Be sober and watch, for your adversary the devil, as a roaring lion, walketh about, seeking whom he may devour."

13 *return to vasty Tartar back*

   I.e., head back to immense Hell. *Tartar* is a shortened form of *Tartarus*, in classical mythology the deepest part of the underworld.

14 *Show men dutiful?*

   I.e., do men show themselves to be dutiful?

That almost mightst have coined me into gold,[1]
Wouldst thou have practiced on me for thy use?[2]
May it be possible that foreign hire
Could out of thee extract one spark of evil

hurt   That might annoy° my finger? 'Tis so strange   100
That, though the truth of it stands off as gross
As black and white,[3] my eye will scarcely see it.
Treason and murder ever kept together,[4]
As two yoke-devils[5] sworn to either's purpose,
Working so grossly in a natural cause   105
That admiration did not whoop at them.[6]
But thou, 'gainst all proportion, didst bring in
Wonder[7] to wait on treason and on murder;
And whatsoever cunning fiend it was

worked / unnaturally   That wrought° upon thee so preposterously°   110
vote; fame   Hath got the voice° in Hell for excellence.
All other devils that suggest by treasons[8]
Do botch and bungle up damnation
With patches, colors, and with forms being fetched
From glist'ring semblances of piety;[9]   115
But he that tempered thee bade thee stand up,[10]
motive   Gave thee no instance° why thou shouldst do treason,
Unless to dub thee with the name of traitor.[11]
fooled   If that same demon that hath gulled° thee thus
Should with his lion gait[12] walk the whole world,   120
He might return to vasty Tartar back[13]
i.e., legions of demons   And tell the legions,° "I can never win
A soul so easy as that Englishman's."
suspicion   Oh, how hast thou with jealousy° infected
trust   The sweetness of affiance!° Show men dutiful?[14]   125
Why, so didst thou. Seem they grave and learnèd?
Why, so didst thou. Come they of noble family?
Why, so didst thou. Seem they religious?

1   *gross passion or of mirth or anger*
     **Immoderate feelings either of
     mirth or anger**

2   *in modest complement*
     I.e., in total modesty

3   *Not working with the eye without the ear*
     **I.e., not relying solely on appear-
     ances**

4   *but in purgèd judgment trusting neither*
     **I.e., except as guided by clear judg-
     ment, trusting neither sight nor
     sound (or perhaps, as the phrase
     relates to the judgment of people,
     trusting neither appearance nor
     reputation)**

5   *the full-fraught man and best endued*
     **I.e., (even) the man fully loaded and
     most highly endowed (with virtues)**

6   *fall of man*
     **An allusion to Adam and Eve's failure
     to obey God and their subsequent
     expulsion from Eden**

7   *to the answer of*
     So that they may answer to

8   *For me, the gold of France did not seduce*
     **Cambridge denies the accusation of
     having sold his loyalties, claiming
     that the gold was a means to achieve
     his goal rather than the goal itself;**

but he does not name his actual motive. In fact, his motives are political.
He is the son-in-law of Edmund,
Earl of March, a rival claimant
to the throne. His father is the
Duke of York who appears among
Richard's adherents in *Richard II*;
his older brother is the Duke of
Aumerle in that play, later also the
Duke of York, under which name
he appears in *Henry V* at Agincourt:
see 4.3.129–130, 4.6.3–32, and the
note on the latter passage). Scroop
also has a Yorkist connection: he is
the son of the Stephen Scroop who
announces to Richard II the execution of Bushy, Green, and the Earl
of Wiltshire: *Richard II*, 3.2.91–142.
In other words, this act of treason is
almost certainly part of a continuing
Yorkist claim to the throne, and not
the avaricious or demonic act of
betrayal that Henry claims it is; in
Henry VI, Part One, the Earl of March
explains Cambridge's rebellion
and his treason in just these terms
(2.5.88–89).

9   *I did admit it as a motive / The sooner to
     effect what I intended*
     **I.e., I took the money to more
     quickly bring about my actual goal
     (see note 8 above).**

10   *in sufferance*
     In suffering my punishment

frugal   Why, so didst thou. Or are they spare° in diet,
               Free from gross passion or of mirth or anger,[1]   130
passions   Constant in spirit, not swerving with the blood,°
               Garnished and decked in modest complement,[2]
               Not working with the eye without the ear,[3]
               And but in purgèd judgment trusting neither?[4]
sifted (like flour)   Such and so finely bolted° didst thou seem.   135
               And thus thy fall hath left a kind of blot
               To mark the full-fraught man and best endued[5]
               With some suspicion. I will weep for thee,
               For this revolt of thine, methinks, is like
obvious   Another fall of man.[6]—Their faults are open.°   140
               Arrest them to the answer of[7] the law,
               And God acquit them of their practices.

               Exeter
               I arrest thee of high treason, by the name of
               Richard Earl of Cambridge.
               I arrest thee of high treason, by the name of   145
               Henry Lord Scroop of Masham.
               I arrest thee of high treason, by the name of
               Thomas Grey, knight, of Northumberland.

               Scroop
exposed   Our purposes God justly hath discovered,°
               And I repent my fault more than my death,   150
               Which I beseech your Highness to forgive,
               Although my body pay the price of it.

               Cambridge
               For me, the gold of France did not seduce,[8]
               Although I did admit it as a motive
               The sooner to effect what I intended.[9]   155
               But God be thankèd for prevention,
               Which I in sufferance[10] heartily will rejoice,
               Beseeching God and you to pardon me.

1   *to you, as us, like*

     To you, as to us, equally

2   *But every rub is smoothèd on our way*

     That every obstacle has been
     cleared from our path. In the game
     of bowls, the word *rub* names any
     uneven ground that disrupts the
     bowl.

Grey

Never did faithful subject more rejoice

At the discovery of most dangerous treason 160

Than I do at this hour joy o'er myself,

Prevented from a damnèd enterprise.

My fault, but not my body, pardon, sovereign.

King Henry

acquit; absolve God quit° you in His mercy. Hear your sentence.

You have conspired against our royal person, 165

Joined with an enemy proclaimed, and from his coffers

payment in advance Received the golden earnest° of our death,

Wherein you would have sold your king to slaughter,

His princes and his peers to servitude,

His subjects to oppression and contempt, 170

And his whole kingdom into desolation.

In regard to Touching° our person seek we no revenge,

care for But we our kingdom's safety must so tender,°

Whose ruin you have sought, that to her laws

We do deliver you. Get you therefore hence, 175

Poor miserable wretches, to your death,

The taste whereof God of His mercy give

You patience to endure, and true repentance

grievous Of all your dear° offences.—Bear them hence.

[**Cambridge**, **Scroop**, *and* **Grey**, *guarded,*] *exit.*

Now, lords, for France, the enterprise whereof 180

Shall be to you, as us, like ¹ glorious.

We doubt not of a fair and lucky war,

Since God so graciously hath brought to light

This dangerous treason lurking in our way

To hinder our beginnings. We doubt not now 185

But every rub is smoothèd on our way.²

Then forth, dear countrymen! Let us deliver

army Our puissance° into the hand of God,

1   *straight in expedition*

     Promptly into motion

2   *The signs of war advance!*

     I.e., raise the banners!

Putting it straight in expedition.[1]

Heartily; With resolve Cheerly° to sea! The signs of war advance![2]   190

No king of England, if not king of France!

Flourish. [They exit.]

1 *Staines*

A town west of London, a crossing point of the river Thames on the route to Southampton

2 *earn*

Grieve (as in line 3) but also with the sense of "make money," more necessary now after Falstaff's death

3 *Arthur's bosom*

The Hostess intends "Abraham's bosom" (i.e., Heaven). In the Bible, Abraham is the progenitor of the Jewish people; the phrase "Abraham's bosom" first appears in Luke 16:22.

4 *christom child*

A newly baptized child; i.e., one wearing a *chrisom*, or baptismal robe. The Hostess's *christom* may be a mistaken pronunciation or, perhaps, her conflation of "chrisom" and "Christian" / "christened."

5 *e'en just*

Precisely

6 *flowers*

Flowers spread in the sick room

7 *'a babbled of green fields*

This is a notorious textual crux. In the Folio, the phrase reads "a Table of green fields," which seems to make little sense, although it has had its occasional defenders. Lewis Theobald famously proposed that *Table* was a misreading of the word "babbled," in the manuscript from which the Folio was printed; on the other hand, other editors have argued that we can't know this for certain and so should emend the sentence to its simplest possible form, "he talked of green fields." The real reading is, of course, unrecoverable; here, as in many other places in Shakespeare, all we have are our own best guesses. The dying Falstaff seems to have been thinking of the opening of Psalm 23, although the Hostess does not appear to realize this: "The Lord is my shepherd; I shall not want. / He maketh me to rest in green pasture" (Geneva version). In the *Henry IV* plays, Falstaff showed a fondness for quoting scripture, often with comic inappropriateness. Here, he speaks directly to the point: he is in fact in the valley of the shadow of death.

8 *sack*

A dry Spanish wine, a favorite of Falstaff's in *Henry IV, Parts One* and *Two*

Act 2, Scene 3

Enter **Pistol**, **Nym**, **Bardolph**, **Boy**, *and* **Hostess**.

Hostess

Prithee, honey-sweet husband, let me bring thee to
Staines.[1]

Pistol

grieve   No, for my manly heart doth earn.° Bardolph, be blithe;

boasting   Nym, rouse thy vaunting° veins; Boy, bristle thy courage

up; for Falstaff he is dead, and we must earn[2] therefore.   5

Bardolph

Would I were with him, wheresome'er he is, either in
Heaven or in Hell!

Hostess

Nay, sure, he's not in Hell! He's in Arthur's bosom,[3]

He   if ever man went to Arthur's bosom. 'A° made a finer

as if   end, and went away an° it had been any christom   10

departed   child.[4] 'A parted° e'en just[5] between twelve and one,

e'en at the turning o' the tide. For after I saw him
fumble with the sheets and play with flowers[6] and
smile upon his fingers' end, I knew there was but one
way; for his nose was as sharp as a pen, and 'a babbled   15
of green fields.[7] "How now, Sir John?" quoth I. "What,
man? Be o' good cheer!" So 'a cried out, "God, God,
God!" three or four times. Now I, to comfort him, bid

he   him 'a° should not think of God; I hoped there was no

need to trouble himself with any such thoughts yet.   20
So 'a bade me lay more clothes on his feet. I put my
hand into the bed and felt them, and they were as cold
as any stone; then I felt to his knees, and so up'ard and
upward, and all was as cold as any stone.

Nym

against   They say he cried out of° sack.[8]   25

1   *carnation*

A shade of light pink. The Hostess mishears, perhaps intentionally, *incarnate* (i.e., in human form).

2   *handle*

(1) discuss; (2) touch; fondle

3   *rheumatic*

Probably her mistake for "lunatic" (i.e., suffering from delirium)

4   *Whore of Babylon*

A monstrous female figure associated with evil, decadence, and lust (described in Revelation 17:1–6). In Shakespeare's time, *Whore of Babylon* had become an abusive Protestant epithet for the Roman Catholic Church. Here, the phrase is suggested by *rheumatic*, as *rheum* and *Rome* were pronounced similarly.

5   *my chattels and my movables*

My personal property

6   *Let senses rule.*

I.e., stay alert; be careful.

7   *The word is "Pitch and pay."*

Your slogan should be "Cash only, no credit."

8   *men's faiths are wafer cakes*

I.e., men's promises are brittle (and thus easy to break)

9   *Holdfast is the only dog*

Referring to the proverb "Brag is a good dog, but Holdfast is better," where a *brag* is a nail or spike and a *holdfast* is a clamp or hook (i.e., something better at holding things). Pistol means that the Hostess needs to be steadfast in holding onto his property and following his advice while he is away.

Hostess

he Ay, that 'a° did.

Bardolph

And of women.

Hostess

Nay, that 'a did not.

Boy

Yes, that 'a did and said they were devils incarnate.

Hostess

'A could never abide carnation;[1] 'twas a color he never   30
liked.

Boy

because of 'A said once the devil would have him about° women.

Hostess

'A did in some sort, indeed, handle[2] women; but then he
was rheumatic,[3] and talked of the Whore of Babylon.[4]

Boy

Do you not remember, 'a saw a flea stick upon Bar-   35
dolph's nose, and 'a said it was a black soul burning in
Hell?

Bardolph

i.e., alcohol Well, the fuel° is gone that maintained that fire. That's
all the riches I got in his service.

Nym

move on Shall we shog?° The King will be gone from South-   40
ampton.

Pistol

Come, let's away. My love, give me thy lips.   [*They kiss.*]
Look to my chattels and my movables.[5]
Let senses rule.[6] The word is "Pitch and pay."[7]
Trust none,   45
For oaths are straws, men's faiths are wafer cakes,[8]
dear And Holdfast is the only dog,[9] my duck.°

1   *Let huswifery appear.*

   I.e., be thrifty as you manage the
   household.

2   *Keep close*

   (1) stay inside; (2) be discreet; don't
   gossip; (3) remain chaste

beware (Latin)   Therefore, *caveto*° be thy counselor.

i.e., eyes / Companions   Go; clear thy crystals.°—Yokefellows° in arms,

Let us to France, like horse leeches, my boys,   50

To suck, to suck, the very blood to suck!

Boy

And that's but unwholesome food, they say.

Pistol

Touch her soft mouth and march.

Bardolph

Farewell, hostess.   [*Kissing her.*]

Nym

I cannot kiss, that is the humor of it; but adieu.   55

Pistol

Let huswifery appear.[1] Keep close,[2] I thee command.

Hostess

Farewell! Adieu!   *They exit* [*separately*].

1   *late*

Recent. These *late examples* include
French losses at Crécy (1346) and
Poitiers (1356).

2   *the fatal and neglected English*

I.e., the fatally underestimated
English

3   *As were a war in expectation*

As if a war were anticipated

4   *Whitsun morris dance*

Whitsunday (Pentecost) comes
seven weeks after Easter and marks
the beginning of the festive week of
Whitsuntide. A *morris dance* is a type
of folk dance, often performed during Whitsuntide to celebrate the
arrival of summer.

Act 2, Scene 4

Flourish. Enter the French **King**, *the* **Dauphin**, *the Dukes of Berri and Britaine,* [*the* **Constable**, *and others*].

King of France

Thus comes the English with full power upon us,
And more than carefully it us concerns
To answer royally in our defenses.
Therefore the Dukes of Berri and of Britaine,
Of Brabant and of Orléans, shall make forth,   5
And you, Prince Dauphin, with all swift dispatch,

reinforce To line° and new-repair our towns of war
defensive; of defense With men of courage and with means defendant,°
i.e., Henry For England° his approaches makes as fierce
whirlpool As waters to the sucking of a gulf.°   10
It fits us then to be as provident
As fear may teach us out of late [1] examples
Left by the fatal and neglected English [2]
battlefields Upon our fields.°

Dauphin

respected   My most redoubted° father,
fitting; proper It is most meet° we arm us 'gainst the foe,   15
For peace itself should not so dull a kingdom,
Even if Though° war nor no known quarrel were in question,
i.e., troops But that defenses, musters,° preparations,
Should be maintained, assembled, and collected
As were a war in expectation. [3]   20
Therefore I say 'tis meet we all go forth
To view the sick and feeble parts of France.
And let us do it with no show of fear—
No, with no more than if we heard that England
Were busied with a Whitsun morris dance. [4]   25
irresponsibly For, my good liege, she is so idly° kinged,

1   *fear attends her not*

    There is no reason to fear her.

2   *exception*

    Taking exception; disagreement

3   *vanities forespent*

    Earlier frivolous behavior

4   *the outside of the Roman Brutus*

    While plotting to overthrow Tarqu-
    inius Superbus, the King of Rome,
    Lucius Junius Brutus (c. 6th century
    B.C.) pretended to be stupid to allay
    the king's suspicions; the Latin
    word *brutus* in fact means "stupid."
    An *outside* is a deceiving appear-
    ance.

5   *But though we think it so*

    But even if we were to believe that

6   *So the proportions of defense are filled*

    I.e., thereby is an adequate defense
    prepared.

7   *Which of a weak and niggardly
    projection / Doth, like a miser, spoil his
    coat with scanting / A little cloth*

    Which, if prepared feebly and on
    the cheap, will be useless, just as a
    miser ruins a coat when he provides
    the tailor with too little cloth

8   *look you*

    Look (to it that) you; be careful to

9   *kindred*

    I.e., Edward III and his son Edward
    the Black Prince

10 *hath been fleshed upon us*

    Have developed a liking for our
    blood. Literally, a reference to the
    practice of feeding hunting animals
    meat from freshly killed game in
    order to encourage their eagerness
    to pursue prey.

11 *Crécy battle*

    An English victory over the French
    in 1346

strangely Her scepter so fantastically° borne
capricious By a vain, giddy, shallow, humorous° youth,
That fear attends her not.[1]

Constable
                              Oh peace, Prince Dauphin!
You are too much mistaken in this king.   30
recent —Question your Grace the late° ambassadors,
dignity With what great state° he heard their embassy,
How well supplied with noble counselors,
in addition How modest in exception,[2] and withal°
terrifying How terrible° in constant resolution,   35
And you shall find his vanities forespent[3]
Were but the outside of the Roman Brutus,[4]
Covering discretion with a coat of folly,
manure As gardeners do with ordure° hide those roots
That shall first spring and be most delicate.   40

Dauphin
Well, 'tis not so, my Lord High Constable;
But though we think it so,[5] it is no matter.
judge In cases of defense 'tis best to weigh°
The enemy more mighty than he seems,
So the proportions of defense are filled,[6]   45
Which of a weak and niggardly projection
Doth, like a miser, spoil his coat with scanting
A little cloth.[7]

King of France
                              Think we King Harry strong,
And, princes, look you[8] strongly arm to meet him.
The kindred[9] of him hath been fleshed upon us,[10]   50
breed And he is bred out of that bloody strain°
That haunted us in our familiar paths.
Witness our too-much-memorable shame
fought When Crécy battle[11] fatally was struck,°

1   *mountain sire*

I.e., Edward III, who was either (1) as
tall as or built like a mountain; (2)
born in the mountains of Wales; (3)
immovable, as a mountain

2   *The patterns that by God and by French
fathers / Had twenty years been made*

I.e., twenty-year-old French
soldiers. The King laments that the
finest examples (*patterns*) of young
Frenchmen were cut down in the
Battle of Crécy.

3   *native mightiness and fate*

Inherited strength and destiny (to
conquer)

4   *Turn head and stop pursuit*

Turn and face (the pursuer) and
(thus) end the chase by taking up
the fight.

5   *Most spend their mouths*

Bark the most

6   *Take up the English short*

Give a sharp, decisive response to
the English.

And all our princes captived by the hand   55
Of that black name, Edward, Black Prince of Wales,
Whiles that his mountain sire,[1] on mountain standing,
Up in the air, crowned with the golden sun,
progeny; child   Saw his heroical seed° and smiled to see him
Mangle the work of nature and deface   60
The patterns that by God and by French fathers
Had twenty years been made.[2] This is a stem
Of that victorious stock, and let us fear
The native mightiness and fate[3] of him.

Enter a **Messenger**.

Messenger
Ambassadors from Harry, King of England,   65
Do crave admittance to your Majesty.
King of France
immediate   We'll give them present° audience. Go and bring them.
                                   [**Messenger** *exits*.]
You see this chase is hotly followed, friends.
Dauphin
Turn head and stop pursuit,[4] for coward dogs
Most spend their mouths[5] when what they seem to
         threaten   70
Runs far before them. Good my sovereign,
Take up the English short,[6] and let them know
Of what a monarchy you are the head.
Self-love, my liege, is not so vile a sin
As self-neglecting.   75

Enter **Exeter** [*and other lords*].

1   *the ordinance of times*

    I.e., tradition

2   *no sinister nor no awkward*

    Neither an irregular nor an oblique

3   *wormholes*

    **I.e., worm-eaten books or
    documents**

4   *memorable line*

    Notable *line* of descent

5   *Willing you overlook this pedigree*

    **Bidding you to read over this family
    tree**

6   *Jove*

    **In Roman mythology, the king of
    the gods**

King of France
From our brother of England?

Exeter
From him, and thus he greets your Majesty:
He wills you, in the name of God Almighty,

aside That you divest yourself and lay apart°
The borrowed glories that, by gift of Heaven,   80
belong By law of nature and of nations, 'longs°
To him and to his heirs, namely, the crown
far-reaching And all wide-stretchèd° honors that pertain
By custom and the ordinance of times [1]
Unto the crown of France. That you may know   85
'Tis no sinister nor no awkward [2] claim,
Picked from the wormholes [3] of long-vanished days,
dug up Nor from the dust of old oblivion raked,°
He sends you this most memorable line, [4]
                                             [*Handing a document*]
conclusive In every branch truly demonstrative,°   90
Willing you overlook this pedigree. [5]
directly And when you find him evenly° derived
From his most famed of famous ancestors,
Edward the Third, he bids you then resign
wrongfully Your crown and kingdom, indirectly° held   95
rightful / claimant From him, the native° and true challenger.°

King of France
Or else what follows?

Exeter
i.e., battle Bloody constraint,° for if you hide the crown
dig Even in your hearts, there will he rake° for it.
Therefore in fierce tempest is he coming,   100
In thunder and in earthquake, like a Jove, [6]
demanding That if requiring° fail, he will compel,

1   *in the bowels of the Lord*
    I.e., the mercy of God (cf. Philip-
    pians 1:8)

2   *on your head / Turning the widows' tears*
    I.e., make you answerable for the
    tears of the women widowed by it

3   *privy maidens' groans*
    Maidens' private grievings (though
    it is possible *privy* is an error for
    "privèd," i.e., deprived or "pining"
    as in the Quarto)

4   *may not misbecome*
    I.e., may not be unflattering to

5   *doth he prize you at*
    Does he think you are worth

6   *an if*
    If

7   *in grant of all demands at large*
    By agreeing to all (our) *demands* in
    full

8   *womby vaultages*
    Womblike caverns

9   *In second accent of his ordnance*
    In the echo of his artillary

10 *render fair return*
    Make a pleasant reply

And bids you, in the bowels of the Lord,[1]
Deliver up the crown and to take mercy
On the poor souls for whom this hungry war   105
vast Opens his vasty° jaws, and on your head
Turning the widows' tears,[2] the orphans' cries,
The dead men's blood, the privy maidens' groans,[3]
For husbands, fathers, and betrothèd lovers
That shall be swallowed in this controversy.   110
This is his claim, his threatening, and my message—
Unless the Dauphin be in presence here,
To whom expressly I bring greeting too.

King of France

For us, we will consider of this further.
Tomorrow shall you bear our full intent   115
Back to our brother England.

Dauphin

                          For the Dauphin,
I stand here for him. What to him from England?

Exeter

Scorn and defiance, slight regard, contempt,
And anything that may not misbecome[4]
The mighty sender, doth he prize you at.[5]   120
royalty Thus says my King: an if[6] your father's highness°
Do not, in grant of all demands at large,[7]
Sweeten the bitter mock you sent his Majesty,
for He'll call you to so hot an answer of° it
That caves and womby vaultages[8] of France   125
Shall chide your trespass and return your mock
In second accent of his ordnance.[9]

Dauphin

Say, if my father render fair return,[10]
It is against my will, for I desire
conflict Nothing but odds° with England. To that end,   130

1   *Even to the utmost grain*

    I.e., to the very last second (*grain*
    refers to the sand in an hourglass)

2   *Dispatch us with all speed*

    I.e., quickly give us your response.
    Exeter disregards royal protocol
    by addressing the King after the
    flourish (trumpet fanfare), which
    is intended to mark the end of the
    meeting.

3   *is footed*

    Has set foot (i.e., has landed)

idleness As matching to his youth and vanity,°

i.e., tennis balls I did present him with the Paris balls.°

Exeter

royal palace He'll make your Paris Louvre° shake for it,

foremost Were it the mistress° court of mighty Europe.

And be assured, you'll find a difference, 135

As we his subjects have in wonder found,

younger Between the promise of his greener° days

And these he masters now. Now he weighs time

Even to the utmost grain.¹ That you shall read

In your own losses, if he stay in France. 140

King of France

Tomorrow shall you know our mind at full.

Flourish.

Exeter

Dispatch us with all speed,² lest that our King

Come here himself to question our delay;

For he is footed³ in this land already.

King of France

You shall be soon dispatched with fair conditions. 145

breathing space A night is but small breath° and little pause

To answer matters of this consequence.

Flourish. They exit.

1   *with imagined wing*

     On the wings of imagination

2   *Dover*

     Likely a mistake for "Hampton"
     (i.e., Southampton), though Dover
     is also a port from which one might
     sail to France.

3   *Embark his royalty*

     I.e., take himself aboard

4   *With silken streamers the young Phoebus*
     fanning

     I.e., its silken banners waving
     across the morning sun. In Roman
     mythology Phoebus is the sun god;
     the young Phoebus is the rising sun,
     imagined here as being cooled by
     the fleet's banners.

5   *whistle*

     The whistle of the ship master or
     boatswain

6   *threaden sails*

     Sails woven of thread

7   *surge*

     Swell of the waves

8   *Grapple your minds to sternage*

     Fasten your imaginations (as with
     grappling hooks) to the sterns

9   *as dead midnight still*

     I.e., as silent as midnight

10   *choice-drawn*

     (1) carefully picked; (2) present by
     choice (i.e., volunteer)

11   *carriages*

     Wooden support structures for
     cannon (*ordnance*)

12   *girded*

     (1) surrounded, besieged; (2) ready
     for action

Act 3, Prologue

Enter **Chorus**.

Chorus

     Thus with imagined wing[1] our swift scene flies

speed   In motion of no less celerity°

     Than that of thought. Suppose that you have seen

well-equipped   The well-appointed° King at Dover[2] pier

gallant   Embark his royalty,[3] and his brave° fleet   5

     With silken streamers the young Phoebus fanning.[4]

imaginations   Play with your fancies° and in them behold

     Upon the hempen tackle shipboys climbing;

     Hear the shrill whistle,[5] which doth order give

     To sounds confused; behold the threaden sails,[6]   10

     Borne with th' invisible and creeping wind,

ship's hulls   Draw the huge bottoms° through the furrowed sea,

     Breasting the lofty surge.[7] Oh, do but think

shore   You stand upon the rivage° and behold

     A city on th' inconstant billows dancing,   15

     For so appears this fleet majestical,

(a French port)   Holding due course to Harfleur.° Follow, follow!

     Grapple your minds to sternage[8] of this navy

     And leave your England as dead midnight still,[9]

     Guarded with grandsires, babies, and old women,   20

vigor / power   Either past or not arrived to pith° and puissance;°

     For who is he whose chin is but enriched

     With one appearing hair that will not follow

selected / soldiers   These culled° and choice-drawn[10] cavaliers° to France?

     Work, work your thoughts, and therein see a siege;   25

     Behold the ordnance on their carriages,[11]

     With fatal mouths gaping on girded[12] Harfleur.

     Suppose th' ambassador from the French comes back,

     Tells Harry that the King doth offer him

1   *The offer likes not*

     The offer does not please (Henry).

2   *linstock*

     **Long stick with a match at one end,
     used to light cannon**

3   Alarum, and chambers go off.

     **A call to arms (typically sounded
     with drums and trumpets) followed
     by the offstage firing of small
     cannon**

4   *eke out*

     **Supplement; supply what is
     necessary to complete (see Act 1,
     Prologue, line 23)**

as   Katharine his daughter, and with her, to° dowry,   30
         Some petty and unprofitable dukedoms.
         The offer likes not;[1] and the nimble gunner
         With linstock[2] now the devilish cannon touches,
                     Alarum, and chambers go off.[3]

Continue to   And down goes all before them. Still° be kind,
         And eke out[4] our performance with your mind.   35
                         He exits.

1   *breach*

I.e., gap in Harfleur's fortifications, the result of artillery fire

2   *terrible aspect*

Terrifying look

3   *Let it pry through the portage of the head*

I.e., let it stare out through the eye sockets. *Portage* literally means "portholes."

4   *jutty his confounded base*

Jut over its eroded base

5   *fet from fathers of war-proof*

Derived from fathers (whose valor was) tested in war

6   *Alexanders*

Refers to Alexander the Great (356–323 B.C.) who regretted that he had only one world to conquer

7   *sheathed their swords for lack of argument*

I.e., stopped fighting (only) because they ran out of opponents

8   *Be copy now to men of grosser blood*

Be a model now to men of lesser valor (i.e., the French, whose valor is less, not being the sons of such noble *fathers*).

9   *mettle of your pasture*

Quality of your upbringing (as Englishmen)

Act 3, Scene 1

Enter the **King**, **Exeter**, **Bedford**, *and* **Gloucester**. *Alarum,*
[with soldiers carrying] scaling ladders at Harfleur.

King Henry

Once more unto the breach,[1] dear friends, once more,

Or close the wall up with our English dead!

In peace there's nothing so becomes a man

As modest stillness and humility,

But when the blast of war blows in our ears,   5

Then imitate the action of the tiger:

Stiffen the sinews, conjure up the blood,

natural feeling / ugly   Disguise fair nature° with hard-favored° rage.

Then lend the eye a terrible aspect;[2]

Let it pry through the portage of the head[3]   10

overhang   Like the brass cannon; let the brow o'erwhelm° it

frighteningly / worn   As fearfully° as doth a gallèd° rock

O'erhang and jutty his confounded base,[4]

Washed / destructive   Swilled° with the wild and wasteful° ocean.

Now set the teeth and stretch the nostril wide,   15

Hold hard the breath, and bend up every spirit

its   To his° full height. On, on, you noblest English,

Whose blood is fet from fathers of war-proof,[5]

Fathers that, like so many Alexanders,[6]

evening   Have in these parts, from morn till even,° fought   20

And sheathed their swords for lack of argument.[7]

bastards →

Dishonor not your mothers: now attest

That those whom you called fathers did beget you.

Be copy now to men of grosser blood[8]

commoners   And teach them how to war. And you, good yeomen,°   25

Whose limbs were made in England, show us here

The mettle of your pasture.[9] Let us swear

worthy of   That you are worth° your breeding, which I doubt not,

1 *so mean and base*

   However low in social status

2 *in the slips*

   Held in leashes

3 *The game's afoot!*

   I.e., the quarry is loose; the hunt begins

4 *upon this charge*

   As you charge (these fortifications)

5 *Saint George*

   England's patron saint

For there is none of you so mean and base [1]
That hath not noble luster in your eyes.   30
I see you stand like greyhounds in the slips, [2]
Straining upon the start. The game's afoot! [3]
Follow your spirit and, upon this charge, [4]
Cry "God for Harry, England, and Saint George!" [5]

cannon   *Alarum, and chambers° go off.* [*They exit.*]

1   *Corporal*

    **Bardolph was a lieutenant at 2.1.2.
    His rank here is probably merely an
    oversight on Shakespeare's part.**

2   *knocks are too hot*

    **I.e., fighting is too intense (*knocks* =
    blows)**

3   *God's vassals*

    I.e., men

4   *Avaunt, you cullions!*

    **I.e., begone, you knaves! (*Cullions*
    literally means "testicles.")**

Act 3, Scene 2

Enter **Nym**, **Bardolph**, **Pistol**, *and* **Boy**.

Bardolph

On, on, on, on, on! To the breach, to the breach!

Nym

Pray thee, Corporal,[1] stay. The knocks are too hot,[2]

box   and for mine own part I have not a case° of lives. The

i.e., simple truth   humor of it is too hot; that is the very plainsong° of it.

Pistol

"The plainsong" is most just, for humors do abound.   5

Knocks go and come; God's vassals[3] drop and die,

> [*sings*] And sword and shield
>
> In bloody field
>
> Doth win immortal fame.

Boy

I wish   Would° I were in an alehouse in London; I would give   10

all my fame for a pot of ale and safety.

Pistol

And I:

> [*sings*] If wishes would prevail with me,
>
> My purpose should not fail with me,

hurry   > But thither would I hie.°   15

Boy

> [*sings*] As duly, but not as truly,
>
> As bird doth sing on bough.

Enter **Fluellen**.

Fluellen

Up to the breach, you dogs! Avaunt, you cullions![4]

139

1   *men of mold*

I.e., mere mortals (*mold* meaning "earth")

2   *bawcock*

Fine fellow (from French *beau coq*, "fine bird")

3   *sweet chuck*

Pistol tries to be ingratiating with this term of familiarity; *chuck* is roughly equivalent to "pet."

4   *These be good humors.*

I.e., this is an excellent way to behave. Nym reacts with sarcasm to the spectacle of Fluellen beating his own soldiers.

5   *Your Honor wins bad humors.*

I.e., you (Fluellen) only succeed in demonstrating your bad temper.

6   *swashers*

Braggarts; swaggerers

7   *boy to*

(1) servant to; (2) a boy compared with

8   *could not be man to me*

(1) could not be my manservant; (2) could not be more of a man than I am

9   *white-livered and red-faced*

I.e., cowardly and angry looking

10   *'a faces it out*

I.e., he looks aggressive

11   *breaks words*

Speaks angry words. Pistol's zeal does not extend to actual fighting: he can *break words* but not *swords* (hence he *keeps whole weapons*).

12   *twelve leagues*

Approximately 36 miles

13   *carry coals*

(1) endure insults; (2) undertake dirty work

14   *makes much against my manhood*

Is insulting to my manliness

15   *pocketing up of wrongs*

(1) enduring insults; (2) receiving stolen goods

Pistol

Be merciful, great duke, to men of mold.[1]

Abate thy rage, abate thy manly rage,   20

Abate thy rage, great duke.

Good bawcock,[2] bate thy rage. Use lenity, sweet
   chuck.[3]

Nym

These be good humors.[4] Your Honor wins bad humors.[5]

[*All but* **Boy**] *exit.*

Boy

As young as I am, I have observed these three swash-

ers.[6] I am boy to[7] them all three, but all they three,   25

though they would serve me, could not be man to me,[8]

buffoons   for indeed three such antics° do not amount to a man.

As for   For° Bardolph, he is white-livered and red-faced,[9] by

he   the means whereof 'a° faces it out[10] but fights not. For

Pistol, he hath a killing tongue and a quiet sword, by   30

the means whereof 'a breaks words[11] and keeps whole

weapons. For Nym, he hath heard that men of few

words are the best men, and therefore he scorns to say

his prayers, lest 'a should be thought a coward; but his

few bad words are matched with as few good deeds, for   35

'a never broke any man's head but his own, and that was

against a post when he was drunk. They will steal any-

plunder; booty   thing and call it purchase.° Bardolph stole a lute case,

bore it twelve leagues,[12] and sold it for three halfpence.

thievery   Nym and Bardolph are sworn brothers in filching,° and   40

(port in France)   in Calais° they stole a fire shovel. I knew by that piece

of service the men would carry coals.[13] They would

have me as familiar with men's pockets as their gloves

or their handkerchiefs, which makes much against my

manhood,[14] if I should take from another's pocket to   45

put into mine, for it is plain pocketing up of wrongs.[15]

1   *Their villainy goes against my weak*
    stomach, and therefore I must cast it up.
    Their bad behavior (1) goes against
    my inclinations, and therefore I
    must reject it; (2) nauseates me,
    and therefore makes me vomit.

2   *mines*
    Tunnels excavated beneath enemy
    fortifications and filled with explo-
    sives to cause the fortifications'
    collapse

3   *disciplines of the war*
    Military science

4   *th' athversary*
    "The adversary," as pronounced in
    Fluellen's Welsh accent

5   *is digt himself four yard under the*
    countermines
    I.e., has dug his own tunnels four
    yards beneath the English ones

6   *plow*
    I.e., blow. Fluellen's Welsh accent
    causes him to substitute *p* for *b* (as
    here), *ch* for *j* (as in *Cheshu* in line 64)
    and *f* for *v* (as in *falorous* in line 70).

7   *directions*
    Understanding (of proper military
    procedure)

8   *Captain MacMorris*
    Michael Neill has suggested that

this is an Irish version of the English
name "Fitzmaurice"; if so, it suggests that MacMorris may be one
of the Old English—that is, English
settlers who had occupied parts of
Ireland since as early as the reign
of Henry II and who had over time
adopted the language and customs
of Ireland. The Old English were figures of particular anxiety in English
accounts of Ireland, since their very
existence suggested the precari-
ousness of English identity. See, for
example, Edmund Spenser's *A View
of the Present State of Ireland* (1596).
MacMorris's Irish accent is indicated phonetically in Shakespeare's
text, like Fluellen's Welsh accent
and, later, Jamy's Scottish accent.

9   *in his beard*
    To his face

I must leave them and seek some better service. Their
villainy goes against my weak stomach, and therefore
I must cast it up.[1]   *He exits.*

Enter **Gower** [*and* **Fluellen**].

Gower

immediately   Captain Fluellen, you must come presently° to the   50
mines.[2] The Duke of Gloucester would speak with you.

Fluellen

To the mines? Tell you the Duke it is not so good to
come to the mines, for, look you, the mines is not ac-
i.e., depth   cording to the disciplines of the war.[3] The concavities°
of it is not sufficient, for, look you, th' athversary,[4] you   55
explain   may discuss° unto the Duke, look you, is digt himself
Jesu (Jesus)   four yard under the countermines.[5] By Cheshu,° I think
he (i.e., the enemy)   'a° will plow[6] up all, if there is not better directions.[7]

Gower

command   The Duke of Gloucester, to whom the order° of the
siege is given, is altogether directed by an Irishman, a   60
very valiant gentleman, i' faith.

Fluellen

It is Captain MacMorris,[8] is it not?

Gower

I think it be.

Fluellen

By Cheshu, he is an ass, as any in the world! I will
verify as much in his beard.[9] He has no more direc-   65
tions in the true disciplines of the wars, look you, of
i.e., has   the Roman disciplines, than is° a puppy dog.

Enter **MacMorris** *and Captain* **Jamy**.

1   *great expedition*

    Quick wit; good instincts

2   *pioneers*

    Soldiers assigned to dig tunnels
    (*mines*) and other fortifications

3   *given o'er*

    Stopped

4   *la*

    An emphatic interjection, like
    "indeed"

Gower

he Here 'a° comes, and the Scots captain, Captain Jamy, with him.

Fluellen

i.e., valorous Captain Jamy is a marvelous falorous° gentleman, that 70
is certain, and of great expedition [1] and knowledge in
i.e., ancient th' aunchient° wars, upon my particular knowledge of
his directions. By Cheshu, he will maintain his argument as well as any military man in the world, in the
ancient disciplines of the pristine° wars of the Romans. 75

Jamy

i.e., good I say gud° day, Captain Fluellen.

Fluellen

evening (or afternoon) Good e'en° to your Worship, good Captain James.

Gower

left How now, Captain MacMorris, have you quit° the
mines? Have the pioneers [2] given o'er? [3]

MacMorris

i.e., 'tis By Chrish, la, [4] 'tish° ill done. The work ish give over; the 80
trompet sound the retreat. By my hand I swear, and
my father's soul, the work ish ill done; it ish give over.
I would have blowed up the town, so Chrish save me,
la, in an hour. Oh, 'tish ill done; 'tish ill done! By my
hand, 'tish ill done. 85

Fluellen

Captain MacMorris, I beseech you now, will you
allow / disagreements vouchsafe° me, look you, a few disputations° with
you, as partly touching or concerning the disciplines
of the war, the Roman wars, in the way of argument,
look you, and friendly communication—partly to 90
satisfy my opinion, and partly for the satisfaction,
look you, of my mind—as touching the direction of
the military discipline; that is the point.

1   *It sall be vary gud, gud feith, gud captains*
    bath

    **It shall be very good, good faith,
    good captains both. Jamy's Scottish
    accent is thickly deployed here.**

2   *with gud leve*

    **With good leave (i.e., if you will
    allow)**

3   *marry*

    **Indeed (a mild oath, derived from
    by the Virgin Mary)**

4   *be Chrish*

    By Christ

5   *ay'll de gud service, or I'll lig i' th' grund*
    for it

    **I'll do good service, or I'll lie in the
    ground for it (i.e., die trying).**

6   *I wad full fain heard some question*
    'tween you tway

    **I would very gladly have heard some
    discussion between you two.**

7   *under your correction*

    Unless I'm mistaken

8   *What ish my nation?*

    **What about my nation? This, and
    what follows, has proved notori-
    ously difficult to interpret, partly
    because MacMorris is clearly**
    incensed and so, not fully lucid.
    Philip Edwards has suggested a
    paraphrase for the first question:
    "What is this separate race you're
    implying by using the phrase 'your
    nation'? Who are you, a Welshman,
    to talk of the Irish as though they
    were a separate nation from you?"
    See *Threshold of a Nation: A Study in
    English and Irish Drama* (Cambridge:
    Cambridge University Press, 1979),
    pp. 75–76.

9   *Ish a villain*

    **He is a villain (who makes such a
    statement).**

Jamy

It sall be vary gud, gud feith, gud captains bath,[1] and

requite; answer   I sall quit° you with gud leve,[2] as I may pick occasion.   95

That sall I, marry.[3]

MacMorris

It is no time to discourse, so Chrish save me! The day

is hot, and the weather, and the wars, and the King,

and the dukes. It is no time to discourse. The town

i.e., besieged   is beseeched,° and the trumpet call us to the breach,   100

and we talk, and, be Chrish,[4] do nothing. 'Tis shame

save   for us all. So God sa'° me, 'tis shame to stand still; it is

shame, by my hand. And there is throats to be cut, and

works to be done, and there ish nothing done, so

Chrish sa' me, la!   105

Jamy

i.e., mass   By the mess,° ere these eyes of mine take themselves

to slomber, ay'll de gud service, or I'll lig i' th' grund

for it.[5] I owe God a death, and I'll pay 't as valorously

i.e., brief; short   as I may, that sall I suerly do, that is the breff° and

the long. Marry, I wad full fain heard some question   110

'tween you tway.[6]

Fluellen

Captain MacMorris, I think, look you, under your

correction,[7] there is not many of your nation—

MacMorris

Of my nation? What ish my nation?[8] Ish a villain,[9]

and a bastard, and a knave, and a rascal! What ish my   115

nation? Who talks of my nation?

Fluellen

Look you, if you take the matter otherwise than is

perhaps   meant, Captain MacMorris, peradventure° I shall

treat   think you do not use° me with that affability as in dis-

good judgment   cretion° you ought to use me, look you, being as good   120

1   *you will mistake*

    **You are deliberately misunder-
    standing**

2   parley

    **Trumpet call, inviting the enemy to
    negotiate**

3   *when there is more better opportunity to
    be required*

    **I.e., when we have a *better*
    opportunity**

a man as yourself, both in the disciplines of war and in
the derivation of my birth, and in other particularities.

MacMorris

I do not know you so good a man as myself. So Chrish
save me, I will cut off your head!

Gower

Gentlemen both, you will mistake[1] each other.   125

Jamy

Ah, that's a foul fault!

A parley[2] [is sounded].

Gower

The town sounds a parley.

Fluellen

Captain MacMorris, when there is more better opportunity to be required,[3] look you, I will be so bold as to
tell you I know the disciplines of war, and there is an   130
end.   *[They] exit.*

1   *latest parle*
    Final negotiating session

2   *like to men proud of destruction*
    Like men eager to be destroyed

3   *fleshed soldier*
    Experienced soldier (see 2.4.50 and note)

4   *In liberty of bloody hand*
    I.e., with freedom to kill

5   *wide as Hell*
    I.e., with no restrictions

6   *What is it then to me if impious war, / Arrayed in flames like to the prince of fiends, / Do with his smirched complexion all fell feats / Enlinked to waste and desolation?*
    I.e., what do I care if unholy war, dressed in flames like the devil and wearing a blackened face, does all those savage deeds that bring about devastation and ruin?

7   *holds his fierce career*
    Maintains a high-speed gallop. *Wickedness* is portrayed as a horse plunging uncontrollably downhill.

8   *in their spoil*
    I.e., while they pillage

9   *As send precepts to the leviathan*
    As send written commands to a giant sea monster. The *leviathan* is a massive creature that appears in the Bible (see Job 40:20).

Act 3, Scene 3

*[Enter the **Governor** and some citizens on the walls.] Enter the*
***King** and all his train before the gates.*

King Henry

decides	How yet resolves° the Governor of the town?
allow	This is the latest parle[1] we will admit.°
	Therefore to our best mercy give yourselves,
	Or, like to men proud of destruction,[2]
to do	Defy us to° our worst; for, as I am a soldier,
suits	A name that in my thoughts becomes° me best,
bombardment	If I begin the batt'ry° once again,
	I will not leave the half-achieved Harfleur
	Till in her ashes she lie burièd.
	The gates of mercy shall be all shut up,
	And the fleshed soldier,[3] rough and hard of heart,
	In liberty of bloody hand[4] shall range
	With conscience wide as Hell,[5] mowing like grass
	Your fresh fair virgins and your flow'ring infants.
	What is it then to me if impious war,
	Arrayed in flames like to the prince of fiends,
	Do with his smirched complexion all fell feats
	Enlinked to waste and desolation?[6]
	What is 't to me, when you yourselves are cause,
	If your pure maidens fall into the hand
	Of hot and forcing violation?
	What rein can hold licentious wickedness
	When down the hill he holds his fierce career?[7]
ineffectually / useless	We may as bootless° spend our vain° command
	Upon th' enragèd soldiers in their spoil[8]
	As send precepts to the leviathan[9]
	To come ashore. Therefore, you men of Harfleur,
on	Take pity of° your town and of your people

Line numbers: 5, 10, 15, 20, 25

1   *filthy and contagious*

    **Dark and disease carrying. In
    Shakespeare's time, clouds were
    considered sources of sickness.**

2   *heady*

    (1) violent; (2) impulsive

3   *Defile the locks*

    **(1) drag by the hair; (2) violate the
    chastity**

4   *Jewry*

    **Judea. King Herod's efforts to kill
    the infant Jesus led him to murder
    the children of Bethlehem (see
    Matthew 2:16–18).**

5   *Herod's bloody-hunting slaughtermen*

    **Executioners hunting for blood
    (and covered in it). The entire
    speech is significantly shorter in
    the Quarto, and is often cut down
    in performance, probably because
    these lines complicate any simple
    heroic view of Henry and his war.**

6   *guilty in defense*

    **I.e., blameworthy for having
    defended the city against their
    rightful king (though, of course, it
    is precisely Henry's right to France
    that is being fought over)**

7   *defensible*

    I.e., capable of defending our city

8   *growing / Upon*

    Spreading among

Whiles yet my soldiers are in my command,

mercy Whiles yet the cool and temperate wind of grace° 30

Blows away O'erblows° the filthy and contagious¹ clouds

Of heady² murder, spoil, and villainy.

expect If not, why, in a moment look° to see

indiscriminate The blind° and bloody soldier with foul hand

Defile the locks³ of your shrill-shrieking daughters; 35

Your fathers taken by the silver beards,

And their most reverend heads dashed to the walls;

impaled Your naked infants spitted° upon pikes,

Whiles the mad mothers with their howls confused

Do break the clouds, as did the wives of Jewry⁴ 40

At Herod's bloody-hunting slaughtermen.⁵

What say you? Will you yield and this avoid,

Or, guilty in defense,⁶ be thus destroyed?

Governor

Our expectation hath this day an end.

help The Dauphin, whom of succors° we entreated, 45

Replies to / troops Returns° us that his powers° are yet not ready

end; defeat To raise° so great a siege. Therefore, great King,

We yield our town and lives to thy soft mercy.

Enter our gates, dispose of us and ours,

For we no longer are defensible.⁷ 50

King Henry

Open your gates. [**Governor** *exits.*]

Come, uncle Exeter,

Go you and enter Harfleur; there remain

And fortify it strongly 'gainst the French.

Use mercy to them all. For us, dear uncle,

The winter coming on and sickness growing 55

retreat Upon⁸ our soldiers, we will retire° to Calais.

Tonight in Harfleur will we be your guest;

prepared Tomorrow for the march are we addressed.°

Flourish, and [they] enter the town.

1   *Alice, tu as été en Angleterre, et tu bien parles le langage.*

    Alice, you have been in England and speak the language well.

2   *Un peu, madame.*

    A little, my lady.

3   *Je te prie, m'enseignez; Il faut que j'apprenne à parler. Comment appelez-vous la main en anglais?*

    I pray you teach me; I have to learn to speak it. What do you call *la main* in English?

4   *La main? Elle est appelée de hand.*

    La main? It is called "de hand."

5   *Et les doigts?*

    And the fingers?

6   *Les doigts? Ma foi, j'oublie les doigts; mais je me souviendrai. Les doigts? Je pense qu'ils sont appelés de fingres; oui, de fingres.*

    Les doigts? Dear me, I forget *les doigts*; but I will remember. I think that they are called de fingres; yes, de fingres.

7   *La main, de hand; les doigts, de fingres. Je pense que je suis le bon écolier. J'ai gagné deux mots d'anglais vitement. Comment appelez-vous les ongles?*

    La main, de hand; les doigts, de fingres. I think that I am a good scholar. I have learned two English words quickly. What do you call *les ongles*?

8   *Les ongles? Nous les appelons de nails.*

    Les ongles? We call them "de nails."

9   *De nailes. Écoutez; dites-moi si je parle bien: de hand, de fingres, et de nails.*

    De nails. Listen; tell me whether I speak correctly: de hand, de fingres, and de nails.

10 *C'est bien dit, madame; il est fort bon anglais.*

    That is correct, my lady; it is very good English.

11 *Dites-moi l'anglais pour le bras.*

    Tell me the English for *le bras*.

Act 3, Scene 4

Enter **Katharine** *and* [**Alice**,] *an old gentlewoman.*

Katharine

Alice, tu as été en Angleterre, et tu bien parles le langage.[1]

Alice

Un peu, madame.[2]

Katharine

Je te prie, m'enseignez; il faut que j'apprenne à parler. Comment appelez-vous la main en anglais?[3]   5

Alice

La main? Elle est appelée *de hand*.[4]

Katharine

De hand. Et les doigts?[5]

Alice

Les doigts? Ma foi, j'oublie les doigts; mais je me souviendrai. Les doigts? Je pense qu'ils sont appelés *de fingres*; oui, *de fingres*.[6]   10

Katharine

La main, *de hand*; les doigts, *de fingres*. Je pense que je suis le bon écolier. J'ai gagné deux mots d'anglais vite-ment. Comment appelez-vous les ongles?[7]

Alice

Les ongles? Nous les appelons *de nails*.[8]

Katharine

De nails. Écoutez; dites-moi si je parle bien: *de hand*, *de*   15
fingres, et *de nails*.[9]

Alice

C'est bien dit, madame; il est fort bon anglais.[10]

Katharine

Dites-moi l'anglais pour *le bras*.[11]

155

1   *Et le coude?*

And the elbow?

2   D' elbow. *Je m'en fais la répétition de tous les mots que vous m'avez appris dès à présent.*

"D' elbow." I am going to repeat the words you have taught me thus far.

3   *Il est trop difficile, madame, comme je pense.*

It is too difficult, my lady, I think.

4   *Excusez-moi, Alice; écoutez:* de hand, de fingres, de nails, de arma, de bilbow.

Pardon me, Alice; listen: de hand, de fingres, de nails, de arma, de bilbow.

5   *Ô Seigneur Dieu, je m'en oublie!* D' elbow. *Comment appelez-vous* le col?

O Lord, I cannot remember! D' elbow. What do you call the neck?

6   *Oui. Sauf votre honneur, en vérité, vous prononcez les mots aussi droit que les natifs d'Angleterre.*

Yes. If I may say so, in truth, you pronounce the words just as well as the natives of England.

7   *Je ne doute point d'apprendre, par la grâce de Dieu, et en peu de temps.*

I have no doubt that I will learn, with God's help, and quickly.

Alice

De arma, madame.

Katharine

Et le coude?[1]   20

Alice

D' elbow.

Katharine

D' elbow. Je m'en fais la répétition de tous les mots que
vous m'avez appris dès à présent.[2]

Alice

Il est trop difficile, madame, comme je pense.[3]

Katharine

Excusez-moi, Alice; écoutez: *de hand, de fingres, de nails, de*   25
arma, de bilbow.[4]

Alice

D' elbow, madame.

Katharine

Ô Seigneur Dieu, je m'en oublie! *D' elbow.* Comment
appelez-vous *le col*?[5]

Alice

De nick, madame.   30

Katharine

De nick. Et le menton?

Alice

De chin.

Katharine

De sin. Le col, *de nick*; le menton, *de sin.*

Alice

Oui. Sauf votre honneur, en vérité, vous prononcez les
mots aussi droit que les natifs d'Angleterre.[6]   35

Katharine

Je ne doute point d'apprendre, par la grâce de Dieu, et
en peu de temps.[7]

1 *N'avez vous pas déjà oublié ce que je vous ai enseigné?*

Haven't you already forgotten what I've taught you?

2 *Non, je réciterai à vous promptement:* de hand, de fingre, de mails—

No, I will recite promptly to you: *de hand, de fingre, de mails*—

3 *Sauf votre honneur,* d'elbow.

With all due respect, *d'elbow*.

4 *Ainsi dis-je:* d' elbow, de nick, *et de sin. Comment appelez-vous le pied et la robe?*

That's what I said: *d' elbow, de nick*, et *de sin*. What do you call the foot and the gown?

5 *Le* foot, *madame, et le* count.

"Le *foot*," my lady, and "le *count*." *Count* represents Alice's pronunciation of "gown." Katharine reacts to what she hears as the French *foutre* and *con*, which mean the same (and carry the same vulgar effect) as the English *fuck* and *cunt*. The final t on *count* was likely included in the Folio to emphasize the joke for an English-speaking audience.

6 Le foot et le count! *Ô Seigneur Dieu! Ils sont les mots de son mauvais, corruptible, gros, et impudique, et non pour les dames d'honneur d'user. Je ne voudrais pro-noncer ces mots devant les seigneurs de France pour tout le monde. Foh!* Le foot et le count! *Néanmoins, je réciterai une autre fois ma leçon ensemble:* d' hand, de fingre, de nails, de arma, d' elbow, de nick, de sin, de foot, le count.

Le *foot* and le *count*. O Lord! Those are evil-sounding words, corrupt, coarse, and immodest, and are not proper for ladies to use. I would not pronounce those words before French lords for the whole world. Foh! Le *foot* et le *count*! Nevertheless, I will recite once more my whole lesson: *d' hand, de fingre, de nails, de arma, d' elbow, de nick, de sin, de foot, le count*.

7 *C'est assez pour une fois. Allons-nous à dîner.*

That's enough for one time. Let's go to dinner.

Alice

N'avez vous pas déjà oublié ce que je vous ai enseigné?[1]

Katharine

Non, je réciterai à vous promptement: *de hand, de fingre,*
de mails[2]—   40

Alice

De nails, madame.

Katharine

De nails, de arma, de ilbow.

Alice

Sauf votre honneur, *d' elbow.*[3]

Katharine

Ainsi dis-je: *d' elbow, de nick*, et *de sin*. Comment appelez-
vous le pied et la robe?[4]   45

Alice

Le *foot*, madame, et le *count*.[5]

Katharine

Le *foot* et le *count*! Ô Seigneur Dieu! Ils sont les mots de
son mauvais, corruptible, gros, et impudique, et non
pour les dames d'honneur d'user. Je ne voudrais pro-
noncer ces mots devant les seigneurs de France pour   50
tout le monde. Foh! Le *foot* et le *count*! Néanmoins, je
réciterai une autre fois ma leçon ensemble: *de hand,*
de fingre, de nails, de arma, d' elbow, de nick, de sin, de foot, le
count.[6]

Alice

Excellent, madame!   55

Katharine

C'est assez pour une fois. Allons-nous à dîner.[7]

She exits [with **Alice***].*

1   *River Somme*

     Located almost midway between
     Harfleur (3.3) and Calais

2   *Shall a few sprays of us, / The emptying of*
     our fathers' luxury, / Our scions, put in wild
     and savage stock, / Spirt up so suddenly into
     the clouds / And overlook their grafters?

     Shall a few offshoots from our
     (French) stock—the result of
     our forebears' lust—shall these
     branches, grafted onto the wild
     and savage trunk (of native English
     Saxons), sprout up so quickly to
     such heights that they look down
     on (us, who are) the source of the
     grafted shoots? The Dauphin uses
     a grafting metaphor to describe
     the approaching Englishmen, who
     are the descendents of the Saxons
     (English natives) and the Normans,
     who invaded and conquered
     England in 1066.

3   Mort de ma vie

     Death to my life (an oath)

4   *but I will*

     I.e., if I don't

5   *nook-shotten*

     Misshapen; irregular; i.e., having
     a coast filled with indentations
     (*nooks*) but with a sense of moral
     irregularity as well

6   *isle of Albion*

     The island that now comprises
     Great Britain, and includes Eng-
     land, Scotland, Wales

7   Dieu de batailles

     God of battles

8   *Is not their climate foggy, raw, and dull*

     Classical climate theory distin-
     guished between three habitable
     zones, a hot one that made its
     inhabitants intelligent but lecherous
     and inactive, a cold one that made its
     inhabitants active but stupid and in-
     capable of good government, and a
     temperate one that moderated both
     extremes, making its inhabitants
     most capable of self-government
     and therefore also of empire; see,
     for example, Aristotle's *Politics*. From
     such sources, the English inherited
     an anxiety about their northern and
     marginal position vis à vis the clas-
     sical Mediterranean; see Milton's
     worry that England's northerly
     climate will be inhospitable for
     producing true epic poetry (*Paradise
     Lost*, 9.44–45).

9   *as in despite*

     As though with contempt

10   *Can sodden water, / A drench for sur-*
     reined jades, their barley broth

     I.e., can boiled water, (which the
     English use as) a medicinal treat-
     ment for overworked horses, (and
     which also serves as) their ale

11   *roping*

     Hanging (like an uncoiled rope)

Act 3, Scene 5

Enter the **King of France**, *the* **Dauphin**, [*the Duke of* **Bourbon**,] *the* **Constable** *of France, and others.*

King of France

'Tis certain he hath passed the River Somme.[1]

Constable

with   And if he be not fought withal,° my lord,

Let us not live in France; let us quit all

And give our vineyards to a barbarous people.

Dauphin

i.e., O living God!   *Ô Dieu vivant!*° Shall a few sprays of us,   5

lust   The emptying of our fathers' luxury,°

Our scions, put in wild and savage stock,

Sprout   Spirt° up so suddenly into the clouds

And overlook their grafters?[2]

Bourbon

merely   Normans, but° bastard Normans, Norman bastards!   10

Mort de ma vie,[3] if they march along

Unfought withal, but I will[4] sell my dukedom

sloppy; muddy   To buy a slobb'ry° and a dirty farm

In that nook-shotten[5] isle of Albion.[6]

Constable

from where   *Dieu de batailles,*[7] where° have they this mettle?   15

Is not their climate foggy, raw, and dull,[8]

On whom, as in despite,[9] the sun looks pale,

Killing their fruit with frowns? Can sodden water,

hard-ridden   A drench for sur-reined° jades, their barley broth,[10]

Boil   Decoct° their cold blood to such valiant heat?   20

lively / inspired   And shall our quick° blood, spirited° with wine,

Seem frosty? Oh, for honor of our land,

Let us not hang like roping[11] icicles

Upon our houses' thatch, whiles a more frosty people

1 *Sweat drops of gallant youth*

   I.e., shed the blood of their brave young

2 *"Poor" we may call them in their native lords.*

   We should call them (*our rich fields*) poor, for having such cowardly owners (the French aristocracy).

3 *bred out*

   Exhausted; used up

4 *bid us*

   Tell us to attend

5 *lavoltas high and swift corantos*

   A *lavolta* was a dance marked by spinning and jumping (hence *high*); a *coranto* involved running (hence *swift*).

6 *our grace is only in our heels*

   We excel only in (1) dancing; (2) fleeing

7 *most lofty runaways*

   (1) high-jumping dancers; (2) high-born cowards

8 *Montjoy*

   Used as a proper name here, Montjoy was historically the title of France's royal herald.

9 *For your great seats now quit you of great shames*

   For the sake of your noble titles, keep yourselves from terrible disgrace.

10 *low vassal seat*

   I.e., lowly position

11 *void his rheum*

   Spit out his phlegm (an inelegant metaphor for the run-off of melting snow)

Sweat drops of gallant youth[1] in our rich fields.   25
"Poor" we may call them in their native lords.[2]

Dauphin
By faith and honor,
wives   Our madams° mock at us and plainly say
Our mettle is bred out[3] and they will give
Their bodies to the lust of English youth   30
restock   To new-store° France with bastard warriors.

Bourbon
They bid us[4] to the English dancing schools
And teach lavoltas high and swift corantos,[5]
Saying our grace is only in our heels[6]
And that we are most lofty runaways.[7]   35

King of France
Where is Montjoy[8] the herald? Speed him hence.
i.e., King Henry Let him greet England° with our sharp defiance.
Up, princes, and, with spirit of honor edged
hurry / battlefield More sharper than your swords, hie° to the field!°
Charles Delabret, High Constable of France,   40
You Dukes of Orléans, Bourbon, and of Berri,
Alençon, Brabant, Bar, and Burgundy,
Jacques Chatillion, Rambures, Vaudemont,
Beaumont, Grandpré, Roussi, and Fauconbridge,
Foix, Lestrelles, Boucicault, and Charolais,   45
High dukes, great princes, barons, lords, and knights,
For your great seats now quit you of great shames.[9]
Stop   Bar° Harry England, that sweeps through our land
pennants With pennons° painted in the blood of Harfleur.
army   Rush on his host° as doth the melted snow   50
Upon the valleys, whose low vassal seat[10]
The Alps doth spit and void his rheum[11] upon.
Go down upon him—you have power enough—

1   *captive chariot*

     **A chariot (or other vehicle) used to
     display a prisoner publicly, as in
     ancient Rome**

2   *Rouen*

     **Capital of Normandy, in northern
     France**

3   *This becomes the great.*

     **Your resolution suits your great-
     ness.**

4   *for achievement*

     I.e., as his only achievement

5   *haste on Montjoy*

     I.e., send Montjoy quickly

And in a captive chariot[1] into Rouen[2]
Bring him our prisoner.   55

Constable
This becomes the great.[3]
Sorry am I his numbers are so few,
His soldiers sick and famished in their march,
For I am sure, when he shall see our army,

cesspool   He'll drop his heart into the sink° of fear   60
And for achievement[4] offer us his ransom.

King of France
Therefore, Lord Constable, haste on Montjoy,[5]
And let him say to England that we send
To know what willing ransom he will give.
Prince Dauphin, you shall stay with us in Rouen.   65

Dauphin
Not so, I do beseech your Majesty.

King of France
Be patient, for you shall remain with us.
Now forth, Lord Constable and princes all,
And quickly bring us word of England's fall.   *They exit.*

1   *the bridge*

Probably the bridge over the Ter-
noise River at Blagny; the bridge's
capture in October 1415 was crucial
to the English army's progress
against France.

2   *Agamemnon*

Ancient Mycenaean general, who
commanded the Greek army during
the Trojan War

3   *live*

"Life" in Fluellen's Welsh accent

4   *aunchient lieutenant*

Pistol's rank is ensign ("ancient" or
aunchient, as Fluellen pronounces
it), so the phrase could be merely
the result of *lieutenant* having been
written in error and not deleted, or,
as has been suggested, the phrase
is equivalent to "sublieutenant." In
the theater the first word is likely
to be heard as "ancient" meaning
"old," but it is most likely the military sense that is intended.

5   *Mark Antony*

Ancient Roman general and politi-
cian, who, along with Lepidus and
Octavianus (later Augustus Caesar),
established the Second Triumvi-
rate, which ruled Rome from 43 B.C.
to 33 B.C.

6   *as gallant service*

I.e., service as gallant (as Mark
Antony performed)

Act 3, Scene 6

Enter Captains, English and Welsh: **Gower** *and* **Fluellen**.

Gower
How now, Captain Fluellen? Come you from the
bridge?[1]

Fluellen
soldierly feats I assure you, there is very excellent services° commit-
performed ted° at the bridge.

Gower
Is the Duke of Exeter safe?   5

Fluellen
The Duke of Exeter is as magnanimous as Agamemnon,[2] and a man that I love and honor with my soul,
and my heart, and my duty, and my live,[3] and my living,
i.e., has and my uttermost power. He is° not—God be praised
injury and blessed!—any hurt° in the world, but keeps the   10
bridge most valiantly, with excellent discipline. There
i.e., bridge is an aunchient lieutenant[4] there at the pridge.° I think
in my very conscience he is as valiant a man as Mark
standing; reputation Antony,[5] and he is a man of no estimation° in the
world, but I did see him do as gallant service.[6]   15

Gower
What do you call him?

Fluellen
i.e., Ancient; Ensign He is called Aunchient° Pistol.

Gower
I know him not.

Enter **Pistol**.

1   *furious*

     (1) rapid; (2) destructive

2   *pax*

     A tablet (often of metal but also of
     other materials) on which Christ's
     crucifixion was typically depicted
     or some other sacred image; an ob-
     ject of devotion kissed by the priest
     and congregation at Mass. *Pax* is
     also the Latin word for "peace."

3   *Let gallows gape for dog*

     In Shakespeare's time, animals
     were sometimes punished by
     hanging.

Fluellen

Here is the man.

Pistol

Captain, I thee beseech to do me favors.   20

The Duke of Exeter doth love thee well.

Fluellen

Ay, I praise God, and I have merited some love at his

hands.

Pistol

Bardolph, a soldier, firm and sound of heart

lively; full   And of buxom° valor, hath, by cruel fate   25

dizzying   And giddy° Fortune's furious¹ fickle wheel,

That goddess blind,

That stands upon the rolling restless stone—

Fluellen

By your patience, Aunchient Pistol: Fortune is painted

blindfold   blind, with a muffler° afore her eyes, to signify to   30

you that Fortune is blind; and she is painted also with

a wheel, to signify to you, which is the moral of it,

that she is turning and inconstant, and mutability and

variation; and her foot, look you, is fixed upon

a spherical stone, which rolls and rolls and rolls.   35

In good truth, the poet makes a most excellent

symbolic figure   description of it. Fortune is an excellent moral.°

Pistol

Fortune is Bardolph's foe, and frowns on him;

For he hath stol'n a pax,²

he   And hangèd must 'a° be—a damnèd death!   40

Let gallows gape for dog;³ let man go free,

hempen rope   And let not hemp° his windpipe suffocate.

sentence   But Exeter hath given the doom° of death

For pax of little price.

Therefore, go speak—the Duke will hear thy voice—   45

1   *penny cord*

    Cheap rope

2   fico

    **Italian for "fig." A thumb shoved
    between two closed fingers (or
    placed in the mouth) constitutes
    the *fico*, a contemptuous gesture.
    The fig of Spain in line 57 refers to the
    same gesture.**

3   *a bawd, a cutpurse*

    A pimp, a thief

4   *grace himself*

    Present himself; pass himself off

5   *are perfect in*

    Are word-perfect at reciting

And let not Bardolph's vital thread be cut
With edge of penny cord [1] and vile reproach.

repay Speak, Captain, for his life, and I will thee requite.°

Fluellen

Aunchient Pistol, I do partly understand your meaning.

Pistol

for that Why then, rejoice therefor.°   50

Fluellen

Certainly, Aunchient, it is not a thing to rejoice at. For
if, look you, he were my brother, I would desire the
Duke to use his good pleasure and put him to execution, for discipline ought to be used.

Pistol

Die and be damned! And *fico* [2] for thy friendship!   55

Fluellen

It is well.

Pistol

The fig of Spain!   *He exits.*

Fluellen

Very good.

Gower

absolute Why, this is an arrant° counterfeit rascal! I remember
him now: a bawd, a cutpurse. [3]   60

Fluellen

i.e., brave I'll assure you, 'a uttered as prave° words at the pridge
as you shall see in a summer's day. But it is very well.

guarantee What he has spoke to me, that is well, I warrant° you,
when time is serve.

Gower

simpleton Why, 'tis a gull,° a fool, a rogue, that now and then   65
goes to the wars to grace himself [4] at his return into
London under the form of a soldier. And such fellows
are perfect in [5] the great commanders' names, and they

1   *learn you*

    Learn

2   *stood on*

    Demanded (during negotiations)

3   *the phrase of war, which they trick up*
    with new-tuned oaths

    **The lingo of war, which they deco-
    rate with fashionably new phrases**

4   *a beard of the General's cut*

    **I.e., a beard that mimics the style of
    the General. The *General* here—as,
    probably, at 5.0.30—seems to refer
    to the Earl of Essex, who after sack-
    ing the Spanish city of Cadiz in 1596
    took to wearing a full beard that
    became known as his Cadiz beard.
    On Essex and the dating of this play,
    see LONGER NOTE on p. 333.**

5   *horrid suit of the camp*

    Intimidating military dress

6   *slanders of the age*

    **People who ruin the reputation
    of the current age (by behaving so
    disgracefully)**

7   *a hole in his coat*

    **I.e., a weakness; something to be
    exploited (proverbial)**

8   *from the pridge*

    **I.e., with the latest information
    from the bridge**

will learn you ¹ by rote where services were done—
fortification at such and such a sconce,° at such a breach, at such 70
a convoy; who came off bravely, who was shot, who
disgraced, what terms the enemy stood on ²—and
memorize this they con° perfectly in the phrase of war, which
they trick up with new-tuned oaths.³ And what a beard
of the General's cut ⁴ and a horrid suit of the camp ⁵ 75
drunken will do among foaming bottles and ale-washed° wits
is wonderful to be thought on. But you must learn to
know such slanders of the age,⁶ or else you may be
misled; mistaken marvelously mistook.°

Fluellen

I tell you what, Captain Gower. I do perceive he is not 80
the man that he would gladly make show to the world
he is. If I find a hole in his coat,⁷ I will tell him my
mind. [*Drum heard.*] Hark you, the King is coming, and I
must speak with him from the pridge.⁸

battle-worn   *Drum and colors. Enter the King and his poor°*
        soldiers [with **Gloucester**].

i.e., bless —God pless° your Majesty! 85

King Henry

How now, Fluellen, cam'st thou from the bridge?

Fluellen

Ay, so please your Majesty. The Duke of Exeter has very
gallantly maintained the pridge. The French is gone
off, look you, and there is gallant and most prave
fighting passages.° Marry, th' athversary was have possession 90
of the pridge, but he is enforced to retire, and the
Duke of Exeter is master of the pridge. I can tell your
Majesty, the Duke is a prave man.

1   *His face is all bubukles and whelks and*
     knobs and flames o' fire

     **His face is covered with carbuncles
     and pimples and pustules and
     flaming red cheeks (from drinking).
     Bubukles is a nonce word that con-
     flates *bubo* (Latin for "abscess") and
     carbuncle (boil-like swelling).**

2   *his lips blows at his nose, and it is like a*
     coal of fire, sometimes plue and some-
     times red

     **Bardolph seemingly has an
     underbite—his lower jaw jutting
     out from below the upper—that
     suggests to Fluellen the image of a
     bellows blowing on coal (Bar-
     dolph's nose), which turns *plue* (i.e.,
     blue) and *red* as it cools and heats.**

3   *his nose is executed*

     **His nose (with the rest of him) is
     slated for execution.**

4   Tucket

     Fanfare; trumpet call

5   *habit*

     **Uniform (i.e., a sleeveless coat
     unique to the herald and decorated
     with the French king's coat of arms)**

King Henry

What men have you lost, Fluellen?

Fluellen

losses   The perdition° of th' athversary hath been very great,   95
reasonable great. Marry, for my part, I think the
except   Duke hath lost never a man, but° one that is like to
be executed for robbing a church, one Bardolph, if
your Majesty know the man. His face is all bubukles
and whelks and knobs and flames o' fire;[1] and his   100
lips blows at his nose, and it is like a coal of fire,
sometimes plue and sometimes red.[2] But his nose is
executed,[3] and his fire's out.

King Henry

We would have all such offenders so cut off. And we
give express charge that in our marches through   105
forcibly taken   the country there be nothing compelled° from the
villages, nothing taken but paid for, none of the
French upbraided or abused in disdainful language;
gentleness   for when lenity° and cruelty play for a kingdom, the
player   gentler gamester° is the soonest winner.   110

Tucket.[4] *Enter* **Montjoy**.

Montjoy

You know me by my habit.[5]

King Henry

Well then, I know thee. What shall I know of thee?

Montjoy

My master's mind.

King Henry

Unfold it.

Montjoy

Thus says my King: "Say thou to Harry of England,   115

1   *Advantage*

     I.e., tactical and numerical supe-
     riority

2   *bruise an injury*

     I.e., squeeze a boil

3   *admire our sufferance*

     Marvel at the patience we have
     shown

4   *which in weight to reanswer, his pettiness*
     would bow under

     I.e., which fully to repay would
     overwhelm his slight worth. *His pet-*
     tiness may be a mocking rejoinder to
     the appellation "his Majesty."

5   *th' effusion of our blood*

     The spilling of our blood (i.e., the
     French killed in battle)

6   *the muster of his kingdom too faint a*
     number

     I.e., the total number of English
     soldiers is an inadequate compen-
     sation (for our losses).

7   *whose condemnation is pronounced*

     Whose sentence to death we hereby
     pronounce

8   *So far*

     I.e., this concludes the message of

9   *craft and vantage*

     Cunning and superior resources

though we seemed dead, we did but sleep. Advantage[1]
is a better soldier than rashness. Tell him we could have
i.e., defeated rebuked° him at Harfleur, but that we thought not good
to bruise an injury[2] till it were full ripe. Now we speak
i.e., King Henry upon our cue, and our voice is imperial. England°   120
shall repent his folly, see his weakness, and admire
our sufferance.[3] Bid him, therefore, consider of his
be proportionate to ransom, which must proportion° the losses we have
borne, the subjects we have lost, the disgrace we have
endured digested,° which in weight to reanswer, his pettiness   125
To repay / treasury would bow under.[4] For° our losses, his exchequer° is
too poor; for th' effusion of our blood,[5] the muster of
his kingdom too faint a number;[6] and for our disgrace,
his own person kneeling at our feet but a weak and
worthless satisfaction. To this add defiance, and tell   130
him, for conclusion, he hath betrayed his followers,
whose condemnation is pronounced."[7] So far[8] my
King and master; so much my office.

King Henry
rank What is thy name? I know thy quality.°

Montjoy
Montjoy.   135

King Henry
Thou dost thy office fairly. Turn thee back
And tell thy King I do not seek him now,
But could be willing to march on to Calais
hindrance / truth Without impeachment.° For, to say the sooth, °
Though 'tis no wisdom to confess so much   140
Unto an enemy of craft and vantage,[9]
My people are with sickness much enfeebled,
My numbers lessened, and those few I have
Almost no better than so many French,

1   *Who*

     I.e., *those few* (line 143) remaining
     English soldiers

2   *upon one pair of English legs / Did march*
     three Frenchmen

     I.e., one English soldier equalled
     three French soldiers

3   *blown*

     Made to bloom; aroused

4   *God before*

     God leading us; God willing

5   *well advise himself*

     Deliberate with care

Who,[1] when they were in health, I tell thee, herald,   145
I thought upon one pair of English legs
Did march three Frenchmen.[2] Yet, forgive me, God,
That I do brag thus! This your air of France
Hath blown[3] that vice in me. I must repent.
Go, therefore, tell thy master here I am;   150
body   My ransom is this frail and worthless trunk,°
My army but a weak and sickly guard.
Yet, God before,[4] tell him we will come on,
Though France himself and such another neighbor
Stand in our way. There's for thy labor, Montjoy.   155
                                        [*He gives a purse.*]
Go bid thy master well advise himself.[5]
If we may pass, we will; if we be hindered,
We shall your tawny ground with your red blood
Discolor. And so, Montjoy, fare you well.
The sum of all our answer is but this: 160
We would not seek a battle as we are,
Nor, as we are, we say we will not shun it.
So tell your master.

Montjoy
I shall deliver so. Thanks to your Highness.   [*He exits.*]

Gloucester
I hope they will not come upon us now.   165

King Henry
We are in God's hand, brother, not in theirs.
March to the bridge. It now draws toward night.
Beyond the river we'll encamp ourselves
i.e., the English troops   And on tomorrow bid them° march away.   *They exit.*

1 *but on four pasterns*

I.e., on four hooves. The *pastern* is found between the hoof and the fetlock.

2 *Çà, ha!*

"Now, ha!" or perhaps "That one, ha!" The Folio text reads *Ch'ha!*, which some editors explain as an imitation of a horse's neighing or snorting. Others emend to "Ah ha!" Whatever the intended reading, the phrase clearly represents an outburst of enthusiasm.

3 *hairs*

I.e., light and airy

4 le cheval volant, *the Pegasus*, qui a les narines de feu

The flying horse, the Pegasus, who has nostrils of fire. (In classical mythology, Pegasus is a winged horse.)

5 *basest horn*

Lowest (or perhaps "vilest") bony growth, when it strikes the ground as a hoofbeat (punning on *horn* as the musical instrument and perhaps on *base* = bass in a musical sense)

6 *pipe of Hermes*

In Greek mythology, Hermes invented musical instruments and famously put the hundred-eyed Argus to sleep with the music of his pipe.

7 *Perseus*

In Greek mythology, Pegasus sprang from the spot where the hero Perseus shed the blood of the gorgon Medusa. According to Ovid, Perseus rode Pegasus to save the maiden Andromeda from a sea monster.

8 *pure air and fire*

In Renaissance cosmology, the two lightest of the four elements that combine to form all matter (see lines 20–21 and note)

Act 3, Scene 7

Enter the **Constable** *of France, the Lord* **Rambures**, **Orléans**,
[and the] **Dauphin**, *with others.*

Constable

in Tut, I have the best armor of° the world. Would it were
day!

Orléans

You have an excellent armor, but let my horse have his
due.

Constable

It is the best horse of Europe.   5

Orléans

Will it never be morning?

Dauphin

My Lord of Orléans, and my Lord High Constable, you
talk of horse and armor?

Orléans

You are as well provided of both as any prince in the
world.   10

Dauphin

What a long night is this! I will not change my horse
with any that treads but on four pasterns.[1] *Çà*, ha![2] He
bounds from the Earth as if his entrails were hairs;[3] *le
cheval volant*, the Pegasus, *qui a les narines de feu!*[4] When I
bestride him, I soar; I am a hawk. He trots the air. The   15
Earth sings when he touches it. The basest horn[5] of his
hoof is more musical than the pipe of Hermes.[6]

Orléans

He's of the color of the nutmeg.

Dauphin

And of the heat of the ginger. It is a beast for Perseus.[7]
He is pure air and fire;[8] and the dull elements of earth   20

1   *earth and water*

    I.e., the two heaviest of the four
    elements

2   *vary deserved praise on my palfrey*

    Find various ways of praising my
    worthy horse

3   *for the world, familiar to us and unknown,*
    to lay apart their particular functions and
    wonder at him

    For all the world's peoples—
    from places both known and still
    undiscovered—to set aside their
    various tasks and marvel at him

4   *bears*

    Carries a rider (with sexual innu-
    endo here and following)

5   *Me*

    I.e., only *me*

and water [1] never appear in him, but only in patient
stillness while his rider mounts him. He is indeed a

horses (derogatory) horse, and all other jades° you may call beasts.
Constable

perfect Indeed, my lord, it is a most absolute° and excellent
horse. 25
Dauphin

horses It is the prince of palfreys.° His neigh is like the bid-
ding of a monarch, and his countenance enforces
homage.
Orléans
No more, cousin.
Dauphin
Nay, the man hath no wit that cannot, from the rising 30

lying down of the lark to the lodging° of the lamb, vary deserved

variable praise on my palfrey.[2] It is a theme as fluent° as the

infinite grains of sand sea; turn the sands° into eloquent tongues, and my

subject horse is argument° for them all. 'Tis a subject for a

discourse sovereign to reason° on, and for a sovereign's sover- 35
eign to ride on; and for the world, familiar to us and
unknown, to lay apart their particular functions and
wonder at him.[3] I once writ a sonnet in his praise and
began thus: "Wonder of nature"—
Orléans
I have heard a sonnet begin so to one's mistress. 40
Dauphin
Then did they imitate that which I composed to my

war horse courser,° for my horse is my mistress.
Orléans
Your mistress bears [4] well.
Dauphin

appropriate Me [5] well, which is the prescript° praise and perfection

exclusive of a good and particular° mistress. 45

1 *shrewdly shook your back*

   I.e., severely strained your back.
   Shrewdly also puns on "shrew," a
   common term for a bad-tempered,
   sharp-tongued woman.

2 *Mine was not bridled.*

   I.e., but the mistress who strained
   my back was a woman, not a horse
   (also punning on the fact that
   bridles were sometimes used to
   gag and punish shrews).

3 *kern*

   Light-armed soldier. The conversation at this point turns on a sustained double entendre between
   riding bareback and having sex;
   however, the references to *kerns*
   and to *foul bogs* (55) specifically
   evoke the Irish wars being fought
   when the play was written and
   form part of a continuing web of
   allusions to Ireland throughout
   the play.

4 *French hose*

   Wide, loose breeches

5 *strait strossers*

   Literally, close-fitting trousers. The
   expression very likely means "bare-
   legged" (the skin itself being the
   snug pants that sheathe the legs),
   although it may also refer to a tight
   undergarment.

6 *bogs*

   (1) muddy fields (as in Ireland);
   (2) female genitalia; (3) privies or
   outhouses

7 *jade*

   (1) broken-down horse; (2) whore

8 *wears his own hair*

   I.e., has no need for a wig (because,
   unlike the Constable's mistress,
   he has not lost his hair to venereal
   disease)

9 Le chien est retourné à son propre
   vomissement, et la truie lavée au
   bourbier.

   The dog is returned to his own
   vomit, and the cleansed sow to the
   mire (see 2 Peter 2:22).

Constable

Nay, for methought yesterday your mistress shrewdly shook your back.[1]

Dauphin

So perhaps did yours.

Constable

Mine was not bridled.[2]

Dauphin

most likely Oh, then belike° she was old and gentle, and you rode 50 like a kern[3] of Ireland, your French hose[4] off, and in your strait strossers.[5]

Constable

You have good judgment in horsemanship.

Dauphin

Be warned by me, then: they that ride so, and ride not warily, fall into foul bogs.[6] I had rather have my horse 55

serve as to° my mistress.

Constable

gladly I had as lief° have my mistress a jade.[7]

Dauphin

I tell thee, Constable, my mistress wears his own hair.[8]

Constable

I could make as true a boast as that, if I had a sow to my mistress. 60

Dauphin

"*Le chien est retourné à son propre vomissement, et la truie lavée au bourbier.*"[9] Thou mak'st use of anything.

Constable

Yet do I not use my horse for my mistress, or any such

relevant proverb so little kin° to the purpose.

Rambures

My Lord Constable, the armor that I saw in your tent 65 tonight, are those stars or suns upon it?

1   *a many*

    Many (of them)

2   *'twere more honor some were away*

    I.e., your *honor* (honesty) would be
    greater if there were fewer stars (on
    your armor).

3   *his desert*

    What he deserves

4   *paved with English faces*

    I.e., covered with dead English
    soldiers

5   *faced out of my way*

    (1) intimidated; (2) shamed (for
    lying)

6   *I would fain be about the ears of the
    English*

    I would gladly be striking at the
    heads of the English soldiers.

7   *go to hazard*

    I.e., wager. *Hazard* was a game of
    dice.

8   *go yourself to hazard ere*

    Place yourself at risk before

9   *he will eat all he kills*

    I.e., he won't kill anyone.

Constable

Stars, my lord.

Dauphin

Some of them will fall tomorrow, I hope.

Constable

lack (stars) And yet my sky shall not want.°

Dauphin

That may be, for you bear a many¹ superfluously, and   70

'twere more honor some were away.²

Constable

Ev'n as your horse bears your praises, who would trot

as well were some of your brags dismounted.

Dauphin

Would I were able to load him with his desert!³ Will it

never be day? I will trot tomorrow a mile, and my way   75

shall be paved with English faces.⁴

Constable

I will not say so, for fear I should be faced out of my

wish way.⁵ But I would° it were morning, for I would fain

be about the ears of the English.⁶

Rambures

Who will go to hazard⁷ with me for twenty prisoners?   80

Constable

You must first go yourself to hazard ere⁸ you have them.

Dauphin

'Tis midnight; I'll go arm myself.   *He exits.*

Orléans

The Dauphin longs for morning.

Rambures

He longs to eat the English.

Constable

I think he will eat all he kills.⁹   85

1   *tread out*

Erase by trampling upon

2   *he will still be doing*

"He will continually be (ineffec-
tively) active." (Editors have often
glossed *doing* as "copulating," but
the Dauphin seems far more interested in his horse than in women.)

3   *did harm*

I.e., wounded anybody

4   *Nor will do none tomorrow.*

I.e., Nor will he hurt anyone tomorrow.

5   *He needs not*

(1) he had no need to tell you; (2) he
has no need to care who knows it

6   *Never anybody saw it but his lackey.*

No one has seen his valor except his
servant (the only person he has ever
beaten).

7   *'Tis a hooded valor, and when it appears,
it will bate.*

The imagery is from falconry: a
hawk remained *hooded* (i.e., with
its head covered) until released to
hunt, at which point it would *bate*,
or flap its wings, just prior to taking
flight. *Bate* also puns on "abate"
(i.e., diminish).

Orléans

By the white hand of my lady, he's a gallant prince.

Constable

Swear by her foot, that she may tread out[1] the oath.

Orléans

energetic He is simply the most active° gentleman of France.

Constable

Doing is activity, and he will still be doing.[2]

Orléans

He never did harm,[3] that I heard of.   90

Constable

Nor will do none tomorrow.[4] He will keep that good
name still.

Orléans

I know him to be valiant.

Constable

I was told that by one that knows him better than you.

Orléans

Who's What's° he?   95

Constable

Marry, he told me so himself, and he said he cared not
who knew it.

Orléans

He needs not;[5] it is no hidden virtue in him.

Constable

By my faith, sir, but it is. Never anybody saw it but his
lackey.[6] 'Tis a hooded valor, and when it appears, it   100
will bate.[7]

Orléans

Ill will never said well.

Constable

top I will cap° that proverb with "There is flattery in
friendship."

1 *Have at the very eye*

   I.e., I'll strike at the heart

2 *by how much "a fool's bolt is soon shot"*

   **I.e., just as a fool is quicker in his
   replies than a wise man**

3 *You have shot over.*

   **You have missed (the target); i.e.,
   that doesn't follow.**

4 *overshot*

   (1) wrong; (2) drunk

5 *so far out of his knowledge*

   **(1) so far beyond his capabilities;
   (2) so far beyond what is prudent**

Orléans

And I will take up that with "Give the devil his due."   105

Constable

i.e., the Dauphin Well placed. There stands your friend° for the devil.

on Have at the very eye [1] of that proverb with "A pox of°
the devil."

Orléans

You are the better at proverbs by how much "a fool's

thick, short arrow bolt° is soon shot." [2]   110

Constable

You have shot over. [3]

Orléans

'Tis not the first time you were overshot. [4]

Enter a **Messenger**.

Messenger

My Lord High Constable, the English lie within fifteen
hundred paces of your tents.

Constable

Who hath measured the ground?   115

Messenger

The Lord Grandpré.

Constable

A valiant and most expert gentleman. Would it were
day! Alas, poor Harry of England. He longs not for the
dawning as we do.

Orléans

foolish; obstinate What a wretched and peevish° fellow is this King of   120

meander England to mope° with his fat-brained followers so far
out of his knowledge! [5]

1   *Russian bear*

    **An allusion to bearbaiting, an Eliza-
    bethan spectator sport in which a
    bear, secured by the neck to a pole,
    was attacked by dogs (*mastiffs*).**

2   *the men do sympathize with the mastiffs
    in robustious and rough coming on*

    **The men resemble the mastiffs in
    (their) violent and rough attack.**

3   *shrewdly out*

    Terribly short

Constable

understanding If the English had any apprehension,° they would run
away.

Orléans

That they lack, for if their heads had any intellectual   125
armor, they could never wear such heavy headpieces.

Rambures

That island of England breeds very valiant creatures;
dogs their mastiffs° are of unmatchable courage.

Orléans

with eyes closed Foolish curs, that run winking° into the mouth of a
Russian bear¹ and have their heads crushed like rot-   130
ten apples. You may as well say "That's a valiant flea
that dare eat his breakfast on the lip of a lion."

Constable

Exactly Just,° just! And the men do sympathize with the
mastiffs in robustious and rough coming on,² leaving
if you give their wits with their wives; and then, give° them great   135
meals of beef, and iron and steel, they will eat like
wolves and fight like devils.

Orléans

Ay, but these English are shrewdly out³ of beef.

Constable

appetites Then shall we find tomorrow they have only stomachs°
to eat and none to fight. Now is it time to arm. Come;   140
shall we about it?

Orléans

It is now two o'clock; but, let me see, by ten
We shall have each a hundred Englishmen.   *They exit.*

1   *entertain conjecture of*

     Imagine

2   *poring dark*

     (1) darkness in which a person must
     strain (*pore*) to see; (2) pouring
     (deepening) darkness

3   *overlusty*

     (1) excessively merry; (2) overcon-
     fident

4   *the low-rated English play at dice*

     Gamble on the underrated English
     (i.e., play for the prisoners they
     believe they will capture)

5   *their gesture sad, / Investing lank-lean
     cheeks*

     Their solemn demeanor, filling
     their gaunt cheeks

Act 4, Prologue

[*Enter*] **Chorus**.

Chorus

Now entertain conjecture of [1] a time
When creeping murmur and the poring dark [2]
Fills the wide vessel of the universe.
From camp to camp, through the foul womb of night,

softly The hum of either army stilly° sounds,   5
So that That° the fixed sentinels almost receive
The secret whispers of each other's watch.
pale Fire answers fire, and through their paly° flames
army / shadowed Each battle° sees the other's umbered° face.
Steed threatens steed in high and boastful neighs   10
Piercing the night's dull ear, and from the tents
equipping The armorers, accomplishing° the knights,
With busy hammers closing rivets up,
sound Give dreadful note° of preparation.
The country cocks do crow, the clocks do toll,   15
And the third hour of drowsy morning name.
self-assured Proud of their numbers and secure° in soul,
The confident and overlusty [3] French
Do the low-rated English play at dice, [4]
slow-moving And chide the cripple tardy-gaited° night,   20
Who, like a foul and ugly witch, doth limp
So tediously away. The poor condemnèd English,
Like sacrifices, by their watchful fires
inwardly Sit patiently and inly° ruminate
The morning's danger; and their gesture sad,   25
Investing lank-lean cheeks [5] and war-worn coats,
Presenteth them unto the gazing moon
As so / whoever So° many horrid ghosts. Oh, now, who° will behold
The royal captain of this ruined band

1   *Nor doth he dedicate one jot of color /*
    Unto the weary and all-watchèd night

    I.e., his complexion has lost none
    of its color despite his having spent
    the night awake and watchful.

2   *freshly looks and overbears attaint*

    I.e., looks wide awake and ignores
    his exhaustion

3   *largess universal*

    Generosity offered to all

4   *that mean and gentle all*

    So that low- and high-born both

5   *as may unworthiness define*

    (1) as much as I (the Chorus), as
    unworthy as I am, can describe it;
    (2) as best as we worthy actors can
    perform it.

6   *most vile and ragged foils, / Right ill-*
    disposed in brawl ridiculous

    I.e., very shabby swords, poorly
    handled in ridiculous-looking
    fighting

7   *mockeries*

    Shabby imitations

sentry post	Walking from watch° to watch, from tent to tent,	30
	Let him cry, "Praise and glory on his head!"	
army	For forth he goes and visits all his host,°	
	Bids them good morrow with a modest smile,	
	And calls them brothers, friends, and countrymen.	
	Upon his royal face there is no note	35
encircled	How dread an army hath enrounded° him;	
	Nor doth he dedicate one jot of color	
	Unto the weary and all-watchèd night,¹	
	But freshly looks and overbears attaint²	
appearance	With cheerful semblance° and sweet majesty,	40
So that	That° every wretch, pining and pale before,	
	Beholding him, plucks comfort from his looks.	
	A largess universal³ like the sun	
generous	His liberal° eye doth give to everyone,	
	Thawing cold fear, that mean and gentle all⁴	45
	Behold, as may unworthiness define,⁵	
	A little touch of Harry in the night.	
	And so our scene must to the battle fly,	
	Where—Oh, for pity!—we shall much disgrace	
	With four or five most vile and raggèd foils,	50
	Right ill-disposed in brawl ridiculous,⁶	
	The name of Agincourt. Yet sit and see,	
Being reminded of	Minding° true things by what their mockeries⁷ be.	

He exits.

1   *Would men*

     If men would

2   *good husbandry*

     Good management

3   *they*

     I.e., enemies (*our bad neighbor*)

4   *dress us fairly*

     Prepare ourselves suitably

5   *make a moral of*

     I.e., derive a lesson from

6   *to love their present pains / Upon example*

     **To embrace their current suffering
     by following the example (of Henry
     and his nobles)**

7   *out of doubt*

     Undoubtedly

8   *Break up their drowsy grave and newly
     move / With casted slough and fresh
     legerity*

     **I.e., emerge from their torpor and
     move anew, casting off their old
     skin and acting with renewed
     energy. King Henry likens the
     organs to a snake that has shed
     its skin (the *casted slough*) and then
     is able to move easily.**

Act 4, Scene 1

Enter the **King**, **Bedford** [*separately*], *and* **Gloucester**.

King Henry

Gloucester, 'tis true that we are in great danger;
The greater therefore should our courage be.
—Good morrow, brother Bedford. God Almighty,
There is some soul° of goodness in things evil,   *i.e., essential piece*
Would men ¹ observingly distill it out,   5
For our bad neighbor makes us early stirrers,
Which is both healthful and good husbandry.²
Besides, they³ are our outward consciences
And preachers to us all, admonishing
That we should dress us fairly⁴ for our end.   10
Thus may we gather honey from the weed
And make a moral of ⁵ the devil himself.

Enter **Erpingham**.

—Good morrow, old Sir Thomas Erpingham.
A good soft pillow for that good white head
Were better than a churlish° turf of France.   *rough; inhospitable*   15

Erpingham

Not so, my liege, this lodging likes° me better,   *pleases*
Since I may say, "Now lie I like a king."

King Henry

'Tis good for men to love their present pains
Upon example; ⁶ so the spirit is eased.
And when the mind is quickened,° out of doubt ⁷   *cheered up*   20
The organs, though defunct and dead before,
Break up their drowsy grave and newly move
With casted slough and fresh legerity.⁸

199

1   *Brothers both*

     I.e., Gloucester and Bedford

2   *Do my good morrow to them*

     I.e., tell them "Good morning"
     for me

3   *anon / Desire them all*

     I.e., invite them all to come soon

4   Qui vous là?

     I.e., who goes there (in somewhat
     mangled French)

5   *gentleman of a company*

     A volunteer of noble birth whose
     rank was above a common soldier
     but not a commissioned officer

Lend me thy cloak, Sir Thomas.

[**King Henry** *puts on* **Erpingham**'s *cloak*.]

—Brothers both,[1]

Commend me to the princes in our camp;   25

Do my good morrow to them,[2] and anon

Desire them all[3] to my pavilion.

Gloucester

We shall, my liege.

Erpingham

Shall I attend your Grace?

King Henry

No, my good knight,

Go with my brothers to my lords of England.   30

self; heart I and my bosom° must debate awhile,

And then I would no other company.

Erpingham

The Lord in Heaven bless thee, noble Harry!

[*All but* **King Henry**] *exit*.

King Henry

friend God-a-mercy, old heart!° Thou speak'st cheerfully.

Enter **Pistol**.

Pistol

Qui vous là?[4]   35

King Henry

A friend.

Pistol

Declare Discuss° unto me: art thou officer,

vulgar Or art thou base, common, and popular?°

King Henry

I am a gentleman of a company.[5]

1   *Trail'st thou the puissant pike?*

     I.e., do you serve in the infantry? An
     infantryman's pike was typically
     well over 10 feet long and was thus
     dragged (*trailed*) when not in use.
     The high esteem in which the
     pike was held as a weapon prompts
     Pistol's respectful *pussiant*
     (powerful).

2   *bawcock*

     Fine fellow; from French *beau coq*,
     "fine bird" (as in 3.2.22)

3   *from heartstring / I love the lovely bully*

     I.e., from the bottom of my heart I
     love the good fellow.

4   *le Roy*

     From the French *le roi*, "the king."

5   *I am a Welshman*

     Historically, Henry was born
     at Monmouth, in Wales; see
     also 4.7.102, and his claim to be
     Fluellen's kinsman at 4.1.59. In
     the 16th century, the Tudors also
     claimed Welsh descent, as Henry
     VII was born in Wales and had a
     Welsh grandfather. The arrival of a
     supposedly Welsh dynasty on the
     English throne was celebrated as
     the return to power of the ancient
     Britons—the first known inhabit-
     ants of England and the ancestors
     of the modern Welsh—after a
     long exile at the hands of the
     invading Anglo-Saxons: Edmund

Spenser sets out this story of exile
and return as part of his mythical
genealogy of Elizabeth in *The Faerie
Queene*, 3.3. In this play, Henry's
claim to Welshness also seeks
to mitigate the ethnic divisions
among his soldiers: the play may at
times ask us to laugh at Fluellen's
earnest pedantry, but it also shows
us a King who both recognizes his
loyalty and claims kinship with him.

6   *leek*

     The national emblem of Wales; see
     note 7 below.

7   *Saint Davy's day*

     Saint David, the patron saint of
     Wales, commanded an army that
     defeated the invading Saxons in
     A.D. 540. According to legend, the
     decisive battle took place in a leek
     field, and Saint David's soldiers
     camouflaged themselves by attach-
     ing leeks to their helmets. On Saint
     David's feast day (March 1), the
     Welsh wore leeks in their hats to
     commemorate the battle.

Pistol

Trail'st thou the puissant pike?[1]   40

King Henry

Even so. What are you?

Pistol

Holy Roman Emperor   As good a gentleman as the Emperor.°

King Henry

Then you are a better than the King.

Pistol

The King's a bawcock[2] and a heart of gold,

child   A lad of life, an imp° of fame,   45

Of parents good, of fist most valiant.

I kiss his dirty shoe, and from heartstring

I love the lovely bully.[3] What is thy name?

King Henry

Harry le Roy.[4]

Pistol

company   Le Roy? A Cornish name. Art thou of Cornish crew?°   50

King Henry

No, I am a Welshman.[5]

Pistol

Know'st thou Fluellen?

King Henry

Yes.

Pistol

head   Tell him I'll knock his leek[6] about his pate° upon Saint

Davy's day.[7]   55

King Henry

Do not you wear your dagger in your cap that day, lest

he knock that about yours.

Pistol

Art thou his friend?

1   *The* fico

    I.e., the fig, an offensive and defiant
    gesture (see 3.6.55 and note)

2   *sorts*

    Fits; agrees

3   *speak fewer*

    "Speak less" (i.e., you're talking
    too much, a comic complaint given
    Fluellen's own earnest volubility).

4   *the greatest admiration in the universal*
    world

    The greatest wonder in the entire
    world

5   *aunchient prerogatifes*

    I.e., "ancient prerogatives" in
    Fluellen's Welsh pronunciation; the
    traditional rules of war

6   *Pompey the Great*

    Famously successful Roman gen-
    eral, eventually defeated by Julius
    Caesar at Pharsalus in 48 B.C.

7   *tiddle-taddle nor pibble-babble*

    Tittle-tattle nor bibble-babble
    (i.e., idle chit-chat)

8   *prating coxcomb*

    Jabbering fool

King Henry

And his kinsman too.

Pistol

The *fico*[1] for thee, then!   60

King Henry

I thank you. God be with you!

Pistol

My name is Pistol called.   *He exits.*

King Henry

It sorts[2] well with your fierceness.

> *The **King** remains [standing apart].*

> *Enter **Fluellen** and **Gower** [separately].*

Gower

Captain Fluellen!

Fluellen

So; in the name of Jesu Christ, speak fewer.[3] It is the   65
greatest admiration in the universal world,[4] when
the true and aunchient prerogatifes[5] and laws of the
wars is not kept. If you would take the pains but to
examine the wars of Pompey the Great,[6] you shall
guarantee   find, I warrant° you, that there is no tiddle-taddle nor   70
pibble-babble[7] in Pompey's camp. I warrant you, you
shall find the ceremonies of the wars, and the cares of
seriousness it, and the forms of it, and the sobriety° of it, and the
self-control modesty° of it, to be otherwise.

Gower

Why, the enemy is loud; you hear him all night.   75

Fluellen

If the enemy is an ass and a fool and a prating cox-
fitting   comb,[8] is it meet,° think you, that we should also,

look you, be an ass and a fool and a prating coxcomb,
In your own conscience, now?

Gower

I will speak lower.   80

Fluellen

I pray you and beseech you that you will.

[**Gower** and **Fluellen**] exit.

King Henry

Though it appear a little out of fashion,
There is much care and valor in this Welshman.

Enter three soldiers: John **Bates**, *Alexander* **Court**,
and Michael **Williams**.

Court

Brother John Bates, is not that the morning which
breaks yonder?   85

Bates

I think it be. But we have no great cause to desire the
approach of day.

Williams

We see yonder the beginning of the day, but I think we
shall never see the end of it.—Who goes there?

King Henry

A friend.   90

Williams

Under what captain serve you?

King Henry

Under Sir Thomas Erpingham.

Williams

A good old commander and a most kind gentleman. I
situation   pray you, what thinks he of our estate?°

1   *wracked upon a sand*
    Shipwrecked upon a sandbank

2   *conditions*
    Characteristics (i.e., limitations)

3   *ceremonies*
    **I.e., symbols and trappings of
    royalty**

4   *though his affections are higher mounted
    than ours, yet when they stoop they stoop
    with the like wing*
    **Though his emotions are tied to
    loftier issues than ours, yet when
    they sink they do so in similar
    fashion. When applied to falconry,
    to *stoop* means to fly down and
    strike an object of prey; King Henry
    may mean that the King acts on his
    desires as any other person would,
    despite their loftiness (e.g., invad-
    ing France), though the primary
    sense is that the King's spirits sag
    like anyone else's.**

5   *in reason, no man should possess him
    with any appearance of fear*
    **I.e., it makes sense that no one
    should alarm the King by appearing
    afraid.**

6   *Thames*
    **The major river of southern Eng-
    land, which runs through London**

7   *at all adventures, so we were quit here*
    **I.e., whatever the result, just so we
    were no longer here**

8   *speak my conscience of*
    I.e., say what I believe about

King Henry

Even as men wracked upon a sand,[1] that look to be   95
washed off the next tide.

Bates

He hath not told his thought to the King?

King Henry

No, nor it is not meet he should. For, though I speak it
to you, I think the King is but a man, as I am. The vio-

sky let smells to him as it doth to me; the element° shows   100
to him as it doth to me; all his senses have but human
conditions.[2] His ceremonies[3] laid by, in his nakedness
he appears but a man; and though his affections are
higher mounted than ours, yet when they stoop they
stoop with the like wing.[4] Therefore when he sees   105

for reason of° fears, as we do, his fears, out of doubt, be
taste; nature of the same relish° as ours are. Yet, in reason, no man
should possess him with any appearance of fear,[5] lest
he, by showing it, should dishearten his army.

Bates

He may show what outward courage he will, but I   110
believe, as cold a night as 'tis, he could wish himself in
Thames[6] up to the neck—and so I would he were, and
I by him, at all adventures, so we were quit here.[7]

King Henry

faith By my troth,° I will speak my conscience of [8] the King: I
think he would not wish himself anywhere but where   115
he is.

Bates

Then I would he were here alone. So should he be sure
to be ransomed, and a many poor men's lives saved.

King Henry

I dare say you love him not so ill to wish him here
test alone, howsoever you speak this to feel° other men's   120

1   *heavy reckoning*

    **Difficult accounting (to God for his
    conduct)**

2   *Latter Day*

    **The world's last day (i.e., the Day
    of Judgment, when, according to
    Christian belief, the dead are resur-
    rected)**

3   *some upon*

    Some (crying out) about

4   *rawly left*

    **(1) departed from abruptly; (2) left
    behind at a young age; (3) left
    unsupported, hence poor**

5   *blood is their argument*

    **Killing is their theme (i.e., what is
    expected of them).**

6   *were against all proportion of subjection*

    **Would violate all the obligations of
    a subject**

7   *do sinfully miscarry*

    I.e., die in a state of sin

8   *imputation of*

    Responsibility for

9   *in many irreconciled iniquities*

    I.e., with many unabsolved sins

minds. Methinks I could not die anywhere so con-
tented as in the King's company, his cause being just
and his quarrel honorable.

Williams

That's more than we know.

Bates

Ay, or more than we should seek after, for we know   125
enough if we know we are the King's subjects. If his
cause be wrong, our obedience to the King wipes the
crime of it out of us.

Williams

But if the cause be not good, the King himself hath
a heavy reckoning[1] to make when all those legs and   130
arms and heads, chopped off in a battle, shall join together at the Latter Day[2] and cry all, "We died at such
a place"—some swearing, some crying for a surgeon,
some upon[3] their wives left poor behind them, some
upon the debts they owe, some upon their children   135
rawly left.[4] I am afeard there are few die well that die
in a battle, for how can they charitably dispose of
anything when blood is their argument?[5] Now, if
these men do not die well, it will be a black matter
i.e., whom for the king that led them to it, who° to disobey were   140
against all proportion of subjection.[6]

King Henry

So, if a son that is by his father sent about merchan-
business dise° do sinfully miscarry[7] upon the sea, the imputation of[8] his wickedness, by your rule, should be
imposed upon his father that sent him; or if a servant,   145
under his master's command transporting a sum of
money, be assailed by robbers and die in many irreconciled iniquities,[9] you may call the business of the
master the author of the servant's damnation. But this

1   *answer*

    Answer for; be responsible for

2   *there is no king, be his cause never so*
    spotless, if it come to the arbitrament of
    swords, can try it out with all unspotted
    soldiers

    Even if his cause were most just, no
    king could—if the issue had to be
    decided in battle—carry out his
    mission only with sinless soldiers.
    King Henry goes on to explain that
    a king cannot be held responsible
    for the ultimate destiny of his
    soldiers, since *every subject's soul is*
    his own.

3   *the broken seals of perjury*

    I.e., broken promises. The seduc-
    er's promises are imagined as legal
    documents whose waxen seals have
    been broken, thereby rendering the
    documents invalid.

4   *making the wars their bulwark, that have*
    before gored the gentle bosom of peace
    with pillage and robbery

    I.e., hiding in the army, who were
    guilty of pillaging and robbing at
    home

5   *native punishment*

    I.e., punishment waiting for them
    at home

6   *beadle*

    In Shakespeare's time, a *beadle* was
    a lay parish officer responsible for
    punishing minor crimes.

7   *here men are punished for before-breach*
    of the king's laws in now the king's
    quarrel

    Men are punished (by God) for their
    previous violations of the law by
    having to serve in this war.

8   *Where they feared the death, they have*
    borne life away

    I.e., where they were afraid of the
    death penalty, they escaped with
    their lives.

9   *advantage*

    A benefit (because well prepared
    for and, so, the means to Heaven)

is not so. The king is not bound to answer[1] the par-   150
ticular endings of his soldiers, the father of his son,
intend   nor the master of his servant, for they purpose° not
their death when they purpose their services. Besides,
there is no king, be his cause never so spotless, if it
come to the arbitrament of swords, can try it out with   155
perhaps   all unspotted soldiers.[2] Some, peradventure,° have on
them the guilt of premeditated and contrived murder;
some, of beguiling virgins with the broken seals of perjury;[3] some, making the wars their bulwark, that have
before gored the gentle bosom of peace with pillage   160
broken   and robbery.[4] Now, if these men have defeated° the
law and outrun native punishment,[5] though they can
outstrip men, they have no wings to fly from God. War
is His beadle;[6] war is His vengeance—so that here men
are punished for before-breach of the king's laws in   165
now the king's quarrel.[7] Where they feared the death,
they have borne life away,[8] and where they would be
prepared (spiritually)   safe, they perish. Then if they die unprovided,° no
more is the king guilty of their damnation than he was
before guilty of those impieties for the which they   170
punished   are now visited.° Every subject's duty is the king's, but
every subject's soul is his own. Therefore should every
soldier in the wars do as every sick man in his bed,
small imperfection   wash every mote° out of his conscience; and, dying so,
death is to him advantage,[9] or, not dying, the time was   175
blessedly lost wherein such preparation was gained.
And in him that escapes, it were not sin to think that,
i.e., God   making God so free an offer, He° let him outlive that
day to see His greatness and to teach others how they
should prepare.   180

Williams

in a state of sin / sin   'Tis certain, every man that dies ill,° the ill° upon his

1   *he would not be ransomed*

    I.e., King Henry will refuse to be
    ransomed (intended as a gesture
    of solidarity with his soldiers); see
    3.6.151.

2   *You pay him then.*

    I.e., you punish him when he breaks
    his word.

3   *elder-gun*

    A toy gun made of a hollowed
    branch from an elder tree

4   *go about*

    Try

own head; the King is not to answer it.

Bates

I do not desire he should answer for me, and yet I
determine to fight lustily for him.

King Henry

I myself heard the King say he would not be ransomed.[1] 185

Williams

Ay, he said so, to make us fight cheerfully, but when
our throats are cut, he may be ransomed and we ne'er
the wiser.

King Henry

If I live to see it, I will never trust his word after.

Williams

You pay him then.[2] That's a perilous shot out of an 190
elder-gun,[3] that a poor and a private displeasure can
do against a monarch. You may as well go about[4] to

its   turn the sun to ice with fanning in his° face with a
peacock's feather. You'll never trust his word after.
Come, 'tis a foolish saying. 195

King Henry

blunt   Your reproof is something too round.° I should be
angry with you, if the time were convenient.

Williams

Let it be a quarrel between us, if you live.

King Henry

I embrace it.

Williams

How shall I know thee again? 200

King Henry

pledge; token Give me any gage° of thine, and I will wear it in my
      bonnet.
    Then, if ever thou dar'st acknowledge it, I will make it
      my quarrel.

1   *take thee a box on the ear*

     I.e., strike you on the ear

2   *if you could tell how to reckon*

     If you knew how to count

3   *crowns*

     (1) coins; (2) heads (suggesting that
     the English army is outnumbered
     by the French twenty to one)

4   *no English treason to cut French crowns*

     In Shakespeare's time, when a
     coin's metal content determined
     its value, "cutting" or "clipping"
     a coin—shaving its edge so as to
     steal the pared gold or silver—
     was a treasonable offense. Henry
     invokes this practice, but also with
     the sense of "to behead French sol-
     diers." *Clipper* in line 219 continues
     the same word play.

5   *careful*

     Filled with cares; anxious

6   *O hard condition, / Twin-born with
     greatness*

     Henry's point is that the *hard condi-
     tion* of kingship, the responsibilities
     and criticism that come with rule,
     comes along with the power and
     authority; but the phrase *twin-born
     with greatness* may also allude to
     Henry's double existence as both
     a private and a public figure. Medi-
     eval and Tudor jurists elaborated
     a legal fiction according to which
     the king had two bodies, one his
     natural body, the other the body
     politic, a mystical, invisible body
     that survives any individual king
     who inhabits it.

Williams

Here's my glove. Give me another of thine.

King Henry

There. *[They exchange gloves.]*

Williams

This will I also wear in my cap. If ever thou come to   205
me and say, after tomorrow, "This is my glove," by this
hand, I will take thee a box on the ear.[1]

King Henry

If ever I live to see it, I will challenge it.

Williams

Thou dar'st as well be hanged.

King Henry

even if / find Well, I will do it, though° I take° thee in the King's   210
company.

Williams

Keep thy word. Fare thee well.

Bates

Be friends, you English fools, be friends. We have
French quarrels enough, if you could tell how to
reckon.[2]   215

King Henry

wager Indeed, the French may lay° twenty French crowns[3] to
one they will beat us, for they bear them on their shoul-
ders; but it is no English treason to cut French crowns,[4]
and tomorrow the King himself will be a clipper.

Soldiers exit.

Upon the king! "Let us our lives, our souls,   220
Our debts, our careful[5] wives,
Our children, and our sins lay on the king!"

i.e., Kings We° must bear all. O hard condition,

chatter Twin-born with greatness,[6] subject to the breath°
Of every fool, whose sense no more can feel   225

1   *whose sense no more can feel / But his own wringing*

    Whose senses recognize no more than his own aches and pains

2   *ceremony*

    I.e., the pomp and ritual that accompany the king's office

3   *rents*

    Income; earnings (synonymous with *comings-in*)

4   *Is thy soul of adoration?*

    (1) Is your essence only the fact of being adored? (2) Is your essence only the things that inspire *adoration*?

5   *aught else but place, degree, and form*

    Anything besides social rank, eminence, and outward appearance

6   *titles blown from adulation*

    (1) spoken only in flattery; (2) inflated by flattery

7   *Will it give place to flexure and low bending?*

    I.e., will this fever subside because of kneeling and deep (or perhaps "base") bowing?

8   *balm*

    Oil used in a coronation ceremony to anoint a king

9   *ball*

    Orb (a symbol of sovereignty)

10 *intertissued robe of*

    Robe interwoven with

But his own wringing![1] What infinite hearts' ease

do without Must kings neglect° that private men enjoy!

private citizens And what have kings that privates° have not too,

Save ceremony,[2] save general ceremony?

And what art thou, thou idol ceremony?   230

What kind of god art thou, that suffer'st more

Of mortal griefs than do thy worshippers?

What are thy rents?[3] What are thy comings-in?

O ceremony, show me but thy worth!

What? Is thy soul of adoration?[4]   235

Art thou aught else but place, degree, and form,[5]

Creating awe and fear in other men,

Wherein thou art less happy, being feared,

Than they in fearing?

What drink'st thou oft, instead of homage sweet,   240

But poisoned flattery? Oh, be sick, great greatness,

And bid thy ceremony give thee cure.

Think'st thou the fiery fever will go out

With titles blown from adulation?[6]

Will it give place to flexure and low bending?[7]   245

Canst thou, when thou command'st the beggar's
     knee,

Command the health of it? No, thou proud dream,

That play'st so subtly with a king's repose.

unmasks; reveals I am a king that find° thee, and I know

'Tis not the balm,[8] the scepter, and the ball,[9]   250

ceremonial staff The sword, the mace,° the crown imperial,

The intertissued robe of[10] gold and pearl,

stuffed; pretentious The farcèd° title running 'fore the king,

The throne he sits on, nor the tide of pomp

That beats upon the high shore of this world—   255

No, not all these, thrice-gorgeous ceremony,

Not all these, laid in bed majestical,

1   *distressful bread*

    Bread earned with painful toil

2   *But like a lackey from the rise to set /
    Sweats in the eye of Phoebus*

    **But (the *wretched slave*), like a foot-
    man, from dawn to dusk sweats
    under the heat of the sun. *Phoebus* is
    the sun god of classical mythology.**

3   *in Elysium*

    **I.e., in happiness. In Greek mythol-
    ogy, the souls of the blessed dead
    resided in the Elysium fields.**

4   *Hyperion*

    **Here synonymous with *Phoebus*
    (though in Greek mythology
    Hyperion is actually the father of
    the sun god; cf note 2)**

5   *Had the forehand*

    Would have the upper hand

6   *in gross brain little wots / What watch the
    King keeps*

    **I.e., in his dull brain (he) has little
    understanding of what wakefulness
    the King endures (*wots* meaning
    "thinks" or "knows")**

7   *Whose hours the peasant best advantages*

    **I.e., the hours (of royal effort) from
    which the peasant benefits most**

8   *jealous of*

    Anxious about

9   *sense of reck'ning*

    Capacity for counting

Can sleep so soundly as the wretched slave
Who, with a body filled and vacant mind,
Gets him to rest, crammed with distressful bread; [1]   260
Never sees horrid night, the child of Hell,
But like a lackey from the rise to set
Sweats in the eye of Phoebus [2] and all night
Sleeps in Elysium; [3] next day after dawn
Doth rise and help Hyperion [4] to his horse,   265
And follows so the ever-running year
With profitable labor to his grave.
And but for ceremony, such a wretch,
Filling   Winding° up days with toil and nights with sleep,
Had the forehand [5] and vantage of a king.   270
sharer   The slave, a member° of the country's peace,
i.e., peace   Enjoys it,° but in gross brain little wots
What watch the king keeps [6] to maintain the peace,
Whose hours the peasant best advantages. [7]

     Enter **Erpingham**.

Erpingham
My lord, your nobles, jealous of [8] your absence,   275
Seek through your camp to find you.
King Henry
                   Good old knight,
Collect them all together at my tent.
be there   I'll be° before thee.
Erpingham
           I shall do't, my lord.   *He exits.*
King Henry
O God of battles, steel my soldiers' hearts;
Possess them not with fear! Take from them now   280
before   The sense of reck'ning, [9] ere° th' opposèd numbers

1   *the fault / My father made in compassing*
    the crown

    Henry's father, Henry IV, seized the
    crown from Richard II, who was
    later murdered (events portrayed in
    Shakespeare's *Richard II*).

2   *I Richard's body have interrèd new*

    Holinshed writes that Richard II
    had been buried by Henry IV with
    a minimum of ceremony on the
    estate of Langley, but that, at the
    start of his reign, Henry V had the
    body moved to Westminster, where
    it was re-interred with the body
    of Richard's first wife, in a tomb
    constructed at Henry's personal
    expense. The ensuing details about
    Henry's penance for the memory
    of his father's usurpation—such as
    the construction of the chantries,
    or chapels endowed to maintain
    a priest or priests who say mass in
    memory of the founder or of some
    other specified individual—are
    taken from another history, by
    Robert Fabyan; there, however, the
    foundations endowed by Henry
    are religious foundations, one a
    monastery, another a nunnery.

3   *chantries*

    Chapels endowed for the purpose
    of holding masses for the dead

4   *after all*

    I.e., after I have accepted every-
    thing that followed from my
    father's actions

Pluck their hearts from them. Not today, O Lord,
Oh, not today, think not upon the fault
My father made in compassing the crown! [1]

buried I Richard's body have interrèd° new, [2]   285
And on it have bestowed more contrite tears
Than from it issued forcèd drops of blood.
Five hundred poor I have in yearly pay,
Who twice a day their withered hands hold up
Toward Heaven to pardon blood; and I have built   290
Two chantries, [3] where the sad and solemn priests

continually Sing still° for Richard's soul. More will I do,
Though all that I can do is nothing worth,
Since that my penitence comes after all, [4]
Imploring pardon.   295

                    Enter **Gloucester**.

Gloucester
My liege!
King Henry
              My brother Gloucester's voice? Ay.
—I know thy errand. I will go with thee.
The day, my friends, and all things stay for me.
                                              They exit.

1   *gild*

     Turn golden (with its rays)

2   Monte à cheval!

     **To horse! (The Folio omits the à,
     seemingly in error.)**

3   *Varlet!* Lacquais!

     **"Groom! Footman!" Many editions
     print "*Varlet lacquis!*" taking *varlet* as
     a derisive adjective.**

4   Via, les eaux et terre!

     Be off, (over) waters and earth!

5   Rien puis? L'air et feu?

     **"No more? (Not) air and fire?"
     (Water, earth, air, and fire are the
     four basic elements.)**

6   Cieux

     **"The heavens." The Dauphin claims
     that he and his beloved horse will
     fly over all the elements.**

7   *superfluous courage*

     **The spurting blood represents an
     excess of *courage* (valor; spirit) in
     the French horses, which they can
     afford to spill on the English. *Su-
     perfluous* may also indicate that the
     horses' blood will be unnecessary,
     since the overwhelmed English will
     be covered in their own.**

Act 4, Scene 2

Enter the **Dauphin**, **Orléans**, **Rambures**, *and* **Beaumont**.

Orléans

Mount up   The sun doth gild¹ our armor. Up,° my lords!

Dauphin

*Monte à cheval!*² My horse! Varlet! *Lacquais!*³ Ha!

Orléans

O brave spirit!

Dauphin

*Via, les eaux et terre!*⁴

Orléans

*Rien puis? L'air et feu?*⁵   5

Dauphin

*Cieux,*⁶ cousin Orléans.

             Enter **Constable**.

Now, my Lord Constable!

Constable

immediate   Hark how our steeds for present° service neigh!

Dauphin

(i.e., with spurs)   Mount them and make incision° in their hides,

spurt   That their hot blood may spin° in English eyes   10

i.e., blind   And dout° them with superfluous courage.⁷ Ha!

Rambures

What, will you have them weep our horses' blood?

How shall we then behold their natural tears?

             Enter **Messenger**.

Messenger

arrayed for battle   The English are embattled,° you French peers.

1 *squares of battle*

   I.e., battle formations

2 *Though we upon this mountain's basis*
   by / Took stand for idle speculation

   Even if we were to stand at the foot
   of this nearby mountain and idly
   watch (the battle)

3 *that our honors must not*

   That (i.e., merely watching) our
   sense of honor would not allow.

4 *tucket sonance*

   Trumpet call (perhaps a signal to
   march)

5 *carrions, desperate of their bones*

   Soon-to-be corpses, helpless to
   preserve their lives

6 *Ill-favoredly become*

   I.e., disgrace (with their
   appearance)

Constable

To horse, you gallant princes, straight to horse!   15
Do but behold yond poor and starvèd band,
appearance   And your fair show° shall suck away their souls,
shells   Leaving them but the shales° and husks of men.
There is not work enough for all our hands,
Scarce blood enough in all their sickly veins   20
cutlass; broad sword   To give each naked curtal-axe° a stain,
That our French gallants shall today draw out
And sheathe for lack of sport. Let us but blow on them,
The vapor of our valor will o'erturn them.
objections   'Tis positive against all exceptions,° lords,   25
footmen   That our superfluous lackeys° and our peasants,
Who, in unnecessary action swarm
About our squares of battle,¹ were enough
contemptible   To purge this field of such a hilding° foe,
Though we upon this mountain's basis by   30
Took stand for idle speculation²—
But that our honors must not.³ What's to say?
A very little little let us do,
And all is done. Then let the trumpets sound
The tucket sonance⁴ and the note to mount,   35
astound; dazzle   For our approach shall so much dare° the field
cower   That England shall couch° down in fear and yield.

Enter **Grandpré**.

Grandpré

Why do you stay so long, my lords of France?
i.e., English   Yond island° carrions, desperate of their bones,⁵
Ill-favoredly become⁶ the morning field.   40
banners   Their raggèd curtains° poorly are let loose,
exceedingly   And our air shakes them passing° scornfully.

1 *Big Mars seems bankrupt in their*
   beggared host

   **I.e., the spirit of proud Mars
   (Roman god of war) seems to be
   lacking in their impoverished army.**

2 *torch staves*

   Staffs topped with torches

3 *gum down-roping*

   Secretions hanging down like ropes

4 *executors*

   **Those who take control of the pos-
   sessions (and bodies) of the dead**

5 *Description cannot suit itself in words / To
   demonstrate the life of such a battle / In
   life so lifeless, as it shows itself.*

   **I.e., there are no suitable words
   accurately to depict an army that
   appears as dead as this one does.**

6 *guard*

   **Escort. Some editions emend
   to "guidon," which explains the
   Constable's desire to take the
   trumpeter's banner (a guidon is a
   pennant).**

Big Mars seems bankrupt in their beggared host[1]

visor And faintly through a rusty beaver° peeps.

The horsemen sit like fixèd candlesticks, 45

With torch staves[2] in their hand, and their poor jades

Hang Lob° down their heads, drooping the hides and hips,

The gum down-roping[3] from their pale-dead eyes,

jointed And in their pale dull mouths the gimmaled° bit

Lies foul with chewed grass, still and motionless; 50

And their executors,[4] the knavish crows,

Fly o'er them all impatient for their hour.

Description cannot suit itself in words

army To demonstrate the life of such a battle°

In life so lifeless, as it shows itself.[5] 55

Constable

wait They have said their prayers, and they stay° for death.

Dauphin

Shall we go send them dinners and fresh suits

oats; feed And give their fasting horses provender°—

afterward And after° fight with them?

Constable

I stay but for my guard.[6] On to the field! 60

trumpeter I will the banner from a trumpet° take

And use it for my haste. Come, come away!

wear out; waste The sun is high, and we outwear° the day.   *They exit.*

1   *threescore thousand*

     Sixty thousand

Act 4, Scene 3

Enter **Gloucester**, **Bedford**, **Exeter**, **Erpingham**, *with all*
army   *his host,°* **Salisbury**, *and* **Westmorland**.

Gloucester
Where is the King?
Bedford
army   The King himself is rode to view their battle.°
Westmorland
Of fighting men they have full threescore thousand.[1]
Exeter
There's five to one. Besides, they all are fresh.
Salisbury
God's arm strike with us! 'Tis a fearful odds.   5
troops   God b' wi' you, princes all; I'll to my charge.°
If we no more meet till we meet in Heaven,
Then joyfully, my noble Lord of Bedford,
My dear lord Gloucester, and my good lord Exeter,
i.e., Westmorland   And my kind kinsman,° warriors all, adieu!   10
Bedford
Farewell, good Salisbury, and good luck go with thee!
Exeter
Farewell, kind lord. Fight valiantly today!
remind   And yet I do thee wrong to mind° thee of it,
built; composed   For thou art framed° of the firm truth of valor.
                                        [**Salisbury** *exits.*]
Bedford
He is as full of valor as of kindness,   15
Princely in both.

Enter the **King**.

1   *To do our country loss*

For our country to lose

2   *feed upon my cost*

Eat at my expense

3   *I would not lose so great an honor / As one man more, methinks, would share from me / For the best hope I have*

I would not give up the share of honor that even a single additional man would, I think, take away from me—(not even) if it would improve my hopes of salvation

4   *crowns for convoy*

Coins to pay his travel

5   *fears his fellowship to die with us*

Is afraid to die along with me

6   *Feast of Crispian*

I.e., October 25. According to tradition, Crispian (Crispianus) and Crispin (Crispinus) were Roman brothers martyred in France in the 3rd century A.D.; they are the patron saints of shoemakers.

Westmorland

                          Oh, that we now had here
But one ten thousand of those men in England
That do no work today!

King Henry

Who is   What's° he that wishes so?
My cousin Westmorland? No, my fair cousin.

destined If we are marked° to die, we are enough   20
To do our country loss,[1] and if to live,
The fewer men, the greater share of honor.
God's will, I pray thee, wish not one man more.
By Jove, I am not covetous for gold,
Nor care I who doth feed upon my cost.[2]   25

grieves It earns° me not if men my garments wear;
Such outward things dwell not in my desires.
But if it be a sin to covet honor,
I am the most offending soul alive.

cousin; kinsman No, faith, my coz,° wish not a man from England.   30
God's peace, I would not lose so great an honor
As one man more, methinks, would share from me
For the best hope I have.[3] Oh, do not wish one more.

army Rather proclaim it, Westmorland, through my host°

appetite That he which hath no stomach° to this fight,   35
Let him depart. His passport shall be made
And crowns for convoy[4] put into his purse.
We would not die in that man's company
That fears his fellowship to die with us.[5]

This day is called the Feast of Crispian.[6]   40
He that outlives this day and comes safe home

i.e., tall (and proud) Will stand a-tiptoe° when the day is named
And rouse him at the name of Crispian.

live to He that shall see this day and live° old age

1   *vigil*

    Evening prior to the saint's day

2   *their flowing cups freshly remembered*

    With their full glasses freshly
    recalled (i.e., toasted)

3   *be he ne'er so vile, / This day shall gentle*
    his condition

    No matter how low born a man
    may be, this day shall make him a
    gentleman.

4   *bestow yourself*

    I.e., ready yourself for battle

5   *bravely in their battles set*

    Gallantly deployed in their battle
    formations

Will yearly on the vigil[1] feast his neighbors   45
And say, "Tomorrow is Saint Crispian."
Then will he strip his sleeve and show his scars
And say, "These wounds I had on Crispin's Day."
Old men forget; yet all shall be forgot,
embellishments   But he'll remember with advantages°   50
What feats he did that day. Then shall our names,
Familiar in his mouth as household words—
Harry the King, Bedford and Exeter,
Warwick and Talbot, Salisbury and Gloucester—
Be in their flowing cups freshly remembered.[2]   55
This story shall the good man teach his son,
And Crispin Crispian shall ne'er go by,
From this day to the ending of the world,
But we in it shall be rememberèd,
We few, we happy few, we band of brothers—   60
For he today that sheds his blood with me
Shall be my brother; be he ne'er so vile,
This day shall gentle his condition.[3]
And gentlemen in England now abed
Shall think themselves accursed they were not here   65
And hold their manhoods cheap whiles any speaks
That fought with us upon Saint Crispin's day.

Enter **Salisbury**.

Salisbury
My sovereign lord, bestow yourself[4] with speed.
The French are bravely in their battles set[5]
speed   And will with all expedience° charge on us.   70
King Henry
All things are ready if our minds be so.

Westmorland

reluctant Perish the man whose mind is backward° now!

King Henry

Thou dost not wish more help from England, coz?

Westmorland

if only God's will, my liege, would° you and I alone,

Without more help, could fight this royal battle!   75

King Henry

Why, now thou hast unwished five thousand men,

pleases Which likes° me better than to wish us one.

—You know your places. God be with you all!

Tucket. Enter **Montjoy**.

Montjoy

Once more I come to know of thee, King Harry,

agree to terms If for thy ransom thou wilt now compound°   80

Before thy most assurèd overthrow,

whirlpool; abyss For certainly thou art so near the gulf°

swallowed up Thou needs must be englutted.° Besides, in mercy,

remind The Constable desires thee thou wilt mind°

so that Thy followers of repentance, that° their souls   85

retreat May make a peaceful and a sweet retire°

From off these fields where, wretches, their poor
  bodies

Must lie and fester.

King Henry

                        Who hath sent thee now?

Montjoy

The Constable of France.

King Henry

I pray thee, bear my former answer back: 90

1   *with hunting him*

I.e., while hunting the lion (an
allusion to one of Aesop's fables,
but replacing Aesop's bear with
a *lion*, the emblem of the English
monarchy)

2   *Find native graves*

Find themselves buried in English
graves (i.e., will not die here on the
French battlefields)

3   *Shall witness live in brass of this day's
work*

Will live as permanent witnesses
to today's accomplishment in their
funeral monuments

4   *abounding valor*

The abundant courage

5   *Killing in relapse of mortality*

I.e., killing even as they turn to dust

6   *warriors for the working day*

(1) soldiers who see battle as a job;
(2) soldiers dressed in battle gear.
Both senses contrast the English
with the French, for whom battle is
an elegant game to which they have
worn their finest attire.

7   *Our gayness and our gilt*

Our bright clothing and shiny armor

8   *in the trim*

(1) in full readiness (like a trimmed
ship); (2) finely dressed

9   *in fresher robes*

I.e., in robes worn in Heaven (a defi-
ant taunt, in keeping with Henry's
earlier threat in lines 105–107 that
even the English dead will help
destroy France)

10 *or they will pluck / The gay new coats
o'er the French soldiers' heads / And turn
them out of service*

I.e., or else they will pull the bright
new coats over the dead French soldiers' heads, as though the corpses
were servants being dismissed
from service (being stripped of
their uniforms)

capture	Bid them achieve° me and then sell my bones.
	Good God, why should they mock poor fellows thus?
	The man that once did sell the lion's skin
	While the beast lived was killed with hunting him.[1]
	A many of our bodies shall no doubt 95
	Find native graves,[2] upon the which, I trust,
	Shall witness live in brass of this day's work.[3]
	And those that leave their valiant bones in France,
	Dying like men, though buried in your dunghills,
	They shall be famed, for there the sun shall greet them 100
wafting	And draw their honors reeking° up to Heaven,
region	Leaving their earthly parts to choke your clime,°
	The smell whereof shall breed a plague in France.
Note	Mark° then abounding valor[4] in our English,
shattering; ricocheting	That, being dead, like to the bullet's crazing° 105
	Break out into a second course of mischief,
	Killing in relapse of mortality.[5]
	Let me speak proudly. Tell the Constable
	We are but warriors for the working day.[6]
	Our gayness and our gilt[7] are all besmirched 110
	With rainy marching in the painful field.
decorative plume / army	There's not a piece of feather° in our host°—
i.e., evidence	Good argument,° I hope, we will not fly—
slovenliness	And time hath worn us into slovenry.°
	But, by the mass, our hearts are in the trim![8] 115
	And my poor soldiers tell me yet ere night
	They'll be in fresher robes,[9] or they will pluck
	The gay new coats o'er the French soldiers' heads
	And turn them out of service.[10] If they do this—
	As, if God please, they shall—my ransom then 120
collected	Will soon be levied.° Herald, save thou thy labor.
	Come thou no more for ransom, gentle herald.
i.e., The French	They° shall have none, I swear, but these my joints,

1   *Shall yield them little*

     **I.e., because Henry plans to fight to
     the death**

Which if they have as I will leave 'em them
Shall yield them little.¹ Tell the Constable.   125

Montjoy
I shall, King Harry. And so fare thee well.
Thou never shalt hear herald anymore.   *He exits.*

King Henry
I fear thou wilt once more come again for a ransom.

         Enter **York**.

York
[*kneeling*] My lord, most humbly on my knee I beg
vanguard   The leading of the vaward.°   130

King Henry
Take it, brave York. Now, soldiers, march away,
And how thou pleasest, God, dispose the day!
            They exit.

1   Alarum. Excursions.

    **Trumpet call to battle and skir-
    mishes, which were likely repre-
    sented by the movement of small
    groups of actors over the stage**

2   Je pense que vous êtes le gentil-
    homme de bonne qualité.

    **I think that you are a gentleman of
    high rank.**

3   Qualtitie calmie custure me!

    **Gibberish French. Pistol is trying
    to say something like "calmly tell
    me your rank," or perhaps merely
    mocking his prisoner's French.**

4   Ô Seigneur Dieu!

    O Lord God!

5   Ô, prenez miséricorde! Ayez pitié
    de moi!

    Oh have mercy! Take pity on me!

6   *"Moy"*

    **Pistol assumes that the French
    soldier is trying to offer him some
    kind of foreign coin.**

7   Est-il impossible d'échapper la
    force de ton bras?

    **Is it impossible to escape the
    strength of your arm?**

8   Ô, pardonnez-moi!

    Oh, pardon me!

Act 4, Scene 4

Alarum. Excursions.[1] *Enter* **Pistol**, **French Soldier**, *[and]* **Boy**.

Pistol

Yield, cur!

French Soldier

Je pense que vous êtes le gentilhomme de bonne qualité.[2]

Pistol

Qualtitie calmie custure me![3]

Art thou a gentleman? What is thy name? Discuss.

French Soldier

Ô Seigneur Dieu![4]   5

Pistol

i.e., is likely to be O Signieur Dew should° be a gentleman.

Consider Perpend° my words, O Signieur Dew, and mark:

sword O Signieur Dew, thou diest on point of fox,°

Unless Except,° O Signieur, thou do give to me

i.e., Enormous Egregious° ransom.   *[He threatens him with his sword.]* 10

French Soldier

Ô, prenez miséricorde! Ayez pitié de moi![5]

Pistol

"Moy"[6] shall not serve. I will have forty moys,

stomach Or I will fetch thy rim° out at thy throat

In drops of crimson blood.

French Soldier

Est-il impossible d'échapper la force de ton bras?[7]   15

Pistol

Brass, cur?

lecherous Thou damnèd and luxurious° mountain goat,

Offer'st me brass?

French Soldier

Ô, pardonnez-moi![8]

1   Écoutez. Comment êtes-vous
    appelé?
    Listen: what is your name?

2   *firk him, and ferret him*
    **Beat him, and tear at him (like a
    ferret)**

3   Que dit-il, monsieur?
    What does he say, sir?

4   Il me commande à vous dire que
    vous faites vous prêt; car ce soldat
    ici est disposé tout à cette heure de
    couper votre gorge.
    **He commands me tell you that you
    must prepare yourself, because this
    soldier intends immediately to cut
    your throat.**

5   Oui, cuppele gorge, permafoy.
    **Pistol continues to mispronounce
    the French: "*Oui* (yes), *couper la gorge*
    (cut the throat), *par me foi* (by my
    faith)."**

6   Ô, je vous supplie, pour l'amour
    de Dieu, me pardoner! Je suis le
    gentilhomme de bonne maison.
    Gardez ma vie, et je vous donnerai
    deux cents écus.
    **Oh, I pray you, for the love of God,
    to pardon me! I am a gentleman of
    a good house. Protect my life, and I
    will give you two hundred crowns.**

Pistol

Say'st thou me so? Is that a ton of moys? 20

for me —Come hither, boy. Ask me° this slave in French

What is his name.

Boy

Écoutez. Comment êtes-vous appelé? [1]

French Soldier

Monsieur le Fer.

Boy

He says his name is Master Fer. 25

Pistol

Master Fer. I'll fer him, and firk him, and ferret him. [2]

Discuss the same in French unto him.

Boy

I do not know the French for "fer," and "ferret," and "firk."

Pistol

Bid him prepare, for I will cut his throat.

French Soldier

Que dit-il, monsieur? [3] 30

Boy

*Il me commande à vous dire que vous faites vous prêt; car ce soldat
ici est disposé tout à cette heure de couper votre gorge.* [4]

Pistol

Oui, cuppele gorge, permafoy. [5]

Peasant, unless thou give me crowns, brave crowns,

Or mangled shalt thou be by this my sword. 35

French Soldier

*Ô, je vous supplie, pour l'amour de Dieu, me pardoner! Je suis le
gentilhomme de bonne maison. Gardez ma vie, et je vous donnerai
deux cents écus.* [6]

Pistol

What are his words?

1   Encore qu'il est contre son jure-
     ment de pardonner aucun prison-
     nier, néanmoins, pour les écus que
     vous l'avez promis, il est content à
     vous donner la liberté, le franchise-
     ment.

     **Although it is contrary to his oath to
     pardon any prisoner, nevertheless,
     for the sake of the crowns you have
     promised, he is satisfied to grant
     you your liberty, your freedom.**

2   Sur mes genoux je vous donne
     mille remercîments; et je m'estime
     heureux que j'ai tombé entre les
     mains d'un chevalier, je pense, le
     plus brave, vaillant, et très-distin-
     gué seigneur d'Angleterre.

     **On my knees I give you a thousand
     thanks, and I consider myself happy
     that I have come to the hands of
     a gentleman, I think, the bravest,
     most valiant, and very distin-
     guished in England.**

3   *As I suck blood*

     **A claim of battlefield ferocity but
     also "as I am a leech" (see 2.3.50–51)**

4   Suivez-vous le grand capitaine.

     Follow the great captain.

Boy

He prays you to save his life. He is a gentleman of a 40
good house, and for his ransom he will give you two
(silver coins) hundred crowns.°

Pistol

Tell him my fury shall abate, and I
The crowns will take.

French Soldier

Petit monsieur, que dit-il? 45

Boy

Encore qu'il est contre son jurement de pardonner aucun prisonnier,
néanmoins, pour les écus que vous l'avez promis, il est content à
vous donner la liberté, le franchisement.[1]

French Soldier

[kneeling] *Sur mes genoux je vous donne mille remercîments; et*
je m'estime heureux que j'ai tombé entre les mains d'un cheva- 50
lier, je pense, le plus brave, vaillant, et très-distingué seigneur
d'Angleterre.[2]

Pistol

Expound unto me, boy.

Boy

He gives you, upon his knees, a thousand thanks, and
he esteems himself happy that he hath fallen into the 55
hands of one, as he thinks, the most brave, valorous,
and thrice-worthy seigneur of England.

Pistol

As I suck blood,[3] I will some mercy show.
Follow me!   [*The* **French Soldier** *rises.*]

Boy

Suivez-vous le grand capitaine.[4] 60

                    [**Pistol** *and* **French Soldier** *exit.*]
I did never know so full a voice issue from so empty a

1   *"The empty vessel makes the greatest
    sound"*

    **Proverbial for "a foolish person
    talks the most"**

2   *roaring devil i' th' old play*

    **In the morality plays that predated
    Shakespeare's time, the Vice char-
    acter would often beat the devil
    with a *wooden dagger*.**

3   *have a good prey of us, if he knew of it*

    **I.e., would easily plunder us, if they
    knew of it**

heart. But the saying is true: "The empty vessel makes
the greatest sound."[1] Bardolph and Nym had ten
times more valor than this roaring devil i' th' old
play,[2] that everyone may pare his nails with a wooden   65

i.e., Pistol dagger, and they are both hanged; and so would this°
rashly be, if he durst steal any thing adventurously.° I must
footmen / baggage stay with the lackeys° with the luggage° of our camp.
The French might have a good prey of us, if he knew of
it,[3] for there is none to guard it but boys.   *He exits.*   70

1   Ô diable!

     Oh, the devil!

2   Ô Seigneur! Le jour est perdu; tout
     est perdu!

     Oh, Lord! The day is lost; all is lost!

3   Mort de ma vie.

     Death of my life!

4   *plumes*

     **I.e., decorative feathers in the
     soldiers' helmets**

5   Ô méchante fortune!

     Oh evil Fortune!

Act 4, Scene 5

Enter **Constable**, **Orléans**, **Bourbon**, [*the*] **Dauphin**, *and*
Rambures.

Constable
Ô diable! [1]
Orléans
Ô Seigneur! Le jour est perdu; tout est perdu! [2]
Dauphin
ruined   *Mort de ma vie!* [3] All is confounded,° all!
Reproach and everlasting shame
Sits mocking in our plumes.[4] *Ô méchante fortune!* [5]   5

                                     A short alarum.

Do not run away.
Constable
                  Why? All our ranks are broke.
Dauphin
everlasting   O perdurable° shame! Let's stab ourselves.
Be these the wretches that we played at dice for?
Orléans
Is this the king we sent to for his ransom?
Bourbon
Shame and eternal shame, nothing but shame!   10
i.e., Into battle   Let us die! In° once more! Back again!
And he that will not follow Bourbon now,
Let him go hence, and with his cap in hand,
sexual procurer; pimp   Like a base pander,° hold the chamber door,
higher born   Whilst by a slave, no gentler° than my dog,   15
violated   His fairest daughter is contaminated.°
Constable
destroyed / befriend   Disorder, that hath spoiled° us, friend° us now!
in   Let us on° heaps go offer up our lives.

1 *We are enough yet*

We have enough soldiers still.

Orléans

We are enough yet[1] living in the field

To smother up the English in our throngs,   20

of If any order might be thought upon.°

Bourbon

The devil take order now! I'll to the throng.

Let life be short, else shame will be too long.

                                        [*They*] *exit.*

1   Alarum

     Trumpet call signaling an attack

2   *yet keep the French the field*

     The French still remain in the field.

3   *The Duke of York commends him to your
     Majesty.*

     **This is Cambridge's older brother;
     he appears briefly at 4.3.129–132,
     kneeling to Henry and receiving a
     commission from him. The long,
     eroticized description of his and
     Suffolk's deaths (see especially
     lines 24–27) presumably shows that
     Henry has fully united England in
     this campaign. But it also reminds
     us that this will not be a lasting
     unity, as the families will be on
     opposing sides in the civil wars that
     will follow King Henry's death (see
     Epilogue, lines 9–12).**

4   *Yokefellow to his honor-owing wounds*

     **Sharing the same honorable
     wounds**

5   *in gore he lay insteeped*

     **In his blood he (Suffolk) lay
     immersed.**

6   *cheered him up*

     Encouraged him

7   *He smiled me in the face, raught me his
     hand*

     **He smiled at me, reached his hand
     out to me**

Act 4, Scene 6

Alarum.[1] *Enter the* **King** *and his train,* [**Exeter**, *and others,*] *with prisoners.*

King Henry
Well have we done, thrice valiant countrymen!
But all's not done; yet keep the French the field.[2]

Exeter
The Duke of York commends him to your Majesty.[3]

King Henry
Lives he, good uncle? Thrice within this hour
I saw him down, thrice up again and fighting.   5
From helmet to the spur all blood he was.

Exeter
In which array,° brave soldier, doth he lie,
Larding° the plain; and by his bloody side,
Yokefellow to his honor-owing wounds,[4]
The noble Earl of Suffolk also lies.   10
Suffolk first died; and York, all haggled° over,
Comes to him where in gore he lay insteeped[5]
And takes him by the beard, kisses the gashes
That bloodily did yawn° upon his face.
He cries aloud, "Tarry,° my cousin Suffolk!   15
My soul shall thine keep company to Heaven.
Tarry, sweet soul, for mine, then fly abreast,
As in this glorious and well-foughten field
We kept together in our chivalry!"
Upon these words I came and cheered him up.[6]   20
He smiled me in the face, raught me his hand,[7]
And, with a feeble grip, says "Dear my lord,
Commend my service to my sovereign."
So did he turn, and over Suffolk's neck
He threw his wounded arm, and kissed his lips,   25

Marginal glosses:
°*ornment (i.e., blood)* — array
Enriching — Larding
hacked — haggled
gape — yawn
Wait — Tarry

1   *And so espoused to death, with blood he*
     sealed / A testament of noble-ending love

     I.e., and, joined to death, thus did
     he with blood testify to his love for
     Suffolk, which ended only with his
     noble death. *Testament* also carries
     the meaning "will," with *blood* here
     acting as the wax seal affixed to the
     document.

2   *Then every soldier kill his prisoners!*

     (See LONGER NOTE on page 332.)

And so espoused to death, with blood he sealed
A testament of noble-ending love.[1]
The pretty and sweet manner of it forced
i.e., tears Those waters° from me which I would have stopped,
But I had not so much of man in me,   30
i.e., pity And all my mother° came into mine eyes
And gave me up to tears.

King Henry

                  I blame you not,
come to terms For, hearing this, I must perforce compound°
flow With mistful eyes, or they will issue° too.   *Alarum.*
But, hark, what new alarum is this same?   35
The French have reinforced their scattered men.
Then every soldier kill his prisoners![2]
Give the word through.   *[They] exit.*

1   *Kill the poys and the luggage?*

    **I.e., kill the boys and steal the
    supplies?**

2   *Alexander the Great.*

    **The conqueror Alexander the Great
    is also alluded to at 1.1.46 and 3.1.19.**

3   *are all one reckonings, save the phrase is a
    little variations*

    **I.e., all mean the same, except the
    words are a bit different**

4   *Macedon*

    **I.e., Macedonia, now a region of
    Northern Greece**

Act 4, Scene 7

Enter **Fluellen** *and* **Gower**.

Fluellen

Kill the poys and the luggage?[1] 'Tis expressly against
absolute the law of arms. 'Tis as arrant° a piece of knavery,
mark you now, as can be offert; in your conscience,
now, is it not?

Gower

'Tis certain there's not a boy left alive, and the cow-   5
ardly rascals that ran from the battle ha' done this
slaughter. Besides, they have burned and carried away
all that was in the King's tent, wherefore the King
most worthily hath caused every soldier to cut his
prisoner's throat. Oh, 'tis a gallant King!   10

Fluellen

i.e., born / (in Wales) Ay, he was porn° at Monmouth,° Captain Gower. What
i.e., Big call you the town's name where Alexander the Pig°
was born?

Gower

Alexander the Great.[2]

Fluellen

Why, I pray you, is not "pig" great? The pig, or the   15
great, or the mighty, or the huge, or the magnanimous, are all one reckonings, save the phrase is a
little variations.[3]

Gower

I think Alexander the Great was born in Macedon.[4] His
father was called Philip of Macedon, as I take it.   20

Fluellen

I think it is in Macedon where Alexander is porn. I tell
you, Captain, if you look in the maps of the 'orld, I
i.e., shall warrant you sall° find, in the comparisons between

259

1   *is come after it indifferent well*

     Matches it reasonably well

2   *Cleitus*

     In 328 B.C. Alexander killed his
     friend Cleitus while they both
     were drunk, in an argument about
     whether or not Alexander had out-
     done his father Philip's deeds.

3   *turned away the fat knight*

     Refers to the rejection of Falstaff at
     the end of *Henry IV, Part Two*

4   *great-belly doublet*

     A tight-fitting jacket, called *great*
     because padded (though, in Fal-
     staff's case, necessary for his large
     stomach)

Macedon and Monmouth, that the situations, look
you, is both alike. There is a river in Macedon, and 25
there is also, moreover, a river at Monmouth. It is

i.e., brains called Wye at Monmouth, but it is out of my prains°
what is the name of the other river; but 'tis all one,
'tis alike as my fingers is to my fingers, and there is
salmons in both. If you mark Alexander's life well, 30
Harry of Monmouth's life is come after it indifferent

comparisons well,[1] for there is figures° in all things. Alexander, God
knows and you know, in his rages, and his furies, and

irritability; anger his wraths, and his cholers,° and his moods, and his
displeasures, and his indignations, and also being a 35

drunk little intoxicate° in his prains, did, in his ales and his
angers, look you, kill his best friend, Cleitus.[2]

Gower
Our King is not like him in that. He never killed any of
his friends.

Fluellen
It is not well done, mark you now, to take the tales out 40
of my mouth ere it is made and finished. I speak but in
the figures and comparisons of it. As Alexander killed
his friend Cleitus, being in his ales and his cups, so
also Harry Monmouth, being in his right wits and his
good judgments, turned away the fat knight[3] with the 45

i.e., gibes great-belly doublet.[4] He was full of jests, and gipes,°
and knaveries, and mocks. I have forgot his name.

Gower
Sir John Falstaff.

Fluellen
That is he. I'll tell you, there is good men porn at
Monmouth. 50

Gower
Here comes his Majesty.

Alarum. Enter **King Henry**, [**Warwick, Gloucester,
Exeter**, *and others*,] *and* **Bourbon** *with* [*other French*]
prisoners. Flourish.

King Henry

I was not angry since I came to France

trumpeter   Until this instant. Take a trumpet,° herald;

Ride thou unto the horsemen on yond hill.

If they will fight with us, bid them come down   55

withdraw from   Or void° the field. They do offend our sight.

If they'll do neither, we will come to them,

scurry   And make them skirr° away as swift as stones

Forced; Hurled   Enforcèd° from the old Assyrian slings.

Besides, we'll cut the throats of those we have,   60

And not a man of them that we shall take

Shall taste our mercy. Go and tell them so. [*Herald exits.*]

Enter **Montjoy**.

Exeter

Here comes the herald of the French, my liege.

Gloucester

His eyes are humbler than they used to be.

King Henry

How now, what means this, herald? Know'st thou not   65

pledged   That I have fined° these bones of mine for ransom?

Com'st thou again for ransom?

Montjoy

                        No, great King.

permission   I come to thee for charitable license°

That we may wander o'er this bloody field

record   To book° our dead and then to bury them,   70

To sort our nobles from our common men,

1   *mercenary blood*

    I.e., the blood of common soldiers
    paid to go to war

2   *peer*

    Show themselves

3   *the day of Crispin Crispianus*

    See 4.3.40 and note.

4   *grandfather*

    I.e., Edward III, Henry's great-
    grandfather

5   *pattle*

    The battle of Crécy (see 1.2.105–106
    and note)

For many of our princes—woe the while!—
Lie drowned and soaked in mercenary blood; [1]

common soldiers So do our vulgar° drench their peasant limbs
In blood of princes; and our wounded steeds   75
Chafe Fret° fetlock-deep in gore and with wild rage
Kick Yerk° out their armèd heels at their dead masters,
Killing them twice. Oh, give us leave, great King,
To view the field in safety and dispose
Of their dead bodies.

King Henry
                              I tell thee truly, herald,   80
I know not if the day be ours or no,
For yet a many of your horsemen peer [2]
And gallop o'er the field.

Montjoy
                              The day is yours.

King Henry
Praised be God, and not our strength, for it!
What is this castle called that stands hard by?   85

Montjoy
They call it Agincourt.

King Henry
Then call we this the field of Agincourt,
Fought on the day of Crispin Crispianus. [3]

Fluellen
if Your grandfather [4] of famous memory, an° 't please
i.e., Black your Majesty, and your great-uncle Edward the Plack°   90
histories Prince of Wales, as I have read in the chronicles,°
fought a most prave pattle [5] here in France.

King Henry
They did, Fluellen.

Fluellen
Your Majesty says very true. If your Majesty is

1   *Monmouth caps*

     Round caps, tall and brimless,
     named for their original place of
     manufacture in Wales

2   *Saint Tavy's Day*

     I.e., Saint David's feast day, men-
     tioned earlier at 4.1.55

3   *I am Welsh*

     King Henry was born in Wales, but
     his only Welsh blood was through a
     maternal great-grandmother.

4   *just notice*

     A precise report

remembered of it, the Welshmen did good service in a   95
garden where leeks did grow, wearing leeks in their
Monmouth caps,[1] which, your Majesty know, to this
hour is an honorable badge of the service; and I do
believe your Majesty takes no scorn to wear the leek
upon Saint Tavy's Day.[2]   100

King Henry
I wear it for a memorable honor,
For I am Welsh,[3] you know, good countryman.

Fluellen
All the water in Wye cannot wash your Majesty's Welsh

i.e., blood / i.e., body plood° out of your pody,° I can tell you that. God pless
it and preserve it, as long as it pleases His Grace—and   105
his Majesty too!

King Henry
Thanks, good my countryman.

Fluellen
By Jeshu, I am your Majesty's countryman. I care not
who know it. I will confess it to all the 'orld. I need
not to be ashamed of your Majesty, praised be God, so   110
long as your Majesty is an honest man.

King Henry
God keep me so!

Enter **Williams** [*with a glove in his cap*].

Our heralds go with him.
Bring me just notice[4] of the numbers dead
On both our parts.   [**Gower, Montjoy**, *and heralds exit.*]
Call yonder fellow hither.

Exeter
Soldier, you must come to the King.   115

1   *a gentleman of great sort, quite from the*
    answer of his degree

    I.e., a gentleman of high rank, too
    elevated to answer a challenge
    from a commoner

2   *Beelzebub*

    Originally the name of a Philistine
    deity, this became the name for the
    "prince of devils" (see Mark 3:22).

3   *sirrah*

    Term of address normally used with
    those of lower rank

King Henry

Soldier, why wear'st thou that glove in thy cap?

Williams

If/pledge An° 't please your Majesty, 'tis the gage° of one that I
with should fight withal,° if he be alive.

King Henry

An Englishman?

Williams

An 't please your Majesty, a rascal that swaggered with 120
me last night, who, if alive and ever dare to challenge
give this glove, I have sworn to take° him a box o' th' ear;
or if I can see my glove in his cap, which he swore as
he was a soldier he would wear if alive, I will strike it
out soundly. 125

King Henry

What think you, Captain Fluellen? Is it fit this soldier
keep his oath?

Fluellen

coward He is a craven° and a villain else, an 't please your
Majesty, in my conscience.

King Henry

It may be his enemy is a gentleman of great sort, quite 130
from the answer of his degree.[1]

Fluellen

Though he be as good a gentleman as the devil is, as
Lucifer and Beelzebub[2] himself, it is necessary, look
your Grace, that he keep his vow and his oath. If he be
absolute perjured, see you now, his reputation is as arrant° 135
impudent (saucy) fellow a villain and a jack-sauce° as ever his black shoe trod
upon God's ground and His Earth, in my conscience, la!

King Henry

Then keep thy vow, sirrah,[3] when thou meet'st the
fellow.

1   *is good knowledge and literatured in the*
    wars

    **I.e., is smart about and well read in
    military history and tactics**

2   *Alençon and myself were down together*

    **Alençon (a French duke) and I were
    fighting each other on the ground.**

Williams

So I will, my liege, as I live. 140

King Henry

Who serv'st thou under?

Williams

Under Captain Gower, my liege.

Fluellen

Gower is a good captain, and is good knowledge and
literatured in the wars.[1]

King Henry

Call him hither to me, soldier. 145

Williams

I will, my liege. *He exits.*

King Henry

Here, Fluellen, wear thou this favor for me and stick it
in thy cap. [*He gives him* **Williams**'s *glove*.] When
Alençon and myself were down together,[2] I plucked
this glove from his helm.° If any man challenge this, 150
he is a friend to Alençon and an enemy to our person.
If thou encounter any such, apprehend him, an° thou
dost me love.

helmet° / if°

Fluellen

[*putting the glove in his cap*] Your Grace doo's° me as great
honors as can be desired in the hearts of his subjects. 155
I would fain° see the man that has but two legs that
shall find himself aggrieved at this glove, that is all.
But I would fain see it once, an 't please God of His
grace that I might see.

i.e., does° / gladly°

King Henry

Know'st thou Gower? 160

Fluellen

He is my dear friend, an 't please you.

1   *For I do know Fluellen valiant /And*
     touched with choler

     For I know Fluellen to be valiant and
     hot tempered

2   *return an injury*

     Retaliate for an insult

King Henry

Pray thee, go seek him and bring him to my tent.

Fluellen

I will fetch him.   *He exits.*

King Henry

My Lord of Warwick and my brother Gloucester,

Follow Fluellen closely at the heels.   165

The glove which I have given him for a favor

perhaps   May haply° purchase him a box o' th' ear.

It is the soldier's; I by bargain should

Wear it myself. Follow, good cousin Warwick.

If that the soldier strike him, as I judge   170

By his blunt bearing he will keep his word,

Some sudden mischief may arise of it,

For I do know Fluellen valiant

And touched with choler,[1] hot as gunpowder,

And quickly will return an injury.[2]   175

Follow and see there be no harm between them.

—Go you with me, uncle of Exeter.   *They exit [separately].*

1   *I warrant*

I guarantee. The scene begins with the two soldiers in the middle of a conversation.

2   *'Sblood*

I.e., by God's blood (a forceful oath)

3   *be forsworn*

I.e., refuse to honor my vow

4   *I will give treason his payment into plows*

I.e., I will repay (this) treason with blows.

5   *That's a lie in thy throat.*

That's an outrageous lie.

Act 4, Scene 8

Enter **Gower** *and* **Williams**.

Williams
I warrant[1] it is to knight you, Captain.

Enter **Fluellen** [*with soldiers*].

Fluellen
[*to* **Gower**] God's will and his pleasure, Captain, I
speedily beseech you now, come apace° to the King. There is
more good toward you, peradventure, than is in your
knowledge to dream of.   5

Williams
[*to* **Fluellen**] Sir, know you this glove?

Fluellen
Know the glove? I know the glove is a glove.

Williams
I know this, and thus I challenge it.   *strikes him*

Fluellen
absolute 'Sblood,[2] an arrant° traitor as any 's in the universal
world, or in France, or in England!   10

Gower
[*to* **Williams**] How now, sir? You villain!

Williams
Do you think I'll be forsworn?[3]

Fluellen
Stand away, Captain Gower. I will give treason his payment into plows,[4] I warrant you.

Williams
I am no traitor.   15

Fluellen
That's a lie in thy throat.[5]—I charge you in his Majesty's

275

1   *is take*

    Has taken

2   *is pear*

    I.e., will bear

name, apprehend him. He's a friend of the Duke
Alençon's.

Enter **Warwick** *and* **Gloucester**.

Warwick

How now, how now; what's the matter?

Fluellen

My Lord of Warwick, here is—praised be God for it!—   20
a most contagious treason come to light, look you, as
you shall desire in a summer's day. Here is his Majesty.

Enter **King** [**Henry**] *and* **Exeter**.

King Henry

How now, what's the matter?

Fluellen

My liege, here is a villain and a traitor that, look your
Grace, has struck the glove which your Majesty is take[1]   25
out of the helmet of Alençon.

Williams

My liege, this was my glove; here is the fellow of it.
   exchange   [*showing his other glove*] And he that I gave it to in change°
promised to wear it in his cap. I promised to strike
him if he did. I met this man with my glove in his cap,   30
and I have been as good as my word.

Fluellen

Your Majesty, hear now, saving your Majesty's manhood,
   he   what an arrant, rascally, beggarly, lousy knave it° is. I
hope your Majesty is pear[2] me testimony and witness,
   confirm; vouch   and will avouchment° that this is the glove of Alençon   35
that your Majesty is give me, in your conscience now.

1   *lowliness*

(1) low-born appearance; (2) humble
bearing

2   *twelvepence*

A shilling coin (worth *twelvepence*);
see line 67.

King Henry

Give me thy glove, soldier. Look; here is the fellow of it.

[*takes the glove and shows the matching one*]

'Twas I indeed thou promised'st to strike,

words   And thou hast given me most bitter terms.°

Fluellen

If   An° 't please your Majesty, let his neck answer for it, if   40
there is any martial law in the world.

King Henry

How canst thou make me satisfaction?

Williams

All offenses, my lord, come from the heart. Never
came any from mine that might offend your Majesty.

King Henry

It was ourself thou didst abuse.   45

Williams

Your Majesty came not like yourself. You appeared to
me but as a common man—witness the night, your
garments, your lowliness.[1] And what your Highness
suffered under that shape, I beseech you take it for

what   your own fault and not mine, for had you been as ° I   50
took you for, I made no offense. Therefore I beseech
your Highness pardon me.

King Henry

Here, uncle Exeter, fill this glove with crowns
And give it to this fellow. Keep it, fellow,
And wear it for an honor in thy cap   55
Till I do challenge it. Give him the crowns.

[**Exeter** *gives the glove to* **Williams**.]

—And Captain, you must needs be friends with him.

Fluellen

By this day and this light, the fellow has mettle
enough in his belly. Hold; there is twelvepence[2] for

1   *prawls, and prabbles*

     Brawls and brabbles (squabbles)

2   *good sort*

     High rank

3   *bearing banners*

     I.e., with coats of arms

you. [*He offers* **Williams** *a coin.*] And I pray you to serve   60
God, and keep you out of prawls, and prabbles,[1] and
guarantee   quarrels, and dissensions, and I warrant° you it is the
better for you.

Williams

I will none of your money.

Fluellen

i.e., is offered   It is° with a good will. I can tell you it will serve you to   65
why   mend your shoes. Come, wherefore° should you be so
i.e., shilling   pashful? Your shoes is not so good. 'Tis a good silling,°
I warrant you, or I will change it.

Enter **Herald**.

King Henry

counted   Now, herald, are the dead numbered?°

Herald

[*giving a paper*] Here is the number of the slaughtered
French.   70

King Henry

What prisoners of good sort[2] are taken, uncle?

Exeter

Charles Duke of Orléans, nephew to the King;
John Duke of Bourbon, and Lord Boucicault;
Of other lords and barons, knights and squires,
Fully   Full° fifteen hundred, besides common men.   75

King Henry

This note doth tell me of ten thousand French
That in the field lie slain. Of princes, in this number,
And nobles bearing banners,[3] there lie dead
One hundred twenty-six; added to these,
Of knights, esquires, and gallant gentlemen,   80
Eight thousand and four hundred, of the which

1   *of all other men / But five-and-twenty*

The extraordinary disparity in
casualties is taken directly from
Holinshed, where the French are
said to have lost 10,000 men and
the English only the twenty-five
commoners and the four named
aristocrats. Holinshed, however,
adds that this is only as "some do
report" and that others say "that
there were slain above five or six
hundred persons." Even at the
larger figure the victory is of
enormous proportion, and Shakespeare's adoption of the lower
number, coupled with his omission
of Holinshed's account of the
superior English military tactics,
suggests that Shakespeare here
deliberately rejects historical
probability in favor of myth-
making.

2   *plain shock and even play*

The direct clash and straightforward encounter

Five hundred were but yesterday dubbed knights.
So that in these ten thousand they have lost
i.e., common soldiers There are but sixteen hundred mercenaries;°
The rest are princes, barons, lords, knights, squires, 85
And gentlemen of blood and quality.
The names of those their nobles that lie dead:
Charles Delabret, High Constable of France;
Jaques of Chatillion, Admiral of France;
The Master of the Crossbows, Lord Rambures; 90
Great-Master of France, the brave Sir Guichard
　　　Dauphin;
John, Duke of Alençon; Anthony Duke of Brabant,
The brother of the Duke of Burgundy;
powerful And Edward, Duke of Bar; of lusty° earls,
Grandpré and Roussi, Faulconbridge and Foix, 95
Beaumont and Marle, Vaudemont and Lestrelles.
Here was a royal fellowship of death!
Where is the number of our English dead?
　　　　　　　　　　[*He is given another paper.*]
Edward the Duke of York, the Earl of Suffolk,
Sir Richard Keighley, Davy Gam, esquire; 100
e., high or noble birth None else of name,° and of all other men
But five-and-twenty.[1] O God, thy arm was here,
And not to us, but to thy arm alone,
trickery; subterfuge Ascribe we all. When, without stratagem,°
But in plain shock and even play[2] of battle, 105
Was ever known so great and little loss
On one part and on th' other? Take it, God,
For it is none but thine!
Exeter
　　　　　　　　'Tis wonderful.
King Henry
Come; go we in procession to the village,

1   *be it death proclaimèd through our host*

I.e., proclaim throughout our army
that the punishment will be death

2   Non nobis *and* Te Deum

Non nobis refers to the first words
of Psalm 115 ("Not unto us, O Lord,
not unto us, but unto thy name give
glory"); *Te Deum* is a song of thanks
("We praise thee, O God").

3   *The dead with charity enclosed in clay*

The dead given a proper Christian
burial

And be it death proclaimèd through our host[1]   110
To boast of this or take that praise from God
Which is His only.

Fluellen

Is it not lawful, an 't please your Majesty, to tell how
many is killed?

King Henry

Yes, Captain, but with this acknowledgement,   115
That God fought for us.

Fluellen

Yes, in my conscience, He did us great good.

King Henry

Do we all holy rites:
Let there be sung *Non nobis* and *Te Deum*,[2]
The dead with charity enclosed in clay,[3]   120
And then to Calais, and to England then,
fortunate Where ne'er from France arrived more happy° men.

They exit.

1   *admit th' excuse / Of time, of numbers,*
     and due course of things, / Which cannot
     in their huge and proper life / Be here
     presented

     Accept these excuses (for our per-
     formance): because these events
     took place over a long period of
     time, and involved so many people,
     and unfolded in such a complex
     way, they cannot be fully presented
     here.

2   *whiffler*

     Armed attendant who cleared the
     way at the head of a procession

3   *Blackheath*

     Stretch of open land on the south-
     east outskirts of London

4   *Where that his lords desire him to have*
     borne / His bruisèd helmet and his bended
     sword / Before him

     I.e., where his lords want King
     Henry to march, displaying his
     dented helmet and bent sword in
     front of him (in a royal procession
     celebrating the English victory)

5   *Giving full trophy, signal, and ostent /*
     Quite from himself to God

     I.e., giving full credit, honor, and
     ceremonial display not to himself
     but to God

6   *In the quick forge and workinghouse of*
     thought

     I.e., in your imaginations. The
     metaphor is of mental images
     formed as metal is bent and shaped
     in a *forge* or *workinghouse* (work-
     shop). *Quick* means both "rapid"
     and "living."

7   *brethren in best sort*

     Colleagues (i.e., the aldermen of
     London) in their finest dress

Act 5, Prologue

Enter **Chorus**.

Chorus

Allow it	Vouchsafe° to those that have not read the story
with regard to	That I may prompt them; and of° such as have,
	I humbly pray them to admit th' excuse
	Of time, of numbers, and due course of things,
	Which cannot in their huge and proper life 5
	Be here presented.[1] Now we bear the King
i.e., Imagine	Toward Calais. Grant° him there. There seen,
	Heave him away upon your wingèd thoughts
Across	Athwart° the sea. Behold, the English beach
Fences / sea	Pales° in the flood° with men, wives, and boys, 10
	Whose shouts and claps outvoice the deep-mouthed sea,
	Which like a mighty whiffler[2] 'fore the King
	Seems to prepare his way. So let him land,
	And solemnly see him set on to London.
	So swift a pace hath thought that even now 15
	You may imagine him upon Blackheath,[3]
	Where that his lords desire him to have borne
	His bruisèd helmet and his bended sword
	Before him[4] through the city. He forbids it,
	Being free from vainness and self-glorious pride, 20
	Giving full trophy, signal, and ostent
	Quite from himself to God.[5] But now behold,
	In the quick forge and working-house of thought,[6]
	How London doth pour out her citizens.
	The mayor and all his brethren in best sort,[7] 25
	Like to the senators of th' antique Rome,
commoners	With the plebeians° swarming at their heels,
	Go forth and fetch their conqu'ring Caesar in;

1   *by a lower but loving likelihood*

    In comparison with a less grand yet
    dearly wished-for event

2   *the General of our gracious Empress*

    Likely a reference to the Earl of
    Essex, who was sent by Queen
    Elizabeth to put down a rebellion
    in Ireland in March 1599. In these
    lines, the Chorus expresses a wish
    to see the Earl come home in a
    similarly triumphant manner as
    King Henry. (See Longer Note on
    page 333.)

3   *much more cause*

    With much better reason

4   *As yet the lamentation of the French /
    Invites the King of England's stay at home*

    Since the thoroughness of the
    defeat of the French now allows
    the King of England to stay home
    (without military risk)

5   *The Emperor's coming*

    The Holy Roman Emperor Sigis-
    mund came to England in May 1416,
    hoping to broker peace between
    England and France.

6   ...

    A line seems to be missing here.
    The most pertinent piece of
    information conveyed at this point
    in Holinshed concerns the death
    of the Dauphin, the French king's

heir, who is mysteriously absent in
Act Five: the missing line may have
announced his death.

7   *omit / All the occurrences*

    Skip over all the historical events.
    The Chorus announces that the play
    will bypass the events of the five
    years following the King's trium-
    phant return. In the event, there
    was continued fighting and several
    failed negotiations before the
    meeting dramatized in 5.2, which
    took place in May 1420, about four
    and a half years after the battle at
    Agincourt.

8   *Harry's back-return*

    Although Henry returned to France
    in both 1417 and 1419, this refers
    to his return to sign the Treaty of
    Troyes in 1420.

9   *played / The interim*

    Stood in for the intervening events

As by a lower but by loving likelihood,[1]
Were now the General of our gracious Empress,[2]   30
As in good time he may, from Ireland coming,
impaled   Bringing rebellion brochèd° on his sword,
release   How many would the peaceful city quit°
To welcome him! Much more, and much more cause,[3]
Did they this Harry. Now in London place him.   35
As yet the lamentation of the French
Invites the King of England's stay at home;[4]
The Emperor's coming[5] in behalf of France
arrange   To order° peace between them . . .[6] and omit
may have occurred   All the occurrences,[7] whatever chanced,°   40
Till Harry's back-return[8] again to France.
There must we bring him, and myself have played
reminding   The interim,[9] by rememb'ring° you 'tis past.
tolerate   Then brook° abridgment, and your eyes advance
After your thoughts straight back again to France.   45

                                                    He exits.

1 *Nay, that's right.*

A mid-conversation entrance

2 *Saint Davy's day*

Celebrated on March 1 (see 4.1.56 and note). This scene is seemingly set the following day (see line 9).

3 *lousy*

Literally, lice infested, though with the figurative sense, as with *scald* (in this line and in lines 29, 31, and 49) and *scurvy* (line 16), "contemptible" or "worthless"

4 *bid me eat my leek*

Pistol mocked Fluellen, either for participating in the Saint David's day festivities or simply for being Welsh.

5 *I could not breed no contention with him*

I could not start an argument with him.

6 *swelling like a turkey-cock*

A proverbial simile, used to describe someone puffed up with pride.

7 *bedlam*

I.e., crazy (*Bedlam* was a elision of "Bethlehem," a famous insane asylum in London)

8 *fold up Parca's fatal web*

I.e., put an end to your life. The Parcae are the three fates of classical mythology, who spun, measured, and cut the threads that determined individuals' destinies.

Act 5, Scene 1

Enter **Fluellen** *and* **Gower**.

Gower

Nay, that's right.[1] But why wear you your leek today?
Saint Davy's day[2] is past.

Fluellen

There is occasions and causes why and wherefore in all
things. I will tell you ass° my friend, Captain Gower.
The rascally, scald,° beggarly, lousy,[3] pragging°   5
knave, Pistol—which you and yourself and all the
world know to be no petter° than a fellow, look you
now, of no merits—he is come to me and prings me
pread and salt yesterday, look you, and bid me eat my
leek.[4] It was in a place where I could not breed no con-   10
tention with him,[5] but I will be so bold as to wear it in
my cap till I see him once again, and then I will tell
him a little piece of my desires.

Enter **Pistol**.

Gower

Why, here he comes, swelling like a turkey-cock.[6]

Fluellen

'Tis no matter for his swellings, nor his turkey-cocks.   15
—God pless you, Aunchient Pistol! You scurvy, lousy
knave, God pless you!

Pistol

Ha, art thou bedlam?[7] Dost thou thirst, base Trojan,°
To have me fold up Parca's fatal web?[8]
Hence.° I am qualmish° at the smell of leek.   20

Fluellen

I peseech you heartily, scurvy, lousy knave, at my

Marginal glosses:
- *i.e., as* (line 4)
- *scabby / i.e., bragging* (line 5)
- *i.e., better* (line 7)
- *i.e., villain* (line 18)
- *Get away / nauseated* (line 20)

1   *Cadwallader and all his goats*

Cadwallader, the last Welsh king, heroically defended Wales against the Saxons in the 7th century. Because of its mountainous terrain in which goats thrive, Wales was associated (often derisively) with goats and goatherding.

2   *goat*

Probably punning on "goad"

3   *sauce*

Either referring to Fluellen's blows or Pistol's blood (caused by Fluellen's attack)

4   *"mountain squire"*

A reference to the mountainous land in Wales, considered to be of poor quality and little value

5   *I will make you today a squire of low degree*

I.e., I will knock you down flat, a threat playing off Pistol's "mountain" insult in its use of *low*. The *Squire of Low Degree* was a popular medieval romance.

6   *fall to*

Begin; dig in

7   *ploody coxcomb*

I.e., bloody head

desires and my requests and my petitions, to eat,
look you, this leek. Because, look you, you do not love
it, nor your affections and your appetites and your

i.e., does digestions doo's° not agree with it, I would desire you   25
to eat it.

Pistol

Not for Cadwallader and all his goats.[1]

Fluellen

There is one goat[2] for you. (*strikes him*) Will you be so
good, scald knave, as eat it?

Pistol

Base Trojan, thou shalt die.   30

Fluellen

You say very true, scald knave—when God's will is. I
will desire you to live in the meantime and eat your

food victuals.° Come, there is sauce[3] for it. [*strikes him*] You
called me yesterday "mountain squire,"[4] but I will
make you today a squire of low degree.[5] I pray you, fall   35
to.[6] If you can mock a leek, you can eat a leek.

Gower

stunned Enough, Captain. You have astonished° him.

Fluellen

I say I will make him eat some part of my leek, or I will

i.e., beat / head peat° his pate° four days.—Bite, I pray you. It is good

fresh for your green° wound and your ploody coxcomb.[7]   40

Pistol

Must I bite?

Fluellen

Yes, certainly, and out of doubt and out of question,
too, and ambiguities.

Pistol

By this leek, I will most horribly revenge—

1   *Quiet thy cudgel.*

    **Stop hitting me; put down your
    club.**

2   *groat*

    A coin worth four pence

3   *in earnest of*

    As a down payment for

[**Fluellen** *threatens him.*]

I eat and eat, I swear!   45

Fluellen

Eat, I pray you. Will you have some more sauce to your
leek? There is not enough leek to swear by.

Pistol

Quiet thy cudgel.¹ Thou dost see I eat.

Fluellen

Much good do you, scald knave, heartily. Nay, pray you,
throw none away. The skin is good for your broken   50
coxcomb. When you take occasions to see leeks hereafter, I pray you, mock at 'em; that is all.

Pistol

Good.

Fluellen

Ay, leeks is good. Hold you, there is a groat² to heal
your pate.   55

Pistol

Me, a groat?

Fluellen

truly   Yes, verily,° and in truth you shall take it, or I have
another leek in my pocket which you shall eat.

Pistol

I take thy groat in earnest of³ revenge.

Fluellen

If I owe you anything, I will pay you in cudgels. You   60
dealer in wood   shall be a woodmonger° and buy nothing of me but
cudgels. God b' wi' you and keep you, and heal your
head   pate.°   *He exits.*

Pistol

All Hell shall stir for this.

Gower

Go; go. You are a counterfeit cowardly knave. Will you   65

1   *begun upon an honorable respect, and*
    worn as a memorable trophy of prede-
    ceased valour

    **Initiated upon a worthy occasion,
    and worn as a commemorative
    token of bygone gallantry**

2   *play the huswife with me*

    **I.e., play me for a fool; cheat me.
    (*Huswife* literally means "house-
    wife," but the term often is used to
    mean "hussy" or "whore.")**

3   *Doll*

    **Apparently a mistake, as Pistol's
    wife is the Hostess, Nell Quickly (as
    in 2.1 and 2.3). The prostitute Doll
    Tearsheet, an affectionate friend
    of Falstaff, appears in *Henry IV, Part
    Two*, and is mentioned in *Henry V* in
    2.1.73.**

4   *malady of France*

    I.e., syphilis

5   *something lean to cutpurse of quick hand*

    **Devote (myself) to the petty thiev-
    ery of a pickpocket**

6   *To England will I steal, and there I'll*
    steal; / And patches will I get unto these
    cudgeled scars, / And swear I got them in
    the Gallia wars.

    **Through most of the 1590s, England
    was at war in various places—
    Ireland, the Netherlands, and**

France, not to mention the various
sea campaigns against Spain and
the continuous practice of priva-
teering. One result of this nearly
constant state of war was that
England itself was full of discharged
and wounded soldiers, men who
were often deprived by injury or
circumstance of the means to pursue their previous occupations, and
who were said to be roaming the
countryside, begging or stealing.
Various other social phenomena
also contributed to the increasing
prominence of what were called
masterless men, and a whole literature developed around rogues,
vagabonds, beggars, thieves, and
other underworld figures in the late
16th century; ex-soldiers or people
impersonating ex-soldiers played a
part in these anxieties about how to
deal with deserving poor, vagrancy,
criminality, and social upheaval.

mock at an ancient tradition, begun upon an honorable
respect, and worn as a memorable trophy of prede-
prove   ceased valor,[1] and dare not avouch° in your deeds any
insulting / taunting   of your words? I have seen you gleeking° and galling°
at this gentleman twice or thrice. You thought because   70
fashion   he could not speak English in the native garb,° he
could not therefore handle an English cudgel. You find
it otherwise, and henceforth let a Welsh correction
teach you a good English condition. Fare you well.

                                                 He exits.

Pistol
Doth Fortune play the huswife with me[2] now?   75
News have I that my Doll[3] is dead
hospital   I' th' spital° of a malady of France,[4]
refuge   And there my rendezvous° is quite cut off.
grow   Old I do wax,° and from my weary limbs
pimp   Honor is cudgeled. Well, bawd° I'll turn,   80
And something lean to cutpurse of quick hand.[5]
steal away / thieve   To England will I steal,° and there I'll steal;°
And patches will I get unto these cudgeled scars,
French   And swear I got them in the Gallia° wars.[6]   *He exits.*

1 *wherefor we are met*

Which (i.e., peace) is the reason for our meeting

2 *Unto our brother France and to our sister*

A courteous, rather than literal, invocation of kinship; i.e., fellow monarchs

3 *Fairly met!*

I.e., welcome!

4 *brother England*

The Folio reads "Ireland." This would be a plausible title for Henry V—as for Elizabeth—since English monarchs also claimed dominion over Ireland, and on this basis some editions retain the word "Ireland"; but it is strange for the French queen to refer to Henry as "Ireland" rather than "England," his primary title. Probably this was the typesetter's misreading of the manuscript's spelling "Ingland"—a form of the word that, as T. W. Craik points out, twice occurs in the portion of *Sir Thomas More* thought to be in Shakespeare's hand. Another possibility, as John Dover Wilson has speculated, is that this is Shakespeare's slip that shows his "preoccupation with Irish affairs" as he was writing this play.

5 *in their bent*

(1) in the direction they were focused; (2) as they were aimed; (3) in their usual manner

6 *The fatal balls of murdering basilisks*

Literally, the eyeballs of *basilisks*, mythical serpents able to kill with a glance; figuratively, the cannon-balls fired by large cannons known as *basilisks*

7 *thus we appear*

Is the reason I am here

Act 5, Scene 2

Enter at one door **King Henry**, **Exeter**, **Bedford**, [**Glouces-ter**, **Clarence**,] **Warwick**, [**Westmorland**,] *and other lords;
at another,* **Queen Isabel**, *the* [**French**] **King**, *the Duke of* **Burgundy**, [*the princess* **Katharine**, **Alice**,] *and other French.*

King Henry
Peace to this meeting, wherefor we are met![1]
Unto our brother France and to our sister,[2]
Health and fair time of day; joy and good wishes
To our most fair and princely cousin Katharine;
And, as a branch and member of this royalty,°   5
By whom this great assembly is contrived,
We do salute you, Duke of Burgundy;
And princes French, and peers, health to you all!

     royal family — line 5 gloss: royalty° = royal family

King of France
Right joyous are we to behold your face,
Most worthy brother England. Fairly met![3]   10
—So are you, princes English, every one.

Queen Isabel
So happy be the issue,° brother England,[4]
Of this good day and of this gracious meeting,
As we are now glad to behold your eyes—
Your eyes which hitherto have borne in them,   15
Against the French that met them in their bent,[5]
The fatal balls of murdering basilisks.[6]
The venom of such looks, we fairly hope,
Have lost their quality,° and that this day
Shall change all griefs and quarrels into love.   20

     outcome — line 12 gloss: issue° = outcome
     (of poisonousness) — line 19 gloss: quality° = (of poisonousness)

King Henry
To cry "amen" to that, thus we appear.[7]

1   *my office hath so far prevailed / That*

I.e., I have succeeded in my mission
to the point that

2   *put up*

Show

3   *her husbandry doth lie on heaps*

Her (i.e., France's) harvest is now
lying in piles (i.e., it has not been
gathered out of the fields)

4   *Her vine, the merry cheerer of the heart*

A reference to the proverbial
expression, "Good wine makes a
merry heart"

5   *fallow leas*

Unplanted fields

6   *darnel, hemlock, and rank fumitory*

Types of weeds likely to spring up
on uncultivated land (*rank* = over-
abundant)

7   *even mead*

Flat meadow

8   *cowslip, burnet, and green clover*

Herbs and plants good for cattle
grazing

9   *Conceives*

Generates (weeds)

Queen Isabel

You English princes all, I do salute you.

Burgundy

with My duty to you both, on° equal love,
Great Kings of France and England. That I have labored
With all my wits, my pains, and strong endeavors,
To bring your most imperial Majesties
tribunal / conference Unto this bar° and royal interview,°
i.e., Highnesses Your mightiness° on both parts best can witness.
Since then my office hath so far prevailed
That[1] face to face and royal eye to eye
greeted each other You have congreeted,° let it not disgrace me
ask If I demand° before this royal view
obstacle What rub° or what impediment there is
Why that the naked, poor, and mangled peace—
nourisher Dear nurse° of arts, plenties, and joyful births—
Should not in this best garden of the world,
Our fertile France, put up[2] her lovely visage?
i.e., peace Alas, she° hath from France too long been chased,
And all her husbandry doth lie on heaps,[3]
its Corrupting in it° own fertility.
Her vine, the merry cheerer of the heart,[4]
evenly interwoven Unprunèd dies; her hedges, even-pleached,°
Like prisoners wildly overgrown with hair,
Put forth disordered twigs; her fallow leas[5]
The darnel, hemlock, and rank fumitory[6]
take root / plow blade Doth root° upon, while that the coulter° rusts
uproot / wild growth That should deracinate° such savagery.°
formerly The even mead,[7] that erst° brought sweetly forth
The freckled cowslip, burnet, and green clover,[8]
Lacking Wanting° the scythe, all uncorrected, rank,
flourishes Conceives[9] by idleness, and nothing teems°

1   *docks, rough thistles, kecksies, burrs*

   Types of weeds

2   *fallows*

   Plowed but unplanted land

3   *Defective in their natures*

   Naturally degenerate

4   *Even so*

   In the same way

5   *The sciences that should become*

   **The skills and knowledge that
   should exist in**

6   *reduce into*

   Restore to

7   *Whose want*

   The lack of which

8   *tenors and particular effects*

   **General objectives and specific
   requirements**

But hateful docks, rough thistles, kecksies, burrs,[1]
Losing both beauty and utility.
And as our vineyards, fallows,[2] meads, and hedges,
Defective in their natures,[3] grow to wildness,   55
Even so[4] our houses and ourselves and children
lack   Have lost, or do not learn for want° of time,
The sciences that should become[5] our country,
But grow like savages—as soldiers will
That nothing do but meditate on blood—   60
disordered   To swearing and stern looks, diffused° attire,
And everything that seems unnatural.
excellence   Which to reduce into[6] our former favor°
You are assembled, and my speech entreats
impediment   That I may know the let° why gentle peace   65
misfortunes   Should not expel these inconveniences°
And bless us with her former qualities.

King Henry
wish for   If, Duke of Burgundy, you would° the peace,
Whose want[7] gives growth to th' imperfections
Which you have cited, you must buy that peace   70
With full accord to all our just demands,
Whose tenors and particular effects[8]
written out   You have, enscheduled° briefly, in your hands.

Burgundy
The King hath heard them, to the which as yet
There is no answer made.

King Henry
                    Well then, the peace,   75
Which you before so urged, lies in his answer.

King of France
cursory   I have but with a cursitory° eye
If it please   O'erglanced the articles. Pleaseth° your Grace
now   To appoint some of your council presently°

1   *Pass our accept and peremptory answer*

    Deliver my approved and definitive reply

2   *articles too nicely urged be stood on*

    I.e., conditions too strictly insisted upon prevent agreement

3   *comprised / Within the forerank of our articles*

    Included at the top of my list of requirements

4   *good leave*

    Full permission

5   *Will you vouchsafe*

    Are you willing

attention   To sit with us once more, with better heed°   80
quickly   To resurvey them, we will suddenly°
Pass our accept and peremptory answer.[1]

King Henry
Brother, we shall.—Go, uncle Exeter,
And brother Clarence, and you, brother Gloucester,
Warwick, and Huntingdon, go with the King   85
And take with you free power to ratify,
Augment, or alter, as your wisdoms best
advantageous   Shall see advantageable° for our dignity,
Anything in or out of our demands,
agree   And we'll consign° thereto.—Will you, fair sister,   90
Go with the princes or stay here with us?

Queen Isabel
Our gracious brother, I will go with them.
Perhaps   Haply° a woman's voice may do some good,
When articles too nicely urged be stood on.[2]

King Henry
Yet leave our cousin Katharine here with us.   95
primary   She is our capital° demand, comprised
Within the forerank of our articles.[3]

Queen Isabel
She hath good leave.[4]

All except **King** [**Henry**], **Katharine**, [*and* **Alice**] *exit.*

King Henry
Fair Katharine, and most fair,
words   Will you vouchsafe[5] to teach a soldier terms°   100
Such as will enter at a lady's ear
And plead his love suit to her gentle heart?

Katharine
Your Majesty shall mock at me. I cannot speak your
i.e., English   England.°

1   Que dit-il? Que je suis semblable à
    les anges?

    **What does he say? That I am like
    the angels?**

2   Oui, vraiment, sauf votre grâce,
    ainsi dit-il.

    **Yes indeed, begging your Grace's
    pardon, that is what he says.**

3   Ô bon Dieu!

    O good God!

4   Les langues des hommes sont
    pleines de tromperies.

    **Henry translates this phrase
    correctly in lines 115–116.**

5   *The Princess is the better Englishwoman.*

    **Henry compliments Katharine's
    mistrust of flattery, which he char-
    acterizes as an English virtue.**

6   *thy*

    **For the first time, Henry uses the
    more intimate pronoun to address
    Katharine.**

7   *mince it in love*

    Coyly to express my love

8   *I wear out my suit.*

    I exhaust my capacity for courtship.

King Henry

O fair Katharine, if you will love me soundly with your   105
French heart, I will be glad to hear you confess it bro-
kenly with your English tongue. Do you like me, Kate?

Katharine

Excuse me   *Pardonnez-moi,*° I cannot tell wat is "like me."

King Henry

An angel is like you, Kate, and you are like an angel.

Katharine

[*to* **Alice**] *Que dit-il? Que je suis semblable à les anges?*[1]   110

Alice

Oui, vraiment, sauf votre grâce, ainsi dit-il.[2]

King Henry

I said so, dear Katharine, and I must not blush to
affirm it.

Katharine

Ô bon Dieu![3] *Les langues des hommes sont pleines de tromperies.*[4]

King Henry

What says she, fair one? That the tongues of men are   115
full of deceits?

Alice

Oui, dat de tongues of de mans is be full of deceits. Dat
is de Princess.

King Henry

The Princess is the better Englishwoman.[5]—I' faith,
Kate, my wooing is fit for thy[6] understanding. I am   120
glad thou canst speak no better English, for if thou
couldst, thou wouldst find me such a plain king that
thou wouldst think I had sold my farm to buy my
crown. I know no ways to mince it in love[7] but directly to say, "I love you." Then, if you urge me farther   125
than to say, "Do you, in faith?" I wear out my suit.[8]

1   *clap hands and a bargain*
    Shake hands and seal the deal.

2   Sauf votre honneur
    **Literally, "Save your honor," a
    formulaic expression of deference
    and apology**

3   *put me to*
    Have me recite

4   *leapfrog*
    **The *OED* cites this as the first
    printed reference to the game of
    leapfrog. The verb "to leap" also
    carried a sexual connotation, made
    more explicit below.**

5   *under the correction of bragging be it
    spoken*
    **Though I may be criticized for brag-
    ging if I say it**

6   *bound my horse*
    Make my horse jump

7   *lay on*
    Fight fiercely

8   *sit like a jackanapes*
    **Hang on (to the bucking horse) like
    a trained monkey**

9   *look greenly*
    Act like a lovesick boy

10 *cunning in protestation*
    Talent for professions of love

11 *for urging*
    **Even though I may be urged to
    (break my oaths)**

12 *whose face is not worth sunburning*
    **I.e., whose face is so ugly that sun-
    burning could not make it worse**

13 *let thine eye be thy cook*
    **I.e., make me more attractive by
    looking on me with favor**

14 *plain soldier*
    In the simple language of a soldier

15 *uncoined*
    **Unusual (not, like a coin, in com-
    mon currency)**

16 *he perforce must*
    He has no choice but to

17 *a ballad*
    I.e., pointless doggerel

Give me your answer, i' faith, do, and so clap hands
and a bargain.[1] How say you, lady?

Katharine

Sauf votre honneur,[2] me understand well.

King Henry

Marry, if you would put me to[3] verses or to dance for   130
would ruin   your sake, Kate, why you undid° me. For the one, I have
poetic meter   neither words nor measure;° and for the other, I have
rhythm / quantity   no strength in measure,° yet a reasonable measure° in
strength. If I could win a lady at leapfrog[4] or by vault-
ing into my saddle with my armor on my back, under   135
the correction of bragging be it spoken,[5] I should
box   quickly leap into a wife. Or if I might buffet° for my
love, or bound my horse[6] for her favors, I could lay on[7]
like a butcher and sit like a jackanapes,[8] never off. But
before God, Kate, I cannot look greenly,[9] nor gasp   140
out my eloquence, nor I have no cunning in protestation[10]—only downright oaths, which I never use till
urged, nor never break for urging.[11] If thou canst love
character   a fellow of this temper,° Kate, whose face is not worth
sunburning,[12] that never looks in his glass for love of   145
anything he sees there, let thine eye be thy cook.[13] I
speak to thee plain soldier.[14] If thou canst love me for
this, take me. If not, to say to thee that I shall die is
true; but for thy love, by the Lord, no. Yet I love thee
too. And while thou liv'st, dear Kate, take a fellow of   150
plain and uncoined[15] constancy, for he perforce must[16]
do thee right because he hath not the gift to woo in
other places. For these fellows of infinite tongue, that
can rhyme themselves into ladies' favors, they do always reason themselves out again. What? A speaker is   155
chatterer / shapely   but a prater;° a rhyme is but a ballad.[17] A good° leg will
wither   fall,° a straight back will stoop, a black beard will turn

1   Je quand sur le possession de
    France, et quand vous avez le
    possession de moi

    **When I have possession of France,
    and when you have possession
    of me**

2   *Saint Denis be my speed!*

    **Saint Denis (the patron saint of
    France) help me!**

3   donc vôtre est France et vous êtes
    mienne

    **Then France is yours and you are
    mine.**

4   Sauf votre honneur, le français
    que vous parlez, il est meilleur que
    l'anglais lequel je parle.

    **I beg your pardon, the French you
    speak is better than the English that
    I speak.**

head of hair   white, a curled pate° will grow bald, a fair face will
become   wither, a full eye will wax° hollow; but a good heart,
Kate, is the sun and the moon—or rather the sun and   160
not the moon, for it shines bright and never changes
its   but keeps his° course truly. If thou would have such
a one, take me. And take me, take a soldier. Take a
soldier, take a king. And what say'st thou then to my
love? Speak, my fair, and fairly, I pray thee.   165

Katharine

Is it possible dat I sould love de *ennemi* of France?

King Henry

No, it is not possible you should love the enemy of
France, Kate; but, in loving me, you should love the
friend of France, for I love France so well that I will
not part with a village of it. I will have it all mine. And,   170
Kate, when France is mine and I am yours, then yours
is France and you are mine.

Katharine

I cannot tell wat is dat.

King Henry

No, Kate? I will tell thee in French, which I am sure
will hang upon my tongue like a new-married wife   175
about her husband's neck, hardly to be shook off. *Je
quand sur le possession de France, et quand vous avez le possession de moi* [1]—let me see; what then? Saint Denis be
my speed! [2]—*donc vôtre est France et vous êtes mienne.* [3] It is
as easy for me, Kate, to conquer the kingdom as to   180
speak so much more French. I shall never move thee
in French, unless it be to laugh at me.

Katharine

*Sauf votre honneur, le français que vous parlez, il est meilleur que
l'anglais lequel je parle.* [4]

1   *at one*
    Alike

2   *Can any of your neighbors tell*
    **A playful way of saying that if Katha-
    rine can't tell, nobody can.**

3   *the rather*
    Instead

4   *Saint George*
    Patron saint of England

5   *compound a boy*
    I.e., have a son

6   *that shall go to Constantinople and take
    the Turk by the beard*
    **Henry imagines his son as a cru-
    sader, who will take Constantinople
    from the Turks (though in fact Con-
    stantinople was not ruled by the
    Turks until 1453, twenty-three years
    after the events here portrayed).**

7   *flower de luce*
    **Fleur-de-lis (the lily of the French
    emblem)**

8   la plus belle Katharine du monde,
    mon très cher et divin déesse
    **The most beautiful Katharine in
    the world, my very dear and divine
    goddess**

9   fausse
    (1) incorrect; (2) deceptive

King Henry

No, faith, is 't not, Kate, but thy speaking of my 185

sincerely but incorrectly tongue, and I thine, most truly-falsely° must needs

be granted to be much at one.¹ But, Kate, dost thou

understand thus much English: canst thou love me?

Katharine

I cannot tell.

King Henry

Can any of your neighbors tell,² Kate? I'll ask them. 190

Come, I know thou lovest me; and at night, when you

bedroom come into your closet,° you'll question this gentle-

i.e., Alice woman° about me, and, I know, Kate, you will to her

criticize / qualities dispraise° those parts° in me that you love with your

heart. But, good Kate, mock me mercifully the rather,³ 195

extremely gentle princess, because I love thee cruelly.° If ever

thou beest mine, Kate, as I have a saving faith within

struggling me tells me thou shalt, I get thee with scambling,°

and thou must therefore needs prove a good soldier-

breeder. Shall not thou and I, between Saint Denis 200

and Saint George,⁴ compound a boy,⁵ half French, half

English, that shall go to Constantinople and take the

Turk by the beard?⁶ Shall we not? What say'st thou, my

fair flower de luce?⁷

Katharine

I do not know dat. 205

King Henry

No; 'tis hereafter to know, but now to promise. Do but

now promise, Kate, you will endeavor for your French

half part of such a boy, and for my English moiety° take the

word of a king and a bachelor. How answer you, *la plus*

*belle Katharine du monde, mon très cher et devin déesse?*⁸ 210

Katharine

Your majestee 'ave *fausse*⁹ French enough to deceive

1   *got*

    Conceived. Popular belief held that
    the father's state of mind at con-
    ception influenced the resulting
    child's character.

2   *ill layer-up*

    Poor preserver

3   *thou shalt wear me, if thou wear me,*
    better and better

    **I.e., if Katharine will *wear* Henry
    (take on the role of being his wife),
    she will improve him by having
    done so, and at the same time she
    will *wear* him in the sense of break-
    ing him in, conditioning him so
    that he's easier to tolerate.**

4   *Plantaganet*

    **The name of the English royal
    dynasty from the accession of
    Henry II in 1154 to the death of
    Richard III in 1485.**

5   *if he be not fellow with the best king, thou*
    shalt find the best king of good fellows

    **I.e., he may not be the best king
    who ever lived, but she will find him
    to be the best companion.**

6   *broken music*

    Music performed in parts

7   de roi mon père

    The King, my father

maiden de most sage *demoiselle*° dat is *en France*.

King Henry

Now, fie upon my false French! By mine honor, in true

English, I love thee, Kate; by which honor I dare not

swear thou lovest me, yet my blood begins to flatter 215

me that thou dost, notwithstanding the poor and

uningratiating / curse untempering° effect of my visage. Now beshrew° my

father's ambition! He was thinking of civil wars when

he got[1] me; therefore was I created with a stubborn

appearance outside, with an aspect° of iron, that when I come to 220

woo ladies I fright them. But in faith, Kate, the elder I

grow wax° the better I shall appear. My comfort is that old

damage age, that ill layer-up[2] of beauty, can do no more spoil°

upon my face. Thou hast me, if thou hast me, at the

worst, and thou shalt wear me, if thou wear me, better 225

and better.[3] And therefore tell me, most fair Katha-

Cast rine, will you have me? Put° off your maiden blushes;

affirm avouch° the thoughts of your heart with the looks of

an empress. Take me by the hand and say, "Harry of

England, I am thine," which word thou shalt no 230

with sooner bless mine ear withal° but I will tell thee aloud,

"England is thine, Ireland is thine, France is thine, and

Henry Plantagenet[4] is thine"—who, though I speak it

equal before his face, if he be not fellow° with the best

king, thou shalt find the best king of good fellows.[5] 235

Come, your answer in broken music![6] For thy voice is

music and thy English broken. Therefore, Queen of all,

open Katharine, break° thy mind to me in broken English.

Wilt thou have me?

Katharine

Dat is as it sall please *de roi mon père*.[7] 240

1   Laissez, mon seigneur, laissez,
    laissez! Ma foi, je ne veux point
    que vous abaissiez votre grandeur
    en baisant la main d'une—Notre
    Seigneur!—indigne serviteur.
    Excusez-moi, je vous supplie, mon
    très puissant seigneur.

    **Let go, my lord, let go, let go! On
    my word, I woud never want you to
    lower your dignity by kissing the
    hand of an unworthy servant of
    your nobility. Pardon me, I beg you,
    my very mighty lord.**

2   Les dames et demoiselles pour être
    baisées devant leur noces, il n'est
    pas la coutume de France.

    **For ladies and gentleman to kiss
    before marriage is not the custom
    in France.**

3   entendre *bettre* que moi

    **Understands better than I do (the
    Folio's *bettre* indicates Alice's
    French accent for this English word)**

4   Oui, vraiment.

    Yes, truly.

King Henry

Nay, it will please him well, Kate. It shall please him,
Kate.

Katharine

Den it sall also content me.

King Henry

Upon that I kiss your hand, and I call you my queen.

Katharine

Laissez, mon seigneur, laissez, laissez! Ma foi, je ne veux point que 245
vous abaissiez votre grandeur en baisant la main d'une—Notre
Seigneur!—indigne serviteur. Excusez-moi, je vous supplie, mon
très puissant seigneur.[1]

King Henry

Then I will kiss your lips, Kate.

Katharine

Les dames et demoiselles pour être baisées devant leur noces, il 250
n'est pas la coutume de France.[2]

King Henry

Madam my interpreter, what says she?

Alice

Dat it is not be de fashion *pour les* ladies of France—I
cannot tell wat is *baiser* en Anglish.

King Henry

To kiss. 255

Alice

Your majestee *entendre* bettre *que moi.*[3]

King Henry

It is not a fashion for the maids in France to kiss before they are married, would she say?

Alice

Oui, vraiment.[4]

1 *weak list*

   Feeble limits (as in the barriers set
   up for jousting)

2 *the liberty that follows our places*

   The freedoms we have as a result of
   our rank

3 *as I will do yours*

   I.e., stop your mouth by kissing it

4 *My royal cousin*

   A claim of kinship anticipating the
   marriage of Katharine and Henry

5 *Our tongue*

   (1) the English language; (2) Henry's
   own manner of speech (*Our* being
   the royal plural pronoun)

6 *conjure up the spirit of love in her that he*
   will appear in his true likeness

   I.e., I cannot get Cupid to appear
   to her.

King Henry

fastidious O Kate, nice° customs curtsy to great kings. Dear 260
Kate, you and I cannot be confined within the weak
list¹ of a country's fashion. We are the makers of manners, Kate, and the liberty that follows our places²

critics stops the mouth of all find-faults,° as I will do yours³ 265
for upholding the nice fashion of your country in
denying me a kiss. Therefore, patiently and yielding.
[*kissing her*] You have witchcraft in your lips, Kate. There
is more eloquence in a sugar touch of them than in
the tongues of the French Council, and they should
sooner persuade Harry of England than a general peti- 270
tion of monarchs. Here comes your father.

i.e., royal court   *Enter the French power° and the English lords.*

Burgundy

God save your Majesty! My royal cousin,⁴ teach you
our Princess English?

King Henry

I would have her learn, my fair cousin, how perfectly I
love her, and that is good English. 275

Burgundy

a quick learner Is she not apt?°

King Henry

kinsman / personality Our tongue⁵ is rough, coz,° and my condition° is not
smooth, so that, having neither the voice nor the
heart of flattery about me, I cannot so conjure up
the spirit of love in her that he will appear in his true 280
likeness.⁶

Burgundy

Pardon the frankness of my mirth if I answer you for
that. If you would conjure in her, you must make a

1 *If you would conjure in her, you must make a circle*

(1) if you wish to conjure love in her (with enchantments), you must draw a magician's circle around her; (2) if you wish to arouse love in her, you must embrace her; (3) if you wish to breed inside her, you must have her vagina available.

2 *he must appear naked and blind*

Cupid, the god of love, was usually portrayed as a naked, blindfolded youth.

3 *yet rosed over*

Still blushing

4 *deny the appearance of a naked blind boy in her naked seeing self*

Refuses, in her defencelessness, to admit seeing a naked blind boy

5 *hard condition*

Difficult situation (with a sexual innuendo on *hard*)

6 *wink*

close their eyes

7 *consent winking*

Agree to wink (i.e., to marry him)

8 *wink on her to*

Hint to her that she should. This use of *wink* suggests the more contemporary meaning.

9 *teach her to know my meaning*

I.e., teach her about sex

10 *warm kept*

Warm blood was thought to provoke sexual feeling.

11 *Bartholomew-tide*

Bartholomew's day, August 24, falls in the heat of summer, when insects were thought to become sluggish.

12 *they will endure handling*

I.e., like sluggish flies, women will allow themselves to be touched.

13 *ties me over to time*

Puts me at the mercy of time (i.e., means I must wait)

14 *in the latter end*

(1) the end of summer; (2) the lower half of her body

15 *As love is, my lord, before it loves.*

As blind as love is, my lord, when it stands before its beloved.

16 *who cannot see many a fair French city for one fair French maid that stands in my way*

Henry is so preoccupied with his desire for Katharine that he has seemingly forgotten about some French cities still in negotiation (but see lines 314–315).

circle;¹ if conjure up love in her in his true likeness,
he must appear naked and blind.² Can you blame her   285
then, being a maid yet rosed over³ with the virgin
crimson of modesty, if she deny the appearance of a
naked blind boy in her naked seeing self?⁴ It were, my
agree   lord, a hard condition⁵ for a maid to consign° to.

King Henry

i.e., women   Yet they° do wink⁶ and yield, as love is blind and   290
enforces.

Burgundy

They are then excused, my lord, when they see not
what they do.

King Henry

Then, good my lord, teach your cousin to consent
winking.⁷   295

Burgundy

I will wink on her to⁸ consent, my lord, if you will
teach her to know my meaning;⁹ for maids, well
nurtured   summered°and warm kept,¹⁰ are like flies at
Bartholomew-tide:¹¹ blind, though they have their
eyes, and then they will endure handling,¹² which   300
before would not abide looking on.

King Henry

analogy   This moral° ties me over to time¹³ and a hot summer;
and so I shall catch the fly, your cousin, in the latter
end¹⁴ and she must be blind too.

Burgundy

As love is, my lord, before it loves.¹⁵   305

King Henry

It is so; and you may, some of you, thank love for my
blindness, who cannot see many a fair French city for
one fair French maid that stands in my way.¹⁶

1   *perspectively*

Distortedly (as through a lens that
creates optical illusions). This
refers to the kind of anamorphic
painting popular during the Renaissance, in which painted figures
would look like different objects
depending on the angle from
which one viewed them. Perhaps
most famously, Hans Holbein's *The
Ambassadors* contains a strange,
distorted streak running diagonally
across the bottom of the painting;
seen from one side of the painting,
however, the image is foreshort-
ened into a skull, a reminder of our
mortality blazoned across the front
of a painting otherwise occupied
with depicting the accumulation
of expensive and rare objects that
adorn the lives of its two accom-
plished subjects. Shakespeare uses
an image taken from anamorphic
painting in *Richard II*, 2.2.18–20.

2   *wait on her*

Accompany her (as her dowry)

3   *in sequel all*

Everything else that follows

4   *According to their firm proposèd natures*

Exactly as you originally stipulated

5   *for matter of grant*

Documents granting land or
property

6   Notre très cher fils Henri, roi
d'Angleterre, héritier de France

Our very dear son Henry, King of
England, heir to France

7   *let it pass*

Agree to it

French King

Yes, my lord, you see them perspectively,[1] the cities

surrrounded   turned into a maid; for they are all girdled° with   310

reached; unconquered   maiden° walls that war hath never entered.

King Henry

Shall Kate be my wife?

French King

If it   So° please you.

King Henry

I am content, so the maiden cities you talk of may wait

on her.[2] So the maid that stood in the way for my wish   315

shall show me the way to my will.

French King

We have consented to all terms of reason.

King Henry

Is 't so, my lords of England?

Westmoreland

The King hath granted every article:

His daughter first, and then in sequel all,[3]   320

According to their firm proposèd natures.[4]

Exeter

agreed to   Only he hath not yet subscribèd° this:

Where your Majesty demands that the King of France,

having any occasion to write for matter of grant,[5]

shall name your Highness in this form and with this   325

title   addition,° in French: *Notre très cher fils Henri, roi*

d'Angleterre, héritier de France;[6] and thus in Latin: *Praeclaris-*

simus filius noster Henricus, rex Angliae, et haeres Franciae.

French King

so firmly   Nor this I have not, brother, so° denied

But that   But° your request shall make me let it pass.[7]   330

1   *rank with*

     Be included with

2   *whose very shores look pale*

     A reference to white cliffs of Dover
     and of Calais

3   *ill office*

     Unfair dealings

4   *incorporate league*

     Unified alliance

King Henry

I pray you, then, in love and dear alliance,
Let that one article rank with [1] the rest,
And thereupon give me your daughter.

French King

Take her, fair son, and from her blood raise up
Issue° to me, that° the contending kingdoms   335
Of France and England, whose very shores look pale [2]
With envy of each other's happiness,
May cease their hatred, and this dear° conjunction°
Plant neighborhood° and Christian-like accord
In their sweet bosoms, that° never war advance   340
His bleeding sword 'twixt England and fair France.

Lords

Amen!

King Henry

Now welcome, Kate, and bear me witness all
That here I kiss her as my sovereign queen.   [*They kiss.*]
Flourish.

Queen Isabel

God, the best maker of all marriages,   345
Combine your hearts in one, your realms in one.
As man and wife, being two, are one in love,
So be there 'twixt your kingdoms such a spousal°
That never may ill office [3] or fell° jealousy,
Which troubles oft the bed of blessèd marriage,   350
Thrust in between the paction° of these kingdoms
To make divorce of their incorporate league, [4]
That° English may as French, French Englishmen,
Receive° each other. God speak this "Amen"!

All

Amen!   355

Marginal glosses:
- Offspring; Heirs / so that
- loving; costly / alliance
- neighborliness
- so that
- marriage
- destructive
- alliance
- So that
- Acknowledge

1   *we'll take your oath, / And all the peers'*

    I.e., you will formally pledge your
    loyalty to me, as will the rest of the
    nobility of France

2   *for surety of our leagues*

    To uphold our alliance

3   Sennet.

    A trumpet call

King Henry

Prepare we for our marriage, on which day,
My Lord of Burgundy, we'll take your oath,
And all the peers',[1] for surety of our leagues.[2]
Then shall I swear to Kate, and you to me,
And may our oaths well kept and prosp'rous be.   360

Sennet.[3] *They exit.*

1   *bending*

    I.e., stooped by the weight of his task (though perhaps also shaping the history that served as the source)

2   *In little room*

    In a small space (meaning either the theater or the script)

3   *Mangling by starts*

    Misrepresenting by the intermittent treatment (of the history)

4   *Small time*

    A short time. Henry V ruled for nine years and died in 1422 at thirty-five.

5   *infant bands*

    Swaddling clothes. Henry VI was less than a year old when his father died.

6   *Whose state so many had the managing*

    Whose government was managed by so many different people

7   *Which oft our stage hath shown*

    A reference to Shakespeare's three *Henry VI* plays; see "Introduction to *Henry V*."

8   *for their sake, / In your fair minds let this acceptance take*

    I.e., For the sake of the *Henry VI* plays which you have enjoyed in the past, think favorably of this play as well.

Epilogue

Enter **Chorus**.

Chorus

totally inadequate	Thus far, with rough and all-unable° pen,
	Our bending¹ author hath pursued the story,
	In little room² confining mighty men,
	Mangling by starts³ the full course of their glory.
	Small time,⁴ but in that small most greatly lived 5
	This star of England. Fortune made his sword
i.e., France	By which the world's best garden° be achieved,
	And of it left his son imperial lord.
	Henry the Sixth, in infant bands⁵ crowned King
	Of France and England, did this King succeed, 10
	Whose state so many had the managing⁶
	That they lost France and made his England bleed,
	Which oft our stage hath shown;⁷ and for their sake,
	In your fair minds let this acceptance take.⁸ [*He exits.*]

Longer Notes

PAGE 58

1.2.38–39   "In terram Salicam mulieres ne succedant": / "No woman shall succeed in Salic land." This speech has been much debated, the central question being whether we should take it as a serious, if self-serving, exposition of a dynastic claim or as a piece of inscrutable pedantry intended to be laughed at. Many 20th-century productions have played it for comic effect, especially when, in summation, Canterbury claims that everything here is *as clear as is the summer's sun* (86). Henry's response—*May I with right and conscience make this claim?* (96)—might then sound like an impatient eruption; to him, evidently, everything has not seemed so clear. Olivier's film makes the two clergymen appear entirely ridiculous. It should be noted, however, that Shakespeare is here following his source, Holinshed, so closely that he copies Holinshed's errors: like Holinshed, he writes *Louis the Tenth* instead of Louis IX (77), and *Charlemagne* instead of Charles II (75). It is also sometimes pointed out that, in a dynastic and aristocratic state like Elizabethan England, we might expect audiences to follow this kind of detailed genealogical dissection with an interest perhaps lost on modern audiences.

4.6.37   *Then every soldier kill his*
prisoners!

Shakespeare mentions Henry's
order to kill the prisoners no
fewer than three times. Here,
the prisoners are killed because
the French have *reinforced*
their scattered men, and Henry
apparently fears a new attack
in which numerous prisoners
might hamper his soldiers. At
4.7.8–10, Gower seems to assert
that Henry has given the order
to kill the prisoners as an act of
revenge for the French assault
on their camp (although it is
possible that he merely means
that Henry's act turns out to be
justified, retrospectively, in view
of the subsequent behavior of
the French). Finally, at 4.7.60–62,
Henry again orders prisoners to
be killed, this time out of anger
that the French cavalry continue
to hold part of the field. At the
very end of 4.6, the Quarto
text has Pistol shout "Coup à
gorge"—that is, "cut the throat,"
repeating his cry of 2.1.67—and
perhaps then actually cutting
the throat of his prisoner, Le Fer.
By repeatedly mentioning the
killing of the prisoners, and by
multiplying the motives given
for it, Shakespeare makes it
present and significant in a way
that it is not in Holinshed (where
it follows the attack on the camp
and is clearly intended to make
sure that Henry's soldiers are
not occupied with taking care of
the numerous prisoners, in case
there might be another attack).
In his Oxford edition, Gary Taylor
argues that there are in fact two
groups of prisoners, one killed
onstage as the second French
attack arrives at 4.6.35–38, and
the second group—captured
from that French attack—
brought onstage at 4.7.52 and
then threatened with death a
few lines later. Taylor also insists
that some members of the first
group should be killed onstage at
the end of 4.6, arguing that this
is why they have been brought
onstage, and that Shakespeare
intends to confront his audience
with the ruthlessness required by
military victory.

PAGE 288

5.0.30   *the General of our gracious Empress*

On March 27, 1599, the Earl of Essex left England to fight an Irish army led by the Earl of Tyrone. By September, Essex was back in London under house arrest, having signed a treaty with Tyrone against Elizabeth's wishes. He subsequently led an abortive uprising of his own, and finally, in February 1601, was executed for treason. The reference here is notably muted in tone—it is framed as a question—but it nevertheless looks like the kind of thing that would be problematic after September 1599. Most editors have dated the play's first performance to the spring or early summer of that year, assuming that the reference to Essex gives us a basis for dating the play. But there is of course no guarantee that just because we can date these lines with some confidence we can necessarily be certain that the rest of the play was written at the same moment, and in the same form. The allusion to Essex does not appear in the Quarto edition of 1600; this may be a matter of political expediency, but the Quarto also omits other passages—all of the choruses are missing, not just this one—whose absence cannot be attributed confidently to either censorship or self-censorship. It has sometimes been argued that the *general* in this passage is not in fact Essex but his successor in the Irish wars, Charles Blount, and therefore that the play as a whole should be dated after February 1600; this argument has not persuaded many critics, however, especially in view of the other reference to Essex at 3.6.74–75. Shakespeare has sometimes been linked to Essex's rebellion, because some of Essex's associates paid for a command performance of *Richard II* at the Globe the day before the abortive rebellion. The acting company was questioned but was not found to have been involved with the conspirators in the rebellion.

The Life of Henry the Fift.

Enter Prologue.

O For a *Muse* of Fire, that would ascend
The brightest Heauen of Inuention :
A Kingdome for a Stage, Princes to Act,
And Monarchs to behold the swelling Scene.
Then should the Warlike Harry, like himselfe,
Assume the Port of Mars, and at his heeles
(Leasht in, like Hounds) should Famine, Sword, and Fire
Crouch for employment. But pardon, Gentles all :
The flat vnraysed Spirits, that hath dar'd,
On this vnworthy Scaffold, to bring forth
So great an Obiect. Can this Cock-Pit hold
The vastie fields of France ? Or may we cramme
Within this Wooodden O, the very Caskes
That did affright the Ayre at Agincourt ?
O pardon :, since a crooked Figure may
Attest in little place a Million,
And let vs, Cyphers to this great Accompt,

On your imaginarie Forces worke.
Suppose within the Girdle of these Walls
Are now confin'd two mightie Monarchies,
Whose high, vp-reared, and abutting Fronts,
The perillous narrow Ocean parts asunder.
Peece out our imperfections with your thoughts :
Into a thousand parts diuide one Man,
And make imaginarie Puissance.
Thinke when we talke of Horses, that you see them,
Printing their prowd Hoofes i'th' receiuing Earth :
For 'tis your thoughts that now must deck our Kings,
Carry them here and there : Iumping o're Times ;
Turning th' accomplishment of many yeeres
Into an Howre-glasse : for the which supplie,
Admit me Chorus to this Historie ;
Who Prologue-like, your humble patience pray,
Gently to heare, kindly to iudge our Play.   *Exit.*

Actus Primus. Scœna Prima.

Enter the two Bishops of Canterbury and Ely.

Bish. Cant.

MY Lord, Ile tell you, that selfe Bill is vrg'd,
Which in th' eleueth yere of y last Kings reign
Was like, and had indeed against vs past,
But that the scambling and vnquiet time
Did push it out of farther question.
Bish.Ely. But how my Lord shall we resist it now?
Bish.Cant. It must be thought on : if it passe against vs,
We loose the better halfe of our Possession :
For all the Temporall Lands, which men deuout
By Testament haue giuen to the Church,
Would they strip from vs ; being valu'd thus,
As much as would maintaine, to the Kings honor,
Full fifteene Earles, and fifteene hundred Knights,
Six thousand and two hundred good Esquires :
And to reliefe of Lazars, and weake age
Of indigent faint Soules, past corporall toyle,
A hundred Almes-houses, right well supply'd :
And to the Coffers of the King beside,
A thousand pounds by th' yeere   Thus runs the Bill.
Bish.Ely. This would drinke deepe.
Bish.Cant. Twould drinke the Cup and all.
Bish.Ely. But what preuention?

Bish. Cant. The King is full of grace, and faire regard.
Bish.Ely. And a true louer of the holy Church.
Bish.Cant. The courses of his youth promis'd it not.
The breath no sooner left his Fathers body,
But that his wildnesse, mortify'd in him,
Seem'd to dye too : yea, at that very moment,
Consideration like an Angell came,
And whipt th' offending *Adam* out of him ;
Leauing his body as a Paradise,
T' inuelop and containe Celestiall Spirits.
Neuer was such a sodaine Scholler made :
Neuer came Reformation in a Flood,
With such a heady currance scowring faults :
Nor neuer *Hidra*-headed Wilfulnesse
So soone did loose his Seat ; and all at once ;
As in this King.
Bish.Ely. We are blessed in the Change.
Bish.Cant. Heare him but reason in Diuinitie ;
And all-admiring, with an inward with
You would desire the King were made a Prelate :
Heare him debate of Common-wealth Affaires ;
You would say, it hath been all in all his study :
List his discourse of Warre ; and you shall heare
A fearefull Battaile rendred you in Musique.

h   Turne

Editing *Henry V*
by David Scott Kastan

This edition of *Henry V* is a modernized version of the text of the play published in the Folio of 1623, where it is placed fifth in the section of Histories between *2 Henry IV* and *1 Henry VI*. The play had previously appeared in a quarto edition (a small cheap book, like a modern paperback), first in 1600, and with reprints in 1602 and 1619, this last with the title page misdated 1608. These quartos print a version of the play a little less than half the length of the Folio. They lack all the Choruses, three complete scenes present in the Folio, and many individual speeches. The quarto text seems to be some kind of abridgment, perhaps undertaken by actors and designed for touring; thus, while the quarto may indeed preserve authentic readings, the Folio text must be the early printing that most closely represents the play that Shakespeare wrote and upon which a modern edition must be based.

The Folio text was obviously not printed from an earlier quarto but seems to have been printed from a manuscript, likely to have been in Shakespeare's own hand. There are some errors that are clearly misreadings of handwriting (e.g., "name" for "mare" at 2.1.22), while the imprecision in the designations of characters (e.g., the **Hostess** is in speech prefixes variously called "Hostesse," "Quickly," and "Woman") and the inexactness of many stage directions are usually taken as the signs of an authorial manuscript (as opposed to the more exactly specified forms that would be needed in the play-house).

In general, the editorial work of this present edition is conservative, preserving and clarifying the text that appears in the Folio, emending only when it is manifestly in error (and recording these changes in the Textual Notes below). The lines in French, and the various efforts to render accents, however, create difficulty for editors, since it is not always clear if the irregularities are intended or not. Does an error in the French represent Shakespeare's imperfect understanding of the language or the sixteenth-century form of the language (in either case, in accordance with the principles of this edition, it should be rendered as it appears in the Folio) or is it an error in transmission (in which case it should be corrected)? Similar problems stem from the speeches in broken French and broken English by non-native speakers, and from the use of English spelling designed to render Welsh, Irish, and Scottish accents. In general, the principle adopted here is that for characters who are native French speakers minor errors in the representation of their French are silently corrected; for English speakers whose command of French is unlikely to be perfect, as for native French speakers speaking English, their errors are retained in the foreign language, as are all spellings seemingly designed to indicate characteristic local pronunciations. All other changes to the Folio text are in accord with modern practices of editing Shakespeare: normalizing spelling, capitalization, and punctuation, removing superfluous italics, regularizing the names of characters, and rationalizing entrances and exits. Editorial stage directions are kept to a minimum and added always in brackets.

A comparison of the edited text of the Prologue and the first forty-four lines of 1.1. with the facsimile page of the Folio (on p. 334) reveals many of the issues in this process of editing. The speech prefixes throughout are expanded and normalized, so that *Bish. Cant.*

here becomes **Canterbury** (and the fact he is in fact an Archbishop made clear in the bracketed addition to the entry direction). A speech prefix not in the Folio is provided for the **Chorus**, who speaks the Prologue and reappears before each act.

Most of the changes to the Folio text on the facsimile page, however, are matters only of modernization. Spelling throughout the edition is regularized to reflect modern spelling practices. As spelling in Shakespeare's time had not yet been standardized, words were spelled in various ways that indicated their proximate pronunciation, and compositors, in any case, were under no obligation to follow the spelling of their copy. Little, then, is to be gained in an edition such as this by following the spelling of the original printed text. Therefore "himselfe" unproblematically becomes "himself" in line 5 of the Prologue, as "heeles" becomes "heels" in line 6. "Peece" in line 23 becomes "Piece," while "Leasht" in line 7 becomes "Leashed," though the original spelling here confirms that the intended pronunciation is with one syllable rather than with a sounded "ed" (which, where the extra syllable is required and not obvious, is marked with an accent in this edition). As these examples indicate, old spellings are consistently modernized, but old *forms* of words (e.g.,"vastie" in line 12 of the Prologue; i.e., "vasty" for "vast") are retained. In addition, the capitalized first letters of many nouns in the Folio (e.g., "Muse" and "Fire" in line 1 of the Prologue) are here reduced to lowercase, except where modern punctuation would demand them. The superfluous italics of proper names (e.g., *"Adam"* and *"Hidra"* in lines 29 and 35 of 1.1) are all removed—and "Hidra" is rendered Hydra, as modern practice requires. Only when the Folio text is in probable error, as at 3.1.17, where Henry urges his soldiers: "On, on you Noblish English," does this edition make a change, often following the emendations appearing in later editions, but considering carefully what is known about both manuscript and printing practices that might cause the error and suggest the correct reading. Here the word "Noblish" is clearly wrong, and this Barnes & Noble edition emends to "noblest," as indeed does the Second Folio published in 1632.

Punctuation, too, is adjusted to reflect modern practice (which is designed to clarify the logical relations between grammatical units, unlike seventeenth-century punctuation, which was dominated by rhythmical concerns), since the punctuation is no more likely than the spelling or capitalization to be Shakespeare's own. Thus, in the Folio Prologue, the Chorus urges the audience to:

> Thinke when we talke of Horses, that you see them
> Printing their prowd Hoofes i'th' receiuing Earth:

Modernized this reads:

> Think, when we talk of horses, that you see them
> Printing their proud hoofs i' th' receiving earth.
>   (Prologue, lines 26–27)

No doubt there is some loss in this modernization. Clarity and consistency are gained at the expense of some loss of expressive detail, but normalizing spelling, capitalization, and punctuation allows the text to be read with far greater ease than the original, and essentially as it was intended to be understood. Seventeenth-century readers would have been unsurprised to find "u" for "v" in "receiuing" in line 27 (or "v" for "u" in other places; see, for example "vnraysed" (for unraisèd) in line 9 of the Prologue, nor would they have been confused by the spelling "prowd." The intrusive "e"s in words like "Thinke" or "talke" (line 26) would not have seemed odd, nor would the "literary" capitalization of the "Horses" or "Hoofes." The colon at the end of line 27 marks a heavy stop, like the modern period, but doesn't define a different grammatical relation as it would in modern usage. Modernizing in all these cases clarifies rather than alters Shakespeare's intentions. If, unavoidably, in modernization we do lose the histori-cal feel of the text Shakespeare's contemporaries read, it is important to note that Shakespeare's contemporaries would not have thought the Folio in any sense archaic or quaint, as these details inevitably make it seem for a reader today. The text would have looked to them as modern as this one does to us. Indeed, many of the Folio's typo-graphical peculiarities are the result of its effort to make the printed page appear up-to-date for potential buyers.

Modern readers, however, cannot help but be distracted by the different conventions they encounter on the Folio page. While it is indeed of interest to see how orthography and typography have changed over time, these changes are not primary concerns for most readers of this edition. What little, then, is lost in a careful modern-ization of the text is more than made up for by the removal of the ar-tificial obstacle of unfamiliar spelling forms and punctuation habits, which neither Shakespeare nor his publishers could have intended as interpretive difficulties for his readers.

Textual Notes

The list below records all substantive departures in this edition from the Folio text of 1623. It does not record modernizations of spelling, corrections of obvious typographical errors, adjustments of linea-tion, rationalizations of speech prefixes (SP), normalizations of proper names, minor repositioning or rewording of stage directions (SD), or minor correction of the French or the broken English spoken by characters. The adopted reading in this edition is given first in boldface and followed by the original, rejected reading of the Folio, or noted as being absent from the Folio text. If a reading comes from the Quarto, it is followed by [Q]. Editorial stage directions are not collated but are enclosed within brackets in the text. The Latin stage directions are translated (e.g., *They all exit* for *Exeunt omnes*), as are the Latin act and scene designation of the Folio (e.g., Act 1, scene 1 for

Actus primus. Scena Prima) and are supplied where they are missing or misplaced.

Prologue 1SP Chorus [not in F]

1.2.38 succedant succedual; **1.2.45, 1.2.52 Elbe** Elue; **1.2.72 fine** [Q] find; **1.2.94 embare** imbar; **1.2.131 blood** bloods; **1.2.163 her** their; **1.2.166SP Westmoreland** Bish. Ely; **1.2.197 majesty** Maiesties; **1.2.212 End** [Q] And

2.0.1SP Chorus [not in F]; **2.1.22 mare** [Q] name; **2.1.26SP Nym** [not in F]; **2.1.34 drawn** hewne; **2.1.38, 2.1.39 Iceland** Island; **2.1.77–78 you, hostess** your Hostesse; **2.1.108 that's** that; **2.2.29SP Grey** Kni.; **2.2.85 furnish him** furnish; **2.2.105 a** an; **2.2.106 whoop** hoop; **2.2.112 All** And; **2.2.137 mark** make; **2.2.146 Henry** [Q] Thomas; **2.2.157 Which I** Which; **2.2.174 you have** you; **2.3.15 'a babbled** a Table; **2.3.17 'o** a; **2.3.23 up'ard** vp-peer'd; **2.4.116 brother** [Q] brother of; **2.4.133 Louvre** Louer; **2.4.147SD Flourish** [appears in F before 3.0 Entry SD]

3.0.1SP Chorus [not in F]; **3.0.6 fanning** fayning; **3.1.7 conjure** commune; **3.1.17 noblest** Noblish; **3.1.24 men** me; **3.2.64 any** [not in F]; **3.2.108 I owe God a** ay, or goe to; **3.3.32 heady** headly; **3.3.35 Defile** Desire; **3.4.7 Et les doigts?** [assigned to Alice in F]; **3.4.8SP Alice** Kat.; **3.4.11SP Katharine** Alice; **3.4.14 Nous** [not in F]; **3.4.20 le** de; **3.5.7 scions** Syens; **3.5.11 de** du; **3.5.45 Foix** Loys; **3.5.46 knights** Kings; **3.6.30 her** his; **3.6.55 fico** Figo; **3.6.100 'o** a; **3.6.109 lenity** [Q] Leuitie; **3.7.12 pasterns** postures; **3.7.57 lief** lieu; **3.7.61 truie** leuye

4.0.1SP Chorus [not in F]; **4.0.16 name** nam'd; **4.0.27 Presenteth** Presented; **4.1.3 Good** God; **4.1.60 fico** Figo; **4.1.92 Thomas** John; **4.1.235 adoration** Odoration; **4.1.243 Think'st** Thinks; **4.1.281 ere** of; **4.2.2 Monte à** Monte; **4.2.11 dout** doubt; **4.2.35 sonance** Sonuance;

4.2.47 drooping dropping; **4.2.49 gimmaled** lymold; **4.3.13–14 [as in Q]** [in F placed after line11 as part of Bedford's speech]; **4.3.48 And . . . Day [Q]** [not in F]; **4.4.14 Or** for; **4.4.32 à cette heure** asture; **4.4.50 j'ai tombé** le intombe; **4.5.3 Mort de** Mor Dieu; **4.5.15 by a [Q]** a base; **4.6.34 mistful** mixtful; **4.7.36 intoxicate** intoxicates; **4.7.75 our** with; **4.7.94 Majesty** Maiesties; **4.7.110 God [Q]** Good; **4.8.109 we** me; **4.8.117 in my** my

5.01SP Chorus [not in F]; **5.1.66 begun** began; **5.1.77 of** of a; **5.1.84 swear** swore; **5.2.12 England** Ireland; **5.2.50 all** withal; **5.2.54 as** all; **5.2.77 cursitory** curselarie; **5.2.93 Haply** Happily; **5.2.240 sall** shall; **5.2.254 baiser** buisse; **5.2.311 hath** never hath; **5.2.320 then in** in; **5.2.351 paction** Pation

Epilogue 1SP Chorus [not in F]

Henry V on the Early Stage
by Benedict S. Robinson

enry V may have been one of the first plays performed at the Globe. A contemporary historical allusion in the chorus to Act Five appears to establish with reasonable certainty that the play was written between March and September of 1599. (See LONGER NOTE on page 332). From 1594 to 1597, the Lord Chamberlain's Men—Shakespeare's company—had been performing at a playhouse called the Theatre, but the owner of the land on which it stood refused to renew the lease, and so for some time they were forced to rent another theater, the Curtain. Finally, on December 28, 1598, they disassembled the Theatre, transported its timbers across the Thames, and used those timbers to begin building the Globe.

When the Chorus to Act One gestures toward "this unworthy scaffold," "this wooden O," the theater referred to in those (disingenuously) disparaging terms was probably the Globe (1.0.10, 13). That phrase "wooden O" describes the structure most familiar to us as an Elizabethan public theater: roughly circular, constructed out of wood, with two or three tiers of covered galleries surrounding the open yard into which the stage projected. Surrounded by the audience on three sides, the stage was partly covered by a roof supported by two wooden pillars. A winch concealed in the roof enabled actors to ascend to or

Fig 1. In the large London playhouses, the balcony above the stage could be used for staging, seating, or to house musicians.

Fig 2. English Renaissance drama made minimal use of sets or backdrops. In the absence of a set, the stage pillars could be incorporated into the action, standing in for trees and other architectural elements.

Fig 3. The discovery space, located in the middle of the backstage wall, could be used as a third entrance as well as a location for scenes requiring special staging, such as in a tomb or bedchamber.

Fig 4. A trapdoor led to the area below the stage, known as "Hell" (as contrasted with the painted ceiling, known as "Heaven" or the "heavens"). Ghosts or other supernatural figures could descend through the trap, and it could also serve as a grave.

descend from "the heavens"; since the stage was elevated about five feet above the ground, the actors could also ascend from or descend to the space underneath the stage by means of a trapdoor. At the back of the stage were one or two doors, opening into the tiring-house (the dressing rooms), which could serve for entrances or exits or could be opened to reveal an inner performance space. Above the stage, there was another performance space where actors could enter *aloft*. Audience members either stood around the stage in the yard—for which they paid a penny—or, if they paid a second or third penny, sat in one of the galleries.

It should be said that this is a generalized picture, and that the individual Elizabethan theaters all differed from it in various ways—at least one of them, for example, was square. Moreover, Shakespeare's plays had to be adaptable in the demands they made of their stage, since they were not always performed in the same theater: sometimes, as in 1598, the company's arrangements would change. Sometimes the companies would be invited to perform at court, as *Henry V* was, in 1605. At other times, they took their plays on tour, in which case they would be performing in a variety of more or less ad hoc spaces like inn yards. And after 1608, when Shakespeare's company acquired Blackfriars, the plays would have been performed alternately there and at the Globe, depending on the season: in winter they would be at Blackfriars and in summer at the Globe. Blackfriars was a significantly different theater from the Globe: it was a so-called *private* or *hall* theater, indoors, artificially lit, with a structure more like a modern theater.

Theater historians estimate that a public theater like the Globe could hold between 2,000 and 3,000 spectators at a time. In the mid-1590s, perhaps as many as 15,000 Londoners attended the theater every week, a substantial percentage of the population of the city, which was probably in the area of 150,000 to 200,000 people all told. Shakespeare's theater was thus a significantly wide-reaching form of commercial entertainment. By comparison, the print run of most books was legally limited to 1,200 copies per year; a play could reach that many people in an afternoon.[1]

Although the theater companies were all named after aristocratic patrons, this was to some extent a legal fiction designed to protect them from hostile local authorities, who regarded the theaters as flash points for crime, rioting, and disease. Moreover, the theaters also came under religious attacks, for their supposed immorality and perhaps above all for their flagrant violations of the scriptural injunction against cross-dressing. (Until 1660, no women acted professionally in England, so all of the women's parts were played by boys.) But the legal fiction could only partly disguise the fact that the companies were commercial operations of a new sort: the Lord Chamberlain's Men was a joint-stock company, constituted by a group of "sharers" who supplied the capital for running the company. Alongside the sharers, there were the apprentices, the journeymen—actors who were paid a regular wage for their work—and, at least in Shakespeare's company, the housekeepers, those who had contributed capital for the construction of the theater itself. It was as a sharer and a housekeeper—of both the Globe and Blackfriars—that Shakespeare earned his money: a playwright could expect to earn between £5 and £10 for writing a play, but it has been estimated that a sharer and a housekeeper in the early seventeenth century could expect to earn £120 to £150 per year. This at a time when £10 was an acceptable year's wages: if the theater was a disreputable institution, it could clearly also be a lucrative one.[2]

The text of *Henry V* tells us relatively little about how the play was staged. Because of the sparseness of its stage directions, and the occasional inaccuracy of its entrances and exits, editors have speculated that the text of this play, as it appears in the 1623 collection

---

1.   Andrew Gurr, *Playgoing in Shakespeare's London* (Cambridge: Cambridge University Press, 1987).

2.   William Ingram, "The Economics of Playing," in David Scott Kastan, ed., *A Companion to Shakespeare* (London: Blackwell, 1999), 313–327; Andrew Gurr, *The Shakespearean Playing Companies* (Oxford: Clarendon, 1996).

of Shakespeare's plays known as the "First Folio," was printed from Shakespeare's own manuscript rather than from a theatrical document: a theater manuscript would necessarily be more precise about such issues. The notable exception to this general sparseness of information is in the staging of the war. Before Act Three, the Chorus asks us to imagine how "the nimble gunner / With linstock now the devilish cannon touches"—at which point a stage direction reads, "*Alarum, and chambers go off*" (3.0.32–33). We know that the Globe kept a small cannon in the tiring-house to help simulate the chaos of war. (During a performance of *Henry VIII* in 1613, the firing of the cannon ignited the theater's thatch roof, burning the whole structure to the ground. It was rebuilt the following year—with a tile roof.) Act Three, scene one is prefaced by the direction, "*Alarum, scaling ladders at Harfleur*," which presumably means that the soldiers should carry the ladders across the stage, on their way to assault the walls. Later, we may perhaps expect to see those ladders leaning against the tiring-house; when the governor of the city speaks to Henry beginning at Act Three, scene three, line forty-four, it seems clear that he is standing in the gallery above the stage, and that the tiring-house wall represents the walls of the city. Presumably one of the doors serves as the gate through which Henry and his soldiers pass at the end of the scene.

There are few other specific directions in the play, and the text is virtually silent about crucial props such as the casket of tennis balls in Act One, scene two. But we may have one further piece of evidence about how this play was staged: the early Quarto edition, published in 1600. This edition has generally been dismissed by most editors, because the text it contains differs radically from the one included in the Folio: the Quarto is about half the length of the Folio text. Shakespeare took notoriously little care about the publishing of his plays, and we do not have any of his manuscripts, except perhaps for a fragment of a play called *Sir Thomas More* on which he may have collaborated. This seeming carelessness can perhaps be explained by the fact that the plays were not really his property but that of the theater company; moreover, drama was at the time not considered literature, and those professional playwrights who tried to publish their plays as if they were more serious books could be mocked: after the appearance of Ben Jonson's *Works* in 1616, an epigram circulated asking, "Tell us, Ben, where doth the secret lurk, / What others call a play, you call a work?"[3]

For years, the prevailing wisdom was that the Quarto of *Henry V* was one of the editions referred to in the Folio as "stolen, and surreptitious," and editors speculated that either audience members or perhaps members of the theater company had put together a pirated text and sold it to an unscrupulous publisher. But various parts of this theory have turned out to be less tenable than once thought, and other possibilities have been advanced as well. Perhaps the Quarto represents an early draft of the play, as has been argued in the cases of *Hamlet* and *King Lear*. Or perhaps it represents an acting script, shortened for performance purposes, or perhaps for a touring production: it seems clear that Elizabethan plays were routinely cut for performance to come anywhere near the "two hours' traffic of our stage" mentioned in *Romeo and Juliet* (1.0.12). Touring productions probably involved still more significant cuts, enabling plays to be performed with smaller casts.

It has sometimes been argued that the Quarto requires such a smaller cast; it is not clear that this is the case, but it may still be true that the Quarto provides some evidence about the play as it was performed: the title page, certainly, sells itself on its theatrical origins, claiming that it has been "sundry times played" by the Lord Chamberlain's Men. If so, the performed play was significantly different from the play we read: as well as being shorter, the Quarto cuts the choruses and drops much of the more problematic material about the war, including all of Act One, scene one, and much of Henry's violent speech in Act Three, scene three. It thus seems to offer a simpler

3.   *Witts Recreations* (London, 1640), Epigram 269.

and more clearly heroic play, and a play less self-conscious about its presentation of history. It is perhaps interesting to notice that some of these cuts are sometimes duplicated by modern productions, which similarly tend to target the more troubling passages and to cut down some of the longer speeches. We can't know for certain, and the whole truth about the Quarto is clearly more complicated than this, but it is possible that parts of it reflect how the play would have been staged around 1600.

Significant Performances
by Benedict S. Robinson

The stage history of any Shakespeare play is in many ways a kind of snapshot of cultural history: each production speaks both to the interpretive possibilities of Shakespeare's text and to its own historical moment. The list that follows is representative rather than comprehensive.

1599   The Globe. First performance, probably sometime between May and September.

1605   Court of James I. This production, along with the issues of the Quarto text of the play in 1600 and 1602, may indicate *Henry V*'s theatrical popularity in the early years of the seventeenth century.

1738–1782   Covent Garden. The first revival of the play in about 120 years.

1839   Covent Garden, Dir. William Macready. This production inaugurated a Victorian trend toward lavish and spectacular scenery and huge casts. Macready's staging is remarkable for including dioramas painted by Clarkson Stanfield moving in the background to illustrate the Chorus's speeches.

1901 Shakespeare Memorial Theatre, Stratford-upon-Avon, Dir. William Poel. Poel aimed to return the performances of Shakespeare's plays to the conditions of their original staging. This included a diminished emphasis on elaborate sets and a new, anti-illusionistic style of presentation. (One might speculate that the trend toward recovering the conditions of original production and toward emphasizing the sparseness of Elizabethan staging was influenced by the effort to distinguish theater as a medium from the emerging medium of film, which could provide realism and spectacle in a way no theatrical production ever could.)

1937 Old Vic, Dir. Tyrone Guthrie. This production, with Laurence Olivier as Henry, presented a thoughtful, self-doubting Henry, a Henry with touches of Hamlet. Guthrie also staged the Salic Law speech in Act One, scene two, as a partly comic display of pedantry. One critic wrote that the production tried to turn the play into "a pacifist tract," although the war scenes seem to have been staged to elicit a genuine patriotism: see Gordon Crosse, *Shakespearean Playgoing 1890–1952* (London: A. R. Mowbray & Co., 1983), p. 105; quoted from Emma Smith, ed., *King Henry V* (Cambridge: Cambridge University Press, 2002), p. 48.

1944 Film, Dir. Laurence Olivier. A World War II–era film dedicated to "the Commandos and Airborne Troops of Great Britain." The film begins by showing a supposedly Elizabethan performance; we see the first scenes as they might have been seen at the Globe, before Olivier takes us *into* the story with a scene in Act Two illustrating the Hostess's description of Falstaff's death: the shift from theater to film seems to enact the Chorus's injunction on us to create the spectacle in our minds. Olivier offers a staunchly patriotic reading of the play: he dispenses with many of the more troubling passages and uses the Elizabethan setting of Act One, scene one, to undercut the political complications of that scene by showing an audience visibly impatient with the bumbling performance of the actors playing the two bishops.

1951 Shakespeare Memorial Theatre, Stratford-upon-Avon, Dir. Anthony Quayle. This production staged *Henry V* as the conclusion to the second tetralogy, claiming that it needs to be seen in sequence to be fully understood.

1964 Royal Shakespeare Theatre, Stratford-upon-Avon, Dirs. John Barton and Peter Hall. Another performance of the play in sequence. This has also been identified by theater historians as the first genuinely anti-war production, although at the time critics distinguished between its appealing depiction of King Harry and its more critical look at the ugliness of war.

1984 Royal Shakespeare Theatre, Stratford-upon-Avon, Dir. Adrian Noble. This production focused on the interpretive difficulty of the play: the program offered two rival accounts, one headed *hero-king*, the other *scourge of God*. Kenneth Branagh played a Henry described as alternately charming and tormented, and the production emphasized the play's more ethically problematic aspects.

1986 English Shakespeare Company (touring), Dir. Michael Bogdanov. Perhaps the most anti-heroic production, Bogdanov played *Henry V* as part of an enlarged sequence, including eventually not just the "second tetralogy" but also the *Henry VI* plays and *Richard III*. Bogdanov saw in *Henry V* a "war of expedience, ruthless manipulation, bribery and corruption, palpable pacifism": this is not an ambiguous *Henry V* but a thoroughly anti-heroic critique of nationalism.

1989 Film, Dir. Kenneth Branagh. Branagh's film is strikingly different from the 1984 Noble production, with which he was involved.

Although the Branagh film, unlike Olivier's, attempts a realistic rather than idealized depiction of the war itself, it is very much like Olivier's version in minimizing the more difficult passages of the play. Perhaps its key scenes are those around Agincourt, where a mud-spattered Henry stands with his soldiers, as the image of a king who suffers and struggles along with his people.

1997   Shakespeare's Globe, Dir. Richard Olivier. Part of the opening season of the new Globe in London, reconstructed according to the best available research on Shakespeare's theater. The goal of this production was to recover Elizabethan stage conditions as completely as possible, including the use of an all-male cast and the encouragement of audience participation.

Inspired by *Henry V*

Henry as Corporate Executive

One of the more surprising realms in which *Henry V* has made an impact is the contemporary boardroom. The evolution of Prince Hal, the dissolute juvenile delinquent, into Henry V, the sober and committed ruler who galvanizes a nation, has struck many in the business world as an inspiring model of leadership development. A cottage industry of consultants and advice manuals have sprung up in recent years, seeking to draw modern, corporate precepts from Shakespeare's plays.

In 2001, Richard Olivier—a theater director and the son of Lawrence Olivier and Joan Plowright—founded a management consultancy agency called Olivier Mythodrama, whose workshops and seminars teach leadership techniques derived from Shakespeare plays. Olivier's book *Inspirational Leadership: Henry V and the Muse of Fire* (2001) takes the play as an extended allegory for the modern business world. Olivier asks his readers to consider the question, "What is your France?" Henry V's clear sense of mission—his feelings of entitlement to the French kingdom and his determination to recapture it—can serve as an example for any personal or group enterprise, Olivier suggests. The coveted territory might be the top of the sales pyramid, improved interdepartmental communication, or the boss's job. Oliver goes on to develop the analogy, describing Henry's deliberations with Essex, Canterbury, Westmoreland, and the rest of the lords over when and how to invade as an example of consensus building. He quotes Canterbury's lines from the Quarto edition of *Henry V*, in which the archbishop compares the King's supporters to arrows that are shot separately yet reach a single target, and to streams that flow to meet in the same sea. Similarly, Olivier asserts, it is up to the leader to unite multiple agents in a common purpose. Henry does this by proclaiming and later demonstrating his own determination to fulfill his mission. Following the plot and themes of *Henry V*, Olivier goes on to discuss such diverse corporate topics as professional rivalry, self-doubt, fair compensation, and the price of success.

Olivier is not alone in bringing lessons from *Henry V* into the business world, where Shakespeare has become an industry tool. A company called Movers and Shakespeares offers leadership and ethics courses based on *Henry V*, and in 2005 Stanford Business School ran a workshop entitled "Leadership as Performance Art: Lessons from Shakespeare and Beyond." Norman Augustine and Kenneth Adelman's *Shakespeare in Charge: The Bard's Guide to Leading and Succeeding on the Business Stage* (1999) devotes its opening chapter to a discussion of Henry V's leadership qualities, particularly as exemplified in his St. Crispin's Day speech. "Successful corporate leaders inspire people to dig deep within themselves," the authors assert. Thomas Leech also singles out Henry's ability to connect with his troops as his defining leadership quality in 2001's *Say It like Shakespeare: How to Give a Speech like Hamlet, Persuade like Henry V, and Other Secrets from the World's Greatest Communicator.*

Henry in Hollywood

The corporate world isn't the only modern arena where Henry V's skill as an orator has proved inspirational: Hollywood has borrowed liberally from him, as well. Several action movies have used the speech Henry delivers to his vastly outnumbered troops before their historic victory at Agincourt (commonly referred to as the St. Crispin's Day speech) as a template for their own stirring, pre-battle pep talks. Movies that borrow from the St. Crispin's Day speech tend to be about protracted military conflicts in which one side represents a moral good and the opposing side an unambiguous bad. Usually, the enemy vastly overmatches the side of good, in numbers or power. At the height of the action, usually before the decisive battle, the film's leader figure gives a speech to galvanize his troops on behalf of what seems to be a hopeless cause. Directors and screenwriters use the speech strategically both to heighten the audience's attention before the climactic action sequence and to highlight themes of brotherhood, freedom, and honor.

In Mel Gibson's 1995 *Braveheart*, for example, the hero, William Wallace, speaks with one of the Scottish soldiers before the Battle of Stirling Bridge. The soldier, having heard that the great warrior is "seven feet tall" and can "shoot fireballs from his eyes" doubts Wallace's identity. Wallace scoffs at these rumors, much as King Henry rejects the idea that the size of his forces will determine their effectiveness against the French. Rather than size, both men assert, it is courage and righteousness that control outcome. One ingredient necessary for both courage and righteousness, they agree, is freedom. Henry makes this point by offering his men an out, proclaiming that those who have "no stomach to this fight" will be allowed to return home, since "We would not die in that man's company / That fears his fellowship to die with us." Wallace and his men are fighting against the English for their freedom, so Wallace emphasizes even more explicitly that his men are free to choose whether to fight. "I see a whole army of my countrymen here in defiance of tyranny," he says. "You have come to fight as free men, and free men you are. What will you do with that freedom? Will you fight?" Wallace then moves on to another St. Crispin's Day motif: the promise of enduring glory in exchange for the risk of death. "Fight and you may die; run and you'll live," he admits. "And dying in your beds many years from now, would you be willing to trade all the days from this day to that for one chance, just one chance to come back here and tell our enemies that they may take our lives, but they'll never take our freedom?!" These words clearly echo an image in the closing lines of the St. Crispin's speech, when Henry declares that the "gentlemen in England now abed" will consider themselves cursed for not having fought with Henry's army, and will "hold their manhoods cheap" because of it.

Other movies borrow from the St. Crispin's Day speech on a more limited basis. In *Independence Day* (1996), which pits the human race against an alien invasion, the final battle takes place on July 4th, and the president of the United States addresses the people on the new meaning of that date: "From this day on, the fourth day of July will no longer be remembered as an American holiday but as the day that all of mankind declared we will not go quietly into the night. We will not vanish without a fight." Henry makes a similar prediction about the future symbolism of St. Crispin's Day when he swears that any soldier who survives into old age will "strip his sleeve and show his scars" at the annual feast, "And Crispin Crispian shall ne'er go by, / From this day to the ending of the world, / But we in it shall be rememberèd."

Other films draw on the famous moment when Henry addresses his troops as "we happy few, we band of brothers." This line combines two common war-story themes: the special fraternity of men in combat and the notion that the results of that combat lie in the hands of fate (with *happy* having the Elizabethan meaning of "lucky"). Both ideas are present in two adventure films from 2003: *Lord of the Rings: The Return of the King* and *The Matrix Reloaded*. In *The Return of the King*, Aragorn (in a speech adapted from the J. R. R. Tolkien novel on which the movie was based) addresses his army before the Black Gate as "Sons of Gondor—of Rohan . . . my brothers!" and then goes on to portray valor as the result of camaraderie, saying, "The day may come when the courage of men fails; when we forsake our friends and break all bonds of fellowship; but it is not this day. . . . This day we fight!"

Humankind is also shown uniting in rebellion in *The Matrix Reloaded*, this time against enslavement by a race of super-machines. Before the battle of Zion, the last remaining human city, the rebel leader Morpheus rallies the people by framing the coming war as a matter of both personal and group destiny. Like King Henry, he emphasizes the exceptional nature of the historical moment, and that each warrior has been specially chosen by fate. "All of our lives we have fought this war," he says. "Tonight I believe we can end it. Tonight is not an accident . . . I do not see coincidence, I see providence, I see purpose. I believe it is our fate to be here. It is our destiny. I believe this night holds for each and every one of us the very meaning of our lives."

Artistic Adaptations

For all its influence on the corporate world and on Hollywood action sequences, relatively few writers and artists have chosen to draw upon *Henry V*. While its predecessor plays, *Henry IV, Parts One* and *Two*, have inspired a number of plays, novels, and films—particularly focusing on the roguish, charismatic Falstaff—artworks inspired by *Henry V* are limited to a handful of paintings and at least one major musical score.

Henry Fuseli depicted Act Two, scene two, of *Henry V* in a work commissioned for the opening of the Boydell Shakespeare Gallery in London. One of nine paintings that Fuseli created for the Boydell Gallery, *Henry V Reveals the Conspiracy of Cambridge, Scrope and Grey* (1786–1789), places Henry in the center of the canvas flanked by the conspirators on one side and soldiers on the other. Soldiers and attendants also stand behind Henry, who is clothed in fitted gold-colored armor, a blue cape draped over his right arm and a blue and gold cap with two large feathers on his head. Henry rests his left hand on a the back of his throne while he glares down accusingly upon the conspirators with his right arm and index finger extended directly toward them. The painting depicts the moment just after King Henry presents Cambridge, Scrope, and Grey with their supposed commissions and the men discover that the king is aware of their crimes (2.2.69–76). The conspirators are depicted in various stages of realization and remorse: one reads the paper diligently, the second clutches the paper in one hand while covering his face with the other, and the third has dropped the paper underfoot and crosses his arms over his heart as he looks pleadingly at King Henry. The fate of the three men is hinted at, as one of Henry's soldiers is shown stepping forward while drawing his sword.

In *Bardolph* (1853), Henry Stacy Marks recalls King Henry's youth, taking his subject from the tavern where Prince Hal spent so much of his time carousing with the old knight Falstaff in *Henry IV, Parts One* and *Two*. The oil painting is a portrait of Bardolph, one of Falstaff's drinking companions, sitting in a high-backed chair, gazing red-nosed into the bottom of his flask with playing cards and dice strewn on the table next to him and an empty cup dangling in his other hand. In Act Two, scene three, of *Henry V*, Falstaff's friends, Bardolph among them, gather to reflect on his passing. A young boy quotes a delirious, near-death witticism by Falstaff, who "saw a flea stick upon Bardolph's nose, and 'a said it was a black soul burning in Hell." Bardolph retorts that the red nose was all Falstaff ever gave him, and now that the alcohol has run out, he doesn't even have that anymore. Marks's painting is done in heavy reds, browns, and grays, which match the mood of Bardolph's melancholy slouch. The loneliness of the picture contrasts with the boisterous mischief usually associated with the tavern scenes in the *Henry IV* plays.

William Frederick Yeames's engraving *The Wooing of Henry V*, for the *Imperial Edition of the Works of Shakespeare* (1873–1876), shows Henry's attempt to win Katherine's love in Act Five, scene two. In the foreground of the illustration, Katherine sits, her eyes downcast, on the opposite side of a long bench from Henry, who reaches out to her with one arm and presses his other hand to his heart. Alice stands behind Katherine observing, her hand at her throat. In the background, an open door leads to another room containing the shadowy figures of the French king and other noblemen, with whom Henry has just finished negotiating. This adds a note of urgency to the romantic intimacy of the scene, reminding the viewer that many more than two lives depend on the success of this relationship. The engraving suggests both the hasty diplomacy of the marriage contract between Henry and Katherine and the earnest clumsiness of Henry's wooing.

Laura T. Alma-Tadema submitted *Queen Katherine* (1888) for a series of portraits of Shakespeare's heroines commissioned by the London weekly newspaper *Graphic*. Although reviews of the subsequent exhibit were lukewarm, the pictures were popular with the public, and in 1896 *Graphic* offered colored lithographs for sale in various sizes. Alma-Tadema, student and wife of the painter Sir Lawrence Alma-Tedama, depicts the conversation in Act Three, scene four, between Katherine and her attendant, Alice, as Katherine learns the English names for *hand*, *fingers*, and *nails*. Alma-Tadema's painting shows Katherine leaning against a wall, gesturing toward one hand with the other, a sober and attentive expression on her face as she looks to Alice, pictured next to Katherine in profile, for approval. The artist was known for her domestic scenes of families and children at play, and the Katherine portrait, with its up-close angle on a moment of vulnerability, has a similar intimacy. In what was a common Victorian preoccupation with dress, more than half of the painting's area is devoted to the details of the women's clothing, jewelry, and headdress.

In music, William Walton's score for the 1944 film version by Lawrence Olivier has been recognized as a performance-worthy piece in its own right. Olivier listed Walton's name last in the screen credits, with the explanation that "for me, music made the film." Malcolm Sargent arranged Walton's suite for chorus and orchestra in 1945, and Muir Mattheson's 1965 arrangement is still performed and recorded today. Mattheson divides the suite into five movements, beginning with an overture entitled "The Globe Playhouse," alluding to the movie's opening panorama of Elizabethan London, which takes Shakespeare's theater as a focal point. The trill of a solo flute is followed by a series of fanfares. The full orchestra then moves into a jovial dance tune, with the drums and trumpets adding a military flavor. By contrast, the second movement, called "Passacaglia: The Death of Falstaff" is slow, melancholy, and minimalist. It is written for strings alone and features a set of simple melodies borrowed in part from traditional drinking songs. The third movement, more than twice the length of any of the others, is the suite's centerpiece. Called "Charge and Battle," it contains two distinct sections. The first is a musical description of the Battle of Agincourt, with heavy percussion and intermittent rolling fanfare, which builds to a frenzied climax, the strings mimicking the beat of the horses' hoofs and the horns mimicking the clash of steel. The battle noise gives way to an initially hesitant combination of flute, oboe, and strings, which then evolves into a version of the folk song *Bailero*, from the Auvergne region in central France. In Olivier's movie, the song accompanies the Duke of Burgundy's plea for peace between England and France. The very brief fourth movement, "Touch her soft lips," again for strings alone, evokes Pistol's good-bye to Mistress Quickly. "Agincourt Song" brings the piece to a close with a triumphant, full-orchestra rendition of the traditional English folk song commemorating King Henry's victory over the French.

For Further Reading
by Benedict S. Robinson

Altman, Joel B. "'Vile Participation': The Amplification of Violence in the Theater of *Henry V.*" *Shakespeare Quarterly* 42 (1991): 1–32. A rhetorical analysis, aimed at showing how the play solicits violent emotions from the audience and then seeks to manage those emotions and their release.

Baker, David J. "'Wildehirissheman': Colonialist Representation in *Henry V.*" *English Literary Renaissance* 22.1 (1992): 37–61. Baker reads *Henry V* alongside a series of English texts about Ireland, arguing that the depiction of the war in France is a displacement for concern about the war in Ireland, and that the play participates in a wider colonial discourse about Ireland.

Barton, Anne. "The King Disguised: Shakespeare's *Henry V* and the Comical History." In Joseph G. Price and Helen D. Willard, eds., *The Triple Bond: Plays, Mainly Shakespearean, in Performance*, 92–117. University Park: Pennsylvania State University Press, 1975. Barton describes the comic dramatic convention of a king who goes in disguise among his subjects, a story that usually ends with mutual recognition between king and subject; Shakespeare offers a more complex and troubling exploration of this narrative.

Dollimore, Jonathan, and Alan Sinfield. "History and Ideology: The Instance of *Henry V*." In John Drakakis, ed., *Alternative Shakespeares*, 206–227. London: Methuen, 1985. Dollimore and Sinfield read *Henry V* as a play that enacts an English state ideology geared toward the colonization of Ireland and the erasing of all internal differences in England, but one that also reveals the fractures within that ideology.

Donaldson, Peter S. "Taking on Shakespeare: Kenneth Branagh's *Henry V*." *Shakespeare Quarterly* 42.1 (1991): 60–71. A sustained comparison of the Olivier and Branagh film versions of the play and their respective relationships to Shakespeare's text.

Greenblatt, Stephen. "Invisible Bullets." In *Shakespearean Negotiations: The Circulation of Social Energy in Renaissance England*, 21–65. Berkeley: University of California Press, 1988. Greenblatt explores the relationships between theatrical and monarchical power, arguing that "the Henry plays confirm the Machiavellian hypothesis that princely power originates in force and fraud even as they draw their audience toward an acceptance of that power" (65).

Holderness, Graham. "'What Ish My Nation?' Shakespeare and National Identities." *Textual Practice* 5.1 (1991): 74–93. A discussion of the Branagh and Olivier films in terms of their treatment of nationalism.

Howard, Jean E., and Phyllis Rackin. "*Henry V*." In *Engendering a Nation: A Feminist Account of Shakespeare's English Histories*, 186–215. New York: Routledge, 1997. Howard and Rackin argue that the gender is an essential category for understanding Shakespeare's history plays: "in the struggle for power between men of two nations, the sexualized bodies of women become a crucial terrain where this battle is played out" (5).

Kastan, David Scott. "'The King Is a Good King, But It Must Be as It May': History, Heroism, and *Henry V.*" In *Shakespeare and the Shapes of Time*. Hanover: University Press of New England, 1982. Kastan discusses Shakespeare's shaping of his historical material, arguing that the play does in fact offer a heroic narrative but that at the same time it calls attention to the way that heroic narrative is produced by a highly selective treatment of refractory historical material.

Kernan, Alvin B. "The Henriad: Shakespeare's Major History Plays." In Alvin B. Kernan, ed., *Modern Shakespearean Criticism: Essays on Style, Dramaturgy, and the Major Plays*. New York: Harcourt, Brace, and World, 1970. Kernan analyzes the sequence of plays from *Richard II* to *Henry V* as embodying a movement from sacred to pragmatic kingship.

Neill, Michael. "Broken English and Broken Irish: Nation, Language, and the Optic of Power in Shakespeare's Histories," *Shakespeare Quarterly* 45 (1994): 1–32. Neill reads Shakespeare's plays in terms of a contradictory English discourse about Ireland: on the one hand it imagines what it is to be English by opposition to what it is to be Irish, and on the other hand it seeks to incorporate Irishness into Englishness, erasing all signs of Irish cultural difference.

Patterson, Annabel. "Back by Popular Demand: The Two Versions of *Henry V.*" In *Shakespeare and the Popular Voice*, 71–92. Oxford: Blackwell, 1989. Patterson discusses the differences between the Quarto and the Folio texts, arguing that the heroic reading of

the play really finds its best support in the Quarto, while the
Folio complicates any idealizing narrative.

Rabkin, Norman. "Either/Or: Responding to *Henry V*." In *Shakespeare and
the Problem of Meaning*, 33–62. Chicago: University of Chicago Press,
1981. Rabkin seeks to transcend the debate between heroic and
anti-heroic readings of the play by arguing that the play is fundamentally and radically ambiguous: it is designed so that it can be
read in either way, but so that either reading necessarily excludes
significant elements of the play.

Smith, Emma, ed. *Shakespeare in Production: King Henry V*. Cambridge: Cambridge University Press, 2002. An edition of the play focused on
tracing its performance history: it includes both a history of significant performances and a text of the play annotated to show
how various directors have handled it.

Sutherland, John. "Henry V, War Criminal?" In John Sutherland and
Cedric Watts, eds., *Henry V, War Criminal?*, 108–116. Oxford: Oxford
University Press, 2000. A brief discussion, aimed at a general
readership, of the problem of the execution of the prisoners at
Agincourt.

Taylor, Gary. *Three Studies in the Text of Henry V*. In Gary Taylor and Stan-
ley Wells, eds., *Modernizing Shakespeare's Spelling with Three Studies in
the Text of Henry V*. Oxford: Clarendon, 1979. Taylor argues that the
Quarto text of *Henry V* derives from a touring script designed to
enable reduced-cast productions.

Tillyard, E. M. W. *Shakespeare's History Plays*. London: Chatto and Windus, 1944. Tillyard insists on the total design of the history plays, arguing that Shakespeare retells English medieval history as the story of a fall into civil war and a redemptive restoration of order under the Tudors.